Grits to Gourmet

Rosalind Lastinger

*BOOK*LOGIX®
Alpharetta, Georgia

Paperback Edition February 2014

ISBN: 978-1-61005-446-1

(For bulk purchases, please contact the publisher.)

10 9 8 7 6 5 4 3 2   0 9 2 3 1 4

Printed in the United States of America

∞This paper meets the requirements of ANSI/NISO Z39.48-1992 (Permanence of Paper)

It's not age that makes a person old.

— Balma Stephenson Monk

This book is dedicated to my mother, Balma Stephenson Monk, and Truman's mother, Lillie Sue Holland Lastinger. They were both wonderful cooks. I do not remember either of them using a printed recipe or even owning a cookbook. Neither of them had a pantry, but they both cooked fantastic meals with whatever they had in their refrigerators and kitchen cabinets. They both embraced large groups of visitors and family members. I remember their smiles while they were busy in their kitchens as though it was a pleasure and not a chore to be cooking for all of us. This cookbook is a big "thank you" to both of them.

Thank God for dirty dishes;
They have a tale to tell.
While other folks are hungry,
We're eating very well.

– Author Unknown

Contents

Acknowledgments

My heartfelt thank-you goes to my husband, Truman. He has always been my greatest supporter. Whenever I need a critique I can depend on him to give me a fair and honest opinion. He has urged me to complete this book for years. He has helped me to edit, compile, and file my recipes. He made an appointment with the publisher and escorted me to the meeting. He has been with me every step of the way…pulling, tugging, and praising me.

Introduction

When Truman and I were newlyweds, we lived in a tiny, furnished two-room apartment in Atlanta. He was enrolled in pre-pharmacy at Oglethorpe University. It was an exciting time in our lives, which became an odyssey of many twists and turns. I knew how to bake a cake and to fry French fries and that was the extent of my culinary skills. Truman had seen his mama cook grits thousands of times, so he proceeded to teach me how to cook grits. I tell people that they were so thick when they were done the spoon stood up in them. I learned by trial and error that cooking grits requires lots of water. While "we" were in pharmacy school we ate lots of grits. It was not until years later that I could afford the luxury of experimenting with food and recipes. I joined my first bridge club in the late 1960s. Our club had seated luncheons, served on our best china, and the food was always delicious. That set the bar high for me. Several of my bridge buddies in Cairo have published their own cookbooks. In fact, some of my best recipes are scribbled on bridge tallies. This book is a culmination of years of my sharing recipes with friends and family members. It is also a tribute to my husband, Truman, and to my children, Laura, Karen, and Travis, who suffered through my early years of cooking and hopefully are enjoying my later years of cooking. Even today I get excited about a new recipe. My wish is that everyone will enjoy the recipes that I have chosen to share in this book.

Kitchen Equivalency Chart

A pinch...1/8 teaspoon or less

3 teaspoons..1 tablespoon

2 tablespoons.. 1/8 cup

4 tablespoons.. 1/4 cup

16 tablespoons...1 cup

5 tablespoons + 1 teaspoon.................................. 1/3 cup

4 ounces .... 1/2 cup

8 ounces ....1 cup

16 ounces .... 1 pound

1 ounce.................................2 tablespoons of fat or liquid

1 cup of liquid ....1/2 pint

2 cups ....1 pint

2 pints...1 quart

4 cups liquid...1 quart

4 quarts .... 1 gallon

8 quarts .... 1 peck [such as apples, pears, etc.]

1 jigger...1 1/2 fluid ounce

1 jigger... 3 tablespoons

Appetizers

ARTICHOKE MUFFINS

Ingredients for 72 pieces

14 oz	Can of artichokes [not pickled]
1/2 cup	Mayonnaise
1/2 cup	Parmesan cheese, grated
1 pkg	English muffins [I prefer Thomas muffins]

Drain and chop artichokes. Separate muffins and place on a baking tray, inside up. Mix Parmesan cheese, mayonnaise, and artichokes. Spread mixture over muffins and bake in a 400-degree oven until bubbly, 15–20 minutes. Broiler may be turned on the last minute to lightly brown the muffins. [May sprinkle with paprika before browning.] Cut each round into 6 pizza-style wedges and place each round on a serving tray.

These are good leftover, but there are seldom any left.

If two pots become stuck together after stacking, it's not impossible to unstick them. Put ice in the inner pot and dunk the outer pot in hot water. The warm water will expand the outer pot and the ice will contract the inner pot, making the pots separate.

ROSALIND'S ASPARAGUS ROLL-UPS

Ingredients for 2 dozen

24	Asparagus spears [canned]
24 slices	Thin sliced white bread
8 oz	Cream cheese, room temperature
1/3 stick	Butter, melted

Trim the crusts off of the bread. Flatten the bread with a rolling pin. Spread each slice of bread with a thin layer of cream cheese. Roll an asparagus spear in each slice of bread, trimming the stem end if desired. Brush each roll with butter and place on a baking sheet with the seam-side down. Bake in a 350-degree oven until lightly browned.

Helpful hint: These may be halved. Also, they are delicious served [hot or cooled] with chicken salad.

BACON ROLL-UPS

Ingredients for 4 dozen

8 oz	Cream cheese, softened
1 tbsp	Dried chives
1 pkg	Bacon, cut into halves
1 loaf	Whole wheat bread

Trim the crusts from the bread and cut the slices in half. Mix the cream cheese and chives together. Spread a spoonful of the mixture on each bread half and roll up. Wrap a bacon slice around each roll. Place the roll up, seam-side down, on a baking sheet. Bake in a 350-degree oven for 30 minutes or until the bacon is done.

Helpful hint: Toothpicks may be used to secure the wraps.

BACON-DATE WRAPS

Ingredients for 30 servings

12 oz	Bacon [or 1 package]
30	Brazil nuts [or blanched whole almonds]
30	Whole dates, pitted

Cut the bacon strips into 1/3 pieces. Place a nut into each date. Wrap each date with a piece of bacon. Place on a baking tray with the cut side of the bacon on the underside. Bake in a 350-degree oven for 15 minutes.

Helpful hint: A tray with drain slots will work best. Bacon grease will run off.

BARBECUE COCKTAIL SMOKIES

Ingredients for 4 dozen

14 oz	Beef Cocktail Smokies
3/4 cup	Barbecue Sauce [Rosalind's sauce or your choice]
3 tbsp	Brown sugar, heaping

Combine all of the ingredients in a boiler and simmer until the liquid becomes syrup-like, about 20 minutes. Serve warm.

Helpful hint: A 16 oz bottle of Kraft Brown Sugar Barbecue Sauce can be used instead of this cookbook's barbecue sauce and brown sugar.

STUFFED CELERY

Ingredients for 8 servings

8 oz	Cheddar cheese, shredded
4 oz	Pimiento [diced and in a jar]
1/2 cup	Mayonnaise, or to taste
4 grinds	Fresh black peppercorns
	Celery stalks, washed and cut into desired lengths

Mix the cheese, mayonnaise, pimiento [including the liquid], and black pepper together. Stuff the celery sections, cover, and chill. This spread is also good on sandwiches.

Helpful hint: These are pretty on a tray with fresh fruit [such as pineapple, grapes, strawberries, apple slices].

CHEESE BALL

Ingredients for 6 persons

8 oz	Cream cheese, softened
1 cup	Cheddar cheese, grated
1 tbsp	Mayonnaise
1 tbsp	Worcestershire sauce
2 1/2 oz	Dried beef [jar], chopped
	Chopped walnuts, pecans, or grated cheese

Blend the cheese, cream cheese, mayonnaise, sauce, and meat together in a food processor or an electric mixer. Shape into a ball. Roll in nuts or cheese. Serve with crackers. Store in the refrigerator.

CAIRO CHEESE DIP

Ingredients for 6 servings

8 oz	Colby cheese, shredded
1 cup	Onion [I like a sweet onion], chopped small
1 cup	Mayonnaise
4 slices	Bacon, cooked crisp and crumbled

Mix the mayonnaise, cheese, and onion. Bake in a 350-degree oven in a Pyrex serving dish until bubbly [about 30 minutes]. Sprinkle the bacon bits over the top and cook another minute or two. Serve warm with crackers.

CHEESE RING

Ingredients for 10 servings

1 lb	Sharp cheddar cheese, shredded
1 cup	Pecans, chopped and lightly toasted
1 sm	Onion, grated
1 cup	Mayonnaise [scant]
	Black pepper, to taste
1 dash	Cayenne
	Strawberry preserves

Mix all of the ingredients, except for the preserves, together. Mix well and put into a ring mold. Place the mold into the refrigerator until well chilled. Unmold onto a serving plate. Place the preserves in the center of the cheese ring. Serve with crackers.

CHEESE STRAWS

Ingredients for 6 dozen

16 oz	Cheddar cheese [sharp or medium], shredded
1 stick	Butter
2 1/4 cup	Flour, all-purpose
1 1/2 tsp	Baking powder
1 tsp	Salt
1/4 tsp	Cayenne pepper
3 tsp	Water

Let cheese and butter [or oleo] soften to room temperature. Cream cheese and butter until smooth and creamy. Mix flour, baking powder, salt, and cayenne pepper together. Add dry mixture to cheese and butter. Add the cold water and mix well. Use a cookie press with a star plate and pipe mixture out on a cookie sheet. Bake at 325 degrees for about 20 minutes. Bottom of cheese straws will be slightly brown and can be lifted up with a spatula. Cut while hot into desired lengths. Cool and store in an airtight container.

CHARLESTON CHEESE

Ingredients for 8 servings

1/2 cup	Mayonnaise
8 oz	Cream cheese, softened
8 oz	Sharp cheddar cheese, shredded
2	Green onions, chopped
6	Round buttery crackers [I like Ritz], crushed
8 slices	Bacon, fried crisp and crumbled

Mix mayonnaise, cream cheese, onions, and cheddar cheese in a bowl. Pour the mixture into a lightly-oiled quiche dish. Top with the crushed crackers. Bake in a 350-degree oven for 15 minutes or until bubbly. Top with the crumbled bacon and serve with crackers.

CREAM CHEESE AND OLIVE SPREAD

Ingredients for 3 cups

12 oz	Cream cheese, softened
1 tbsp	Olive juice
7 oz	Stuffed olives [jar], thinly sliced or chopped
1/3 cup	Mayonnaise
1/4 tsp	Paprika

Mix all of the ingredients together and spread on bread for sandwiches or a party spread. Refrigerate leftovers.

CREAM-FILLED CHERRY TOMATOES

Ingredients for 4 dozen

2 doz	Cherry tomatoes
8 oz	Cream cheese, softened
4 tbsp	Mayonnaise, or more to taste
1 tbsp	Green onion, chopped fine [or chopped chives]
3 dashes	Worcestershire sauce, or more to taste
	Salt
	Pepper

Cut the cherry tomatoes in half. Scoop out and discard the seeds. Turn them upside down on a paper towel. Mix the remaining ingredients together. Fill the tomato halves with the mixture. Cover and refrigerate for several hours before serving. Garnish with a small sprig of parsley, or a little sprinkle of chopped chives, or a small piece of green onion top.

ROSALIND'S CHEX PARTY MIX

Ingredients for 1 batch

1/4 cup	Butter
1 1/4 tsp	Garlic salt
4 1/2 tsp	Worcestershire sauce
1 tbsp	Lemon juice
4 cups	Chex cereal [corn, rice, or wheat]
3 cups	Cheerios
2 cups	Pretzels
1 cup	Salted mixed nuts
1 cup	Honey-roasted nuts

Melt butter in a small saucepan. Stir in seasonings. Place cereal, nuts, and pretzels in a large roasting pan. Drizzle butter mixture over all and stir to coat evenly. Bake for one hour in a 250-degree oven, stirring every 15 minutes or until the mix is no longer moist and the flavors are blended. Cool. Store in an airtight container.

Helpful hint: Try varying the ingredients. I sometimes use chow mein noodles, small cheese crackers, or pecans left over from the Rolo pretzels. It's fun to experiment.

CHICKEN HORS D'OEUVRE

Ingredients for 2 dozen

2 cups	Chicken [cooked], chopped
1 tbsp	Onion, minced
2 tbsp	Pimiento, chopped small
1 dash	Hot sauce
1/2 cup	Mayonnaise
1 cup	Pecans, chopped small

Mix all of the ingredients together. Roll into small balls. Chill for 4 hours and serve. Garnish with parsley.

MAPLE CHICKEN WINGS

Ingredients for 8 persons

4 lbs	Chicken wings
1/3 cup	Teriyaki sauce
1/2 cup	Soy sauce
2 tbsp	Minced garlic
1 tbsp	Garlic powder
1 tbsp	Onion powder
1/2 tbsp	Black pepper
1 1/2 cups	Maple syrup

Cut off chicken wing tips and cut between joints of the remaining parts. [Your meat market man can do this for you.] Place chicken in a large disposable baking pan and place pan on a baking sheet to reinforce it. Mix the remaining ingredients and coat the chicken. Bake in a 350-degree oven for approximately 1 hour, turning every 15–20 minutes. After 1 hour, increase the oven temperature to 425 degrees. Turn the wings and cook for an additional 45 minutes. The liquid in the pan will evaporate, and a delicious sauce will remain on the wings.

FRUIT DIP

Ingredients for 2 cups

7 oz	Marshmallow Cream [jar]
8 oz	Cream cheese, softened

Mix together and chill. Serve with red and green apple slices for a delicious and colorful appetizer. Dip can be stored in the refrigerator in an airtight container for several days. Apples can be dipped in pineapple juice to prevent discoloration.

GAIL'S FRUIT DIP

Ingredients for 2 cups

16 oz	Sour cream
5 oz	Vanilla pudding mix, NOT instant

Mix the package of vanilla pudding powder [not instant pudding] with the sour cream. Cover and chill. Serve with fresh fruit [pineapple, strawberries, grapes, sliced apples, or your choice]. Dee-lish!

KRISTA'S BAKED GOUDA CHEESE

Ingredients for 8 servings

1 round	Gouda cheese
8 oz	Crescent rolls [in the dairy section]
1	Egg white

Unroll the dough and separate crosswise into 2 sections. Seal the perforations by gently pressing them together. Cut off the corners of the pastry and set them aside. Place one section on a baking sheet. Place the cheese in the center. Place the remaining section over the top and gently press it around the cheese. Gently stretch the bottom section's edges evenly over the top and press to seal completely. Brush the dough with the egg white. At this point, the dough cut from the corners may be used for special designs such as leaves. Top with the cutouts and brush again with the egg white. Bake in a 350-degree oven for 20 minutes or until golden brown. Let the cheese cool for 15 minutes and serve with a favorite wafer or strawberry preserves.

Helpful hint: A natural Brie cheese or any round cheese may be used.

ROSALIND'S HAM AND OKRA ROLL-UPS

Ingredients for 96 pieces

16 slices	Ham [4x6-inch thin slices]
1 oz	Dry ranch dressing mix
2 jars	Pickled okra [16 oz each, hot or mild]
8 oz	Cream cheese, softened

Blot and dry the ham and okra. Mix the cream cheese and dressing mix together. Trim stem ends of okra and discard the crowns. Spread the slices of ham with the cream cheese mixture. Place two pieces of okra on ham lengthwise, with the small ends slightly overlapping in the center. Roll up tightly and place in a container that has been lined with paper towels. Place in a freezer for about one hour or chill overnight. Slice into 1/4-inch slices with a thin, sharp knife [six pieces per roll]. Place on a serving tray, cover, and refrigerate.

HOT DIP

Ingredients for 10 persons

1 lb	Ground beef
1 lb	Sausage, hot
1 med	Onion, chopped
1 can	Mushroom soup
1 lb	Velveeta cheese
8 oz	Picante salsa, jar [hot or mild]

Brown the meats and onion. Drain well. Add the rest of the ingredients to the skillet and let simmer until the cheese is melted.

Helpful hint: A 12 oz jar of salsa can be used. It will make the dip thicker.

KAREN'S QUICK CHILI DIP

Ingredients for 8 servings

15 oz	Chili with beans, can
8 oz	Cream cheese, light or regular
4 oz	Sharp cheddar cheese, grated
	Tortilla chips

Press cream cheese in the bottom of a 9-inch Pyrex pie plate. Cover with chili and top with grated cheese. Cover and microwave 4 or 5 minutes until bubbly. Serve hot with tortilla chips.

Helpful hint: Leftovers can be reheated and served as a topping for baked potatoes.

MINIATURE MUSHROOM PIES

Ingredients for 2 dozen

3 tbsp	Butter or margarine
1 cup	Onions, finely chopped
1/2 lb	Mushrooms, finely chopped
1/4 tsp	Thyme
1/2 tsp	Salt
1/8 tsp	Pepper
2 tbsp	Flour
1/4 cup	Sour cream
	PASTRY
8 oz	Cream cheese
1 cup	Butter or margarine, melted
2 1/2 cups	Flour, all-purpose

For the pastry, combine the flour, butter, and cream cheese. Mix well, roll in plastic wrap, and chill.

For the filling, melt the butter in a frying pan and sauté the onions until tender. Add the mushrooms and cook about 3 minutes while stirring. Add the thyme, salt, and pepper, and sprinkle the flour over the mixture. Stir in the sour cream and cook until thickened. Roll the chilled pastry until 1/4 inch thick. Cut into 2-1/2-inch circles. Place 1/2 teaspoon of the mixture on each circle and fold it over. Press the edges with the tines of a fork. Make a small slit on top with a small, sharp knife and place on a tray. Bake or place in the freezer. When frozen, remove, and place the pies in freezer bags until ready to serve. When ready to bake, place the pies on a cookie sheet, thaw slightly, and bake in a 350-degree oven for 25–30 minutes.

ONION STICKS

Ingredients for 20 sticks

20 slices	White bread
1 stick	Butter, room temperature
1/2 cup	Onion, finely chopped

Trim the crusts off of the bread and roll the bread flat with a rolling pin. Spread the bread with butter. Sprinkle each slice with the minced onion. Roll each slice and secure with a toothpick. Bake in 350-degree oven until golden brown [may turn on the broiler the last couple of minutes]. Serve as an appetizer or with seafood bisque or soups.

Helpful hint: The crusts may be baked slowly in a 250-degree oven until dry and crushed into bread crumbs or freeze until later.

SPICY-PEPPERY NUTS

Ingredients for 4 cups

1 lb	Nut halves [pecans, walnuts, or nuts of your choice]
2 1/2 tbsp	Butter
1/2 tsp	Salt
1/8 tsp	Pepper
2 tsp	Worcestershire sauce
1 dash	Hot pepper sauce

Melt the butter in a black iron skillet [or a heavy bottom skillet]. Add the seasonings and stir. Add the nuts and mix well. Place the iron skillet in a 250-degree oven and toast the nuts for 45 minutes or until the nuts are firm and no longer have a raw taste, stirring occasionally. [I like to stir them with a spatula.]

Helpful hint: The nuts may be toasted on a cookie sheet if using a skillet with a porous handle.

OLIVE-CHEESE BALLS

Ingredients for 2 dozen

3 tbsp	Butter [softened]
1 cup	Sharp cheddar cheese [shredded and softened]
1/2 cup	Flour, all-purpose
1/4 tsp	Salt
1/8 tsp	Pepper
24	Green olives

Mix together the butter and cheese. Add the flour, salt, and pepper. Mix well and knead until well blended. Divide into 24 small portions and wrap around the olives. Place on a baking tray, cover, and freeze for 2 or 3 hours. Remove from the freezer and preheat the oven at 400 degrees. Bake for 15–18 minutes. Small pecans can be substituted for the olives. Use cayenne pepper instead of black pepper.

OLIVE NUT SPREAD

Ingredients for 3 cups

1/2 cup	Mayonnaise
1/2 cup	Pecans, chopped
1 cup	Olives, chopped
2 tbsp	Olive juice
1 dash	Pepper

Mix all of the ingredients together. Cover and refrigerate for 24 hours. Spread on very thin bread or crackers.

PARMESAN CHEESE AND ONION PUFFS

Ingredients for 36 servings

18 slices	Thin, white bread
1/2 cup	Parmesan cheese, freshly shredded
1 cup	Mayonnaise
	Onions [pearl or small boiling], thinly sliced
1 tsp	Yellow mustard
3 tsp	Mayonnaise

Cut 2 rounds out of each slice of bread with a 2-inch cookie cutter. Place the bread on a baking sheet and broil [on a top rack] in a preheated 425-degree oven until lightly browned. Mix 1 teaspoon yellow mustard with 3 teaspoons of mayonnaise in a small bowl and set aside. Whisk together the cheese and one cup of mayonnaise. Flip the bread rounds over and spread with the mustard mixture. Place a thin slice of onion on top and cover with about 1 teaspoon of the cheese mixture, covering the bread. Broil in the hot oven, watching carefully, until golden brown and bubbly.

Helpful hint: I have used the frozen pearl onions. Remove the outer skins and slice while still frozen. They get mushy when thawed, but they still have a lot of flavor. Also, I used 1 1/2 or 2 of these per slice of bread. A very inexpensive sandwich bread works well for this recipe.

SWEET AND SPICY PECANS

Ingredients for 1 cup

1 cup	Pecan halves
1/4 cup	Sugar
1 cup	Warm water
	COATING
1 tsp	Chili powder
1 dash	Red [ground] pepper
2 tbsp	Sugar

Stir together 1/4 cup sugar with 1 cup of warm water until the sugar dissolves. Add the pecans and let them soak for 10 minutes. Drain the pecans and discard the liquid.

Whisk together the 2 tablespoons of sugar, the chili powder, and the red pepper. Add the pecans and toss to coat well. Place on a lightly-oiled baking sheet or non-stick foil. Bake in a 350-degree oven for 10 minutes [stirring once or twice] or until the pecans are golden brown.

Helpful hint: For a spicier pecan, add another dash of red pepper. Also, these pecans are good as an appetizer or as a topping on a spinach and strawberry salad.

PEPPER JELLY/CREAM CHEESE APPETIZER

Ingredients for 8 servings

8 oz	Cream cheese
16 oz	Pepper jelly [red or green]
	Crackers of choice

Place the block of cream cheese on a serving dish. Put as much of the pepper jelly over the top as desired. Place a pâté knife on the plate along with crackers for guests to serve themselves.

PEPPER JELLY DIP

Ingredients for 3 cups

16 oz	Cream cheese, softened
8 oz	Pepper jelly [red or green]
1/4 cup	Pecans [chopped small], lightly toasted

Mix together, cover, and refrigerate until served.

PINEAPPLE CHEESE BALL

Ingredients for 8 servings

24 oz	Philadelphia cream cheese
1 lg	Crushed pineapple [can], drained
1 bunch	Green onions, bottoms and a lot of the tops chopped small
1/2 bag	Craisins
1 cup	Pecans, chopped very small
2 1/2 lbs	Whole pecans
	Fresh pineapple top

Beat the cream cheese well. Add the drained pineapple, chopped pecans, onions, and craisins. Blend well. Shape into the form of a pineapple. Arrange 2 or 3 pounds of whole pecans around the cream cheese to resemble a pineapple. Cut the top off of a fresh pineapple and place it on the top of the cheese ball. Chill and serve with assorted party crackers.

PIZZA STICKS

Ingredients for 32 sticks

1 pkg	Thin and Crispy Four Cheese Pizza, thawed
2 tbsp	Olive oil
1/2 cup	Parmesan cheese, finely shredded
1/8 tsp	Cayenne pepper

Brush the edges of the pizza with olive oil and drizzle the remaining oil over the pizza. Mix half of the Parmesan cheese with the cayenne pepper. Sprinkle the cheese mixture over the pizza, reserving the remaining cheese, and bake in a 350-degree oven until the crust is a golden brown [about 20–25 minutes]. Sprinkle with the remaining cheese. Cut the pizza into quarters and each quarter into 8 thin strips. Serve with warm marinara sauce or salsa.

SALTINE SURPRISES [IN MEMORY OF TISH]

Ingredients for 8 dozen

3 stacks	Saltine crackers
1 1/2 cups	Canola oil [I like Wesson]
1 pack	Dry ranch dressing
1 1/2 tbsp	Red pepper flakes

Place the saltine crackers in a container with a tight-fitting lid. Mix the remaining ingredients together. Drizzle the mixture over the crackers and secure the lid of the container. Flip the container over every 15 minutes. Repeat the flipping procedure for 2 hours. Preheat the oven to 250 degrees and turn the oven off. Spread the cracker on a baking sheet and place the sheet in the oven. Leave the crackers in the oven until the oven is cold. Remove the crackers and place them in an airtight container. Ziplock bags work well. Serve as an appetizer, snack, or with tomato soup.

ROSALIND'S SAUSAGE AND CHEESE SWIRLS

Ingredients for 2 dozen

2 cups	Bisquick
1/2 cup	Water
1 lb	Hot sausage [I like Jimmy Dean]
6 oz	Sharp cheddar cheese, shredded small
3 oz	Cream cheese

Cook the sausage until just done [no more pink]. Stir in the cream cheese and set aside. Mix the Bisquick and water together in a bowl and knead until elastic. Roll the dough out into a 9x24-inch rectangle [on wax paper or a flat surface]. Spread the sausage evenly over the dough. Sprinkle the grated cheese over the sausage. Carefully roll the bottom end of the dough up. Wrap the sausage and cheese roll in plastic wrap and freeze or chill. When ready to bake, partially thaw and slice. Let the slices finish thawing on the baking sheet. Bake in a 400-degree oven for 10 minutes, or until the bread is golden brown.

Helpful hint: Cut an empty paper towel tube lengthwise and place the wrapped roll inside and freeze. The sausage roll will freeze without a flat side. If a paper towel holder is not handy, remove the roll from the freezer several times and reshape.

GRANNIE SUE'S SAUSAGE BALLS

Ingredients for 40

3 cups	Bisquick
1 lb	Hot or mild sausage
16 oz	Shredded cheese [sharp]

Mix ingredients together. Shape into small balls and place on a cookie sheet. Bake in a 350-degree oven for 25 minutes.

Helpful hint: These can be made in advance and frozen. Also, less cheese [10 oz] can be used for a stronger sausage taste.

SAUSAGE DIP

Ingredients for 8 persons

1 lb	Sausage, Jimmy Dean
8 oz	Cream cheese
10 oz	Ro-Tel tomatoes, can
4 oz	Velveeta cheese

Cook sausage. Drain completely, blotting with paper towels. Open tomatoes and drain. Put sausage into a saucepan and add the cream cheese and the tomatoes. Simmer on very low heat, stirring occasionally. Add the Velveeta cheese and heat thoroughly. Serve with Scoops.

SAUSAGE MUFFINS

Ingredients for 1 dozen

16 oz	Sausage [hot]
3 oz	Cream cheese
1 sm	Onion, chopped

| 8 oz | Cheese, sharp [shredded] |
| 6 | English muffins |

Cook the sausage and onion in a skillet. Drain well. Add the cream cheese to the sausage and then add the grated cheddar cheese. Stir until the cheese is melted and blended. Open the muffins and lay them cut-side up on a baking tray. Spoon the sausage mixture over each muffin half. Bake in a 350-degree oven for 10–15 minutes or until bubbly. [At this point, these can be stacked and frozen until ready to serve.] Cut each muffin half into 4 [or more] pizza-like slices. Place each round on a serving dish with a spatula.

SAUSAGE SWIRLS

Ingredients for 2 dozen

2 cups	Bisquick
1/2 cup	Water
1 lb	Hot sausage

Mix the Bisquick and water. Knead until elastic. Roll on wax paper. Wet hands and pat the meat almost to the edge of the dough. Roll up as a jellyroll, using the wax paper to guide the roll. Refrigerate for several hours or wrap and freeze. Slice into 1/4-inch slices. Bake on an ungreased cookie sheet in a 400-degree oven for 10–15 minutes or until lightly brown and the sausage in the center begins to bubble. Great for morning parties and served with the Coffee Punch.

SEAFOOD DIP

Ingredients for 20 servings

1/2 lb	Shrimp [cooked and chopped fine]
3 oz	Cream cheese
1/3 cup	Thousand Island dressing
1/3 cup	Mayonnaise
1/3 cup	Picante sauce [medium or mild]
2 tbsp	Grated onion
1 tsp	Horseradish
	Crackers, chips, or vegetables

Mix all ingredients together and store in the refrigerator. Serve with crackers, chips, or assorted vegetables. May be spread on garlic bread, sprinkled with Parmesan cheese, and baked for 5 minutes for a hot hors d'oeuvre. Crabmeat may be substituted for shrimp. Canned shrimp may be used instead of fresh shrimp.

SEVEN-LAYER DIP

Ingredients for 12 servings

16 oz	Refried beans [can]
1 tbsp	Taco seasoning mix
1 cup	Sour cream
1 cup	Salsa
1 cup	Lettuce, shredded
1 cup	Mexican-style cheese, shredded
1/2 cup	Tomato, peeled and chopped
1/2 cup	Green onion, chopped
3 tbsp	Ripe olives, sliced

Mix the taco seasoning and beans together. Spread into the bottom of a 9-inch glass pie plate. Layer the remaining ingredients in the order listed. Cover and refrigerate. Serve with tortilla chips, Scoops, or crackers.

Helpful hint: Ingredients, such as adding a chopped avocado, can vary according to taste.

SHRIMP COCKTAIL

Ingredients for 6 servings

12 oz	Chili sauce
1 1/2 tbsp	Horseradish
1 tbsp	Lemon juice
1/2 tsp	Worcestershire sauce
1 pinch	Salt
1 dash	Pepper
36 med	Shrimp, cooked

Mix all of the ingredients, except for the shrimp, together. Cover and chill. Arrange the cooked shrimp around a bowl of the sauce. Serve with picks.

Helpful hint: Boil the shrimp for 3–5 minutes [or until the shrimp turns pink] in your favorite seasoning. There are good shrimp and crab seasonings near the seafood in grocery stores.

If the scales of fish are dull and come off easily, reject it. Fish should have bright red gills, clear open eyes, firm flesh, and healthy-looking scales.

SHRIMP DIP

Ingredients for 8 persons

1 cup	Mayonnaise
1 cup	Sour cream
1/2 pkg	Dry onion soup mix [regular or golden]
2 cans	Tiny shrimp, drained

Mix the first three ingredients together, incorporating the onion soup until no lumps remain. Add the shrimp. Keep in an airtight container in the refrigerator. Can be made one day before serving. One can of shrimp and one can of crabmeat can be used. Serve with chips or Scoops.

SHRIMP EN'BROCHETTE

Ingredients for 6 servings

2 lbs	Shrimp [10–16 per pound]
	Salt
	Pepper
	Bacon
	Barbecue sauce

Peel, devein, salt, and pepper the shrimp. Cut slices of bacon in half and cook them in the microwave until half done. Wrap each shrimp in a bacon half and secure with a toothpick. Heat the grill to 300 degrees. Cook the shrimp for 5–8 minutes while brushing with barbecue sauce and turning quickly to prevent burning.

SHRIMP MOUSSE

Ingredients for 16 servings

12 oz	Cooked shrimp, chopped [or 6 oz can crabmeat and 6 oz can of small shrimp, drained]
2	Envelopes of unflavored gelatin
1/2 cup	Hot water
10 oz	Can of tomato soup, undiluted
8 oz	Cream cheese, softened
1 cup	Mayonnaise
1/2 cup	Chopped celery
1/2 cup	Chopped onion
1/2 cup	Chopped green bell pepper [or chopped stuffed green olives]

Heat soup. Soften gelatin in a small amount of cold water. Add hot water, stirring until gelatin is dissolved. Stir in soup. Mix cream cheese and mayonnaise in a small bowl. Add soup and beat with a rotary beater. Add seafood and chopped vegetables, mixing with a spoon. Pour into a round mold and chill. Serve with crackers.

Helpful hint: When removing from the mold, do not use hot or warm water to loosen the mold.

LITTLE SMOKIES IN A BLANKET

Ingredients for 40

40	Cocktail Smokies
2 cans	Pillsbury buttermilk biscuits [in the dairy case]

Pull biscuits apart, making 2 biscuits out of each one. Wrap a Smokie in each half. Place on a lightly-oiled cookie sheet and bake in a 350-degree oven until brown.

SPINACH BALLS

Ingredients for 6 dozen

2 pkgs	Chopped spinach, cooked, drained, and squeezed
2 med	Onions, chopped very small
3/4 cup	Butter, melted
1 tbsp	Garlic salt
1/2 tbsp	Black pepper
2 cups	Herb stuffing mix
6 lg	Eggs, beaten with a fork
1/2 cup	Parmesan cheese
1/2 tsp	Thyme

Mix all of the ingredients together. Shape the mixture into balls of a desired size. Place the balls on a baking sheet and chill or freeze. If freezing, place the frozen balls into freezer bags until needed. Thaw in the refrigerator. Bake the spinach balls in a 350-degree oven for about 20 minutes.

SPINACH DIP

Ingredients for 3 cups

10 oz	Frozen spinach, thawed and squeezed dry
1 pkg	Dry vegetable soup mix
8 oz	Water chestnuts, drained and diced
8 oz	Sour cream
1 cup	Mayonnaise
3	Green onions, finely chopped [optional]

Mix all of the ingredients together, cover, and chill. Serve with a tray of raw veggies of choice, crackers, or corn chips. If desired, add a little chopped onion to the dip.

JANE'S SWEET, HOT, AND SOUR MEATBALL

Ingredients for 50 portions

1 lb	Pork sausage
1 lb	Ground beef
1/2 cup	Plain dry bread crumbs
2	Eggs, beaten
1/4 cup	Milk
1/2 cup	Finely chopped onion
1/2 tsp	Salt
1/2 tsp	Black pepper

SAUCE

1/2 cup	Apple jelly
1/4 cup	Spicy brown mustard
1/4 cup	Jack Daniel's Tennessee Whiskey
1 tsp	Worcestershire sauce
	Hot pepper, to taste

Combine all meatball ingredients in a large mixing bowl. Blend well with hands. Form into 1-1/2-inch balls. Place on an ungreased baking sheet that has sides to catch the grease. Bake in a 375-degree oven for 30 minutes or until browned and cooked through.

SAUCE: Combine all of the sauce ingredients in a large skillet and stir until well blended. Stir in the cooked meatballs, coat with sauce, and cook about 5 minutes. [Sauce will thicken slightly.] Serve with picks. Makes approximately 50 meatballs.

SPINACH SQUARES

Ingredients for 5 dozen

20 oz	Frozen, chopped spinach [2 packs]
1 med	Onion, chopped fine
1/4 lb	Mushrooms, sliced thin
2 tbsp	Butter
4 lg	Eggs, beaten with fork
1/4 cup	Fine bread crumbs
1 can	Cream of mushroom soup, undiluted
1/4 cup	Parmesan cheese
1/2 tsp	Pepper
1 tsp	Salt

Thaw the spinach and press out the water. Sauté the onion and mushrooms in the butter until tender. Combine the spinach, mushrooms, onion, and remaining ingredients in a medium mixing bowl. Pour into an oiled 9x13-inch baking dish. Bake in a 325-degree oven for 35 minutes or until lightly brown. Cool slightly and cut into 1-inch squares.

Helpful hint: After draining the thawed spinach in a colander, place it in a clean cloth or paper towels, roll, and squeeze.

VIDALIA-MOZZARELLA SPREAD

Ingredients for 10 servings

1 cup	Vidalia onions, finely chopped
1 cup	Mozzarella cheese, shredded
1 cup	Mayonnaise

Mix all of the ingredients together and put into a 9-inch Pyrex pie plate. Bake in a 350-degree oven until bubbly. Serve warm with small crackers.

Helpful hint: If Vidalia onions are not available, use another sweet onion. Vidalia onions are grown in Vidalia, Georgia, and are only available in the summer. There are none better.

Eugene's Ultimate Stain Remover:

1 tsp Dawn dishwashing detergent
4 tbsp hydrogen peroxide
2 tbsp baking soda

Mix then apply and scrub with a brush.

Beef

BEEF BOURGUIGNONNE

Ingredients for 6 servings

3 lbs	Filet of beef
2 cups	Beef stock
1 tbsp	Tomato paste
1/2 lb	Pearl onions [in the frozen foods]
9 med	Carrots, peeled and sliced diagonally into 3/4-inch slices
1 sprig	Thyme, fresh
4 tbsp	Butter, room temperature [divided]
2 1/2 tbsp	Flour, all-purpose
1/2 lb	Mushrooms, button [cleaned and cut into 1/4-inch slices]
1/2 cup	Red wine [a good wine and more or less, according to taste]
1/2 tsp	Pepper
1/4 lb	Bacon, diced and fried crisp
	Garlic salt with parsley

Trim the beef and cut into medallions, 1-inch thick each. Cut the bacon into small pieces and cook until crisp. Remove the bacon from pan and set aside. Pour off all of the bacon grease except for 1 or 2 tablespoons. Add 1/2 cup of the beef stock to deglaze the frying pan, saving the flavors from the bacon. Set aside. In a small pan, sauté the mushrooms, which have been cleaned and the stems removed, in 2 tablespoons of the butter until tender. Set aside. Sprinkle a large black iron skillet [using no oil] with the garlic-parsley salt, covering the surface. Heat the skillet until almost smoking and add the beef slices [expect a big sizzle]. When the beef medallions are seared, turn them to sear the other side [you may need a spatula to turn them]. When they are the desired doneness, remove and place them on a platter. Deglaze the pan with the wine and cook on medium-high heat for 1 or 2 minutes, stirring to incorporate the flavors. Add the remaining beef stock, tomato paste, pepper, and sprig of thyme, and continue to boil for about 10 minutes. Mix 2 tablespoons of butter and the flour together to make a paste [may use some of the 1/2 cup of beef stock used to deglaze the bacon to mix]. Strain the wine mixture and return it to the pan, adding the beef broth used to deglaze the bacon fry pan. Add the carrots and onions to the wine sauce and simmer for 25 minutes, or until the vegetables are just tender. Add the flour mixture to the wine and vegetables, slowly stirring until the sauce is thickened. Add the beef, mushrooms, and [if desired] the bacon bits. Reheat for 5 or 10 minutes. Do not cook the meat any longer...just heat it. You do not want to serve boiled meat. Check the seasoning and serve immediately.

Helpful hint: Good with orange rice.

ITALIAN BEEF CASSEROLE

Ingredients for 10 servings

8 oz	Lasagna noodles [flat, no boil]
2 1/2 lbs	Ground beef [chuck]
3 tbsp	Butter
1 lb	Ragu, traditional [or sauce of choice]
1 cup	Cottage cheese, large curd
8 oz	Cream cheese, softened
8 oz	Sour cream
1/2 cup	Onion, chopped small
1/4 cup	Green pepper, chopped small

Brown the ground beef in the butter in a heavy [iron] skillet. Mix the cream cheese, cottage cheese, sour cream, onion, and green pepper in a bowl until well blended. Drain any excess oil from the meat and add the tomato sauce. Spread a little of the meat sauce in the bottom of a 9x13-inch casserole dish. Place the noodles over the dish and spread the cheese mixture over the noodles. Place another layer of noodles over the cheese. Pour the tomato and beef mixture over the noodles. Cover tightly with foil and bake in a 350-degree oven for 1 hour.

Helpful hint: A friend of mine uses regular tomato sauce and thin noodles [which are boiled before baking]. Both are good.

NO-PEEK BEEF CASSEROLE

Ingredients for 6 servings

2 lbs	Stew beef or round steak, cut into small pieces
1 pkg	Onion soup mix, dry
6 oz	Sliced mushrooms [2 cans, 3 oz each], drained
10 oz	Cream of mushroom soup [can], undiluted

Mix all ingredients together and put into a 2-quart casserole dish. Cover tightly with foil. Bake in a 300-degree oven for 3 hours. DO NOT PEEK. Serve over noodles or yellow rice.

BEEF TENDERLOIN WITH MUSHROOM SAUCE

Ingredients for 4 servings

1 lb	Beef tenderloin, cut into 8 slices
1/2 cup	Mushrooms, thinly sliced
2 tbsp	Minced onion
1 tsp	Lemon juice
1 tsp	Worcestershire sauce
1/4 cup	Butter
2 tbsp	Parsley, snipped
	Garlic salt
	Pepper [optional]

Sprinkle a heavy iron skillet with garlic salt. When the skillet is very hot, sear the beef medallions on both sides [3–4 minutes on each side], sealing the juices in the meat. Remove the meat from the skillet and place on a platter, keeping it warm. Melt the butter in the skillet and add the remaining ingredients [except for the parsley] and cook until the mushrooms are tender. Add the beef medallions and the parsley to the sauce and re-warm or serve the sauce separately.

Helpful hint: When re-warming the meat, do not boil. Also, the meat can be cooked in 2 tablespoons of butter. One crushed garlic clove and 1/8 teaspoon of salt can be used in cooking the mushrooms instead of the garlic salt.

CHILI

Ingredients for 6 servings

2 lbs	Ground beef
2 med	Onions, chopped
2	Bell peppers, chopped
4	Stalks of celery, chopped
1 qt	Tomatoes
1 pt	Ragu, extra thick
1 tsp	Chili powder
	Salt, pepper, Worcestershire sauce, and hot sauce to taste

Sauté the onions, peppers, and celery in a small amount of butter or oil. Brown the meat, drain, and add to the vegetables. Add the tomatoes and Ragu. Add as much of the seasonings as preferred. Simmer for 30–45 minutes or until flavors are blended.

ROSALIND'S QUICK CHILI

Ingredients for 8 servings

2 lbs	Ground chuck
1 lg	Onion, chopped
2 pkgs	Chili seasoning mix [1.25 oz each]
1 jar	Ragu, your favorite combination [1 lb 10 oz]
2 cans	Chili beans, drained
	Salt
	Pepper
3 tbsp	Brown sugar

Brown the meat and chopped onion in a heavy skillet. Drain the excess grease. Add the salt, pepper, and chili seasoning mix. Add the Ragu and let the mixture bubble [this is the time to add more Ragu, if desired]. Mash one can of the chili beans. Add the 2 cans of beans and the brown sugar. Bring to bubbling. It is important to bring canned goods to a boil to kill any bacteria. This chili freezes well.

CORN DOGS

Ingredients for 6 servings

1/4 cup	Flour, all-purpose
1/2 cup	Meal, plain
1	Egg
3 tsp	Baking powder
1/2 cup	Milk
	Salt
6	Wieners, beef or other, if preferred

Boil wieners; blot dry. Mix the batter ingredients. Dip the cooked wieners in the batter and drop into deep, hot oil until brown.

LASAGNA

Ingredients for 8 servings

1 1/2 lb	Ground beef [chuck]
32 oz	Spaghetti sauce [thick]
1 1/2 cup	Water [rinse out sauce jar]
2 cups	Ricotta cheese
3 cups	Mozzarella cheese, shredded
1 cup	Cheddar cheese, shredded
1/2 cup	Parmesan cheese, grated
2 lg	Eggs
1 tsp	Salt
1/4 tsp	Pepper
1 tsp	Italian seasoning, optional
8 oz	Lasagna noodles, uncooked

Brown the ground beef in a large [3 quart] heavy saucepan. Drain. Add the sauce and water. Simmer for 10 minutes. Mix the rest of the ingredients [except for the noodles] in a bowl. Spread 1 cup of the sauce into a 9x13-inch baking dish. Layer 3 uncooked noodles over the sauce. Cover with 1 1/2 cups of the sauce. Spread half of the cheese mixture over the sauce. Repeat the layers of the noodles, sauce, and the cheese mixture. Top with a layer of noodles and then the remaining sauce. Cover and seal with aluminum foil. Bake in a 350-degree oven for 60 minutes. Remove the foil and bake an additional 10 minutes. Let the lasagna rest for 10 minutes after removing from the oven before cutting.

LIVER AND ONIONS

Ingredients for 6 servings

1 lb	Calf liver
1 med	Onion [I like white]
1 1/2 cups	Flour, self-rising [more or less]
	Salt
	Pepper
	Oil

Peel and slice the onion into 1/4-inch slices. Trim any membrane from the liver. Sprinkle with salt and pepper. Roll the liver in the flour until it is completely covered. Fry it in the hot oil until brown [this step takes only a minute or so for each side]. Remove from the oil and place on a paper towel-lined plate. Pour off the excess oil, leaving a little to just cover the bottom of the skillet. Place the slices of onion into the skillet and brown on both sides, turning with a spatula. Remove the onion slices and sprinkle about 3 full tablespoons of flour into the skillet and brown lightly, stirring with the spatula. [I use some of the same flour.] Add water slowly while stirring. [I put water into the bowl where I salt the liver and I use this.] After the flour and water have turned into gravy, place the liver back into the skillet and place the onions on top. Simmer a few minutes, adding a little water if needed, to let all of the flavors blend. Add salt and pepper to the gravy during the last step, if desired.

People either love or hate liver. My husband, Truman, loves it. I, on the other hand, do not.

ROSALIND'S MEATLOAF

Ingredients for 8 servings

1 1/2 lbs	Ground beef
6	Slices of day-old bread
1	Egg, lightly beaten
1 tsp	Salt
1/2 tsp	Pepper
1/2 cup	Finely chopped onion
14 1/2 oz	Tomato sauce [can]
2 tbsp	Brown sugar
2 tbsp	Vinegar
1 tbsp	Mustard
1/2 cup	Water

Soak the bread in water and squeeze out excess moisture. Combine the bread, meat, egg, seasonings, onion, and 1/2 can of tomato sauce…mixing well. Shape the meat into a loaf in a baking dish. Combine the remaining tomato sauce, brown sugar, vinegar, mustard, and water. Mix well. Pour the sauce over meat loaf. Bake in a 350-degree oven for 1 hour, basting occasionally.

Let red meat rest for 10 to 15 minutes after cooking before slicing. The meat juices can be absorbed by the meat, and the meat will lose less of its juices.

REBECCA AND TRUMAN'S FAVORITE MEXICAN PIZZAS [THANKS, LAURA]

Ingredients for 6 servings

1 lb	Ground beef, cooked and drained
3/4 cup	Water
1 pkg	Taco mix
1 can	Refried beans
1 can	Ro-Tel or tomatoes
2 cups	Nacho/taco-blend cheese, shredded
	Tostadas
	Optional: sour cream, shredded lettuce, sliced olives [ripe or green], sliced green onions, chopped cilantro, avocado slices

Add the water, Ro-Tel, and taco mix to the cooked and drained ground beef. Cook over medium heat and bring to a boil. Reduce the heat, stirring occasionally, and cook until thickened [5–6 minutes]. Spread the refried beans on each tostada shell. Top with the meat mixture and then some of the cheese. Place in the oven and broil a couple of minutes or until the cheese is melted.

MARINATED EYE-OF-ROUND ROAST

Ingredients for 6 servings

3 lbs	Roast [eye-of-round]
1/4 cup	Soy sauce
1 cup	Orange juice
2 tbsp	Red wine vinegar
	Salt
	Pepper

Combine soy sauce, orange juice, and vinegar. Pour over the meat, cover, and refrigerate overnight, basting and turning the meat in the marinade several times. Drain, saving the marinade. Place the roast in a small roasting pan. Sprinkle with salt and pepper. Roast uncovered at 375 degrees until the roast begins to brown [about 30 minutes]. Pour half of the marinade over the meat and cover. Lower the temperature to 350 degrees and cook until tender [about 2 1/2–3 hours]. Baste occasionally. The remaining marinade can be used to sauté fresh, sliced mushrooms…or it can be thickened with some flour to make a sauce to be served over white rice.

I have known a butcher who would slice the roast and tie it back together with butcher's cord so that when the roast is done, slices are perfect.

BEEF STROGANOFF

Ingredients for 8 servings

3 cups	Leftover Roast Beef, cubed
1/2 stick	Butter
1	Onion, chopped
1 can	Cream of chicken soup [10 3/4 oz]
1 can	Water
8 oz	Sliced water chestnuts, drained and rinsed
3 oz	Mushrooms [can], drained
2 tbsp	Flour
1/4 cup	Wine or chicken broth
8 oz	Sour cream
	Salt

Sauté onion in butter until translucent. Stir in flour and blend. Mix the soup and water. Add to onion. Add the mushrooms and water chestnuts to soup/onion mixture. Add the wine and cubed roast beef. Cover and simmer for 20 minutes. Add sour cream [and salt, if needed]. Serve over cooked white rice or noodles.

If preferred, 1 1/2 lbs of lean ground beef, browned and drained, can be used.

ROSALIND'S ROAST BEEF

Ingredients for 8 servings

3 lbs	Eye-of-round or shoulder roast
1 pkg	Dry onion [or beefy onion] soup mix
	Salt
	Pepper
1 jar	Sliced mushrooms, optional

Place the roast in a deep baking dish with 1 inch of water. Sprinkle with a package of beefy-onion soup mix. Sprinkle with a little salt and pepper. [The soup mix is salty, so be careful adding salt.] Cover with foil or a lid. Bake in a 350–400-degree oven until fork tender. Drain a jar of mushrooms and place them in the juices. Mix 2 tablespoons of flour with a cup of water to make a roux, mixing until there are no more lumps. Add the roux to the water in the dish and stir slightly. Adjust the salt and pepper, if needed. Bake uncovered for 30 minutes or until the flour water turns to gravy.

Helpful hint: You may want to turn the roast over for the last 30 minutes of cooking. Be careful! It's hot.

ROSALIND'S PRIME RIB

Ingredients for 8 servings

4 lbs	Beef tenderloin	10 oz	Beef consommé
3 tbsp	Butter,	1 med	Rosemary sprig
	room temperature	1 bunch	Lemon thyme
	Salt	1	Bay leaf
	Black pepper,	10	Black peppercorns
	freshly ground	1 clove	Garlic [optional]
	Garlic salt	1 tbsp	Cornstarch
	with parsley	1 tbsp	Wine [red or white]
	AU JUS		Trimmings from
14 oz	Beef stock or broth		tenderloin

Pat the beef dry with a paper towel and place it into a baking pan. Spread the butter over the beef and season with the salt and pepper. Place the meat in a 450-degree oven. Bake about 25 minutes for rare, 35 minutes for medium rare, and 55 minutes for medium well. For a more accurate timing, I recommend using a meat thermometer. Remove the meat from the oven and place a sheet of foil over the top and let it rest for 20 minutes before slicing.

AU JUS: Place the broths, herbs, peppercorns, and meat trimmings in a saucepan and cook for an hour or more. Add the wine and boil. Strain the juices and place them back into the saucepan. Spoon a little of the juice over the cornstarch and stir until smooth. Add the mixture to the au jus and boil for 15 minutes. Serve over the slices of meat or serve at the table in a bowl with a gravy spoon.

Helpful hint: If desired, instead of the garlic salt rub the meat with a little fresh garlic before rubbing with the butter.

Beverages

BLOODY MARY

Ingredients for 10 servings

46 oz	V8 juice
2 tbsp	Lemon juice
1 tsp	Black pepper
1 tsp	Celery salt
1 tbsp	Worcestershire sauce
10 oz	Vodka
6 dashes	Hot sauce
2 lg	Celery stalks

Pour the juice into a pitcher. Add the seasonings and stir well. Trim the celery sticks, cut in half, and slice lengthwise. Pour Bloody Mary mixture over ice in a glass. Place a celery stick in each glass to garnish and to use as a stirrer.

CHAMPAGNE PUNCH [ROSALIND'S]

Ingredients for 54 servings

4 qts	Champagne
12 oz	Orange juice, undiluted [2 cans, 6 oz each]
6 oz	Limeade, undiluted [6 oz can]
1 qt	Soda
1 qt	Seven-Up
1 cup	Apricot brandy

Chill all ingredients and mix in a large container. Keep in the refrigerator. A frozen mold can be made with additional orange juice or limeade and placed in punch bowl with the punch.

Helpful hint: Do not place ice mold in an empty glass punch bowl...bowl will crack.

MOCK CHAMPAGNE PUNCH

Ingredients for 24 servings

2 qts	Apple juice
2 qts	Ginger ale
3	Sparkling grape juice [bottles]

Mix equal parts of the ingredients together and serve cold. Make ice molds of extra apple juice or white grape juice.

MOCK PINK CHAMPAGNE

Ingredients for 14 servings

1/2 cup	Sugar
1 1/2 cups	Water
2 cups	Cranberry juice
1 cup	Pineapple juice
1/2 cup	Orange juice
14 oz	Lemon-lime carbonated beverage [bottle]

Boil the sugar in the water until the sugar dissolves. Cool. Stir in the pineapple, orange, and cranberry juices and chill. Add the carbonated beverage just before serving.

COCOA MIX

Ingredients for 15 servings

2 cups	Powdered milk
1/4 cup	Cocoa
1 cup	Confectioners' sugar
1 pinch	Salt

Whisk all of the ingredients together and store in an airtight container. Stir 4 tablespoons of the mixture and 1 cup of boiling water together. Top with a marshmallow or a dollop of whipped cream.

NO EGG EGGNOG

Ingredients for 40 servings

2 gal	Eggnog ice cream
2 qts	Dairy eggnog
2 cups	Bourbon
13 1/2 oz	Cool Whip
	Nutmeg, grated

Put the eggnog and bourbon in the punch bowl. Add the Cool Whip and stir. Add the ice cream. Sprinkle nutmeg over the top.

Helpful hint: The bourbon can be chilled also.

IRISH COFFEE

Ingredients for 4 servings

1 1/3 cups	Coffee, hot
1 1/3 cups	Whiskey
1 1/3 cups	Whipped cream, lightly sweetened
	Cocoa powder, optional

Divide the hot coffee [1/3 cup each] into 4 tall cups. Add 1/3 cup of whiskey to each cup of coffee and mix. Top each cup with 1/4 of the whipped cream and sprinkle a little cocoa powder over the cream, if desired.

COFFEE PUNCH

Ingredients for 70 cups

1 cup	Instant coffee [dry]
3 qts	Boiling water
1/2 cup	Chocolate syrup
1 cup	Sugar
2 tbsp	Rum flavoring
2 qts	Milk
1 gal	Vanilla ice cream

Pour 2 1/2 quarts of boiling water over coffee and stir. Add the other pint of boiling water to the chocolate syrup and sugar. Bring the sugar and syrup to a boil and cook for 2 minutes. Add to hot coffee and cool. Refrigerate at this point. Before serving, add the rum flavoring and milk. Put a little punch into the punch bowl and break the ice cream into small pieces in the bowl. Pour the punch over the ice cream. This punch is great to serve at a morning party.

GREEN LIZARDS

Ingredients for 6 persons

6 oz	Limeade
6 oz	Bourbon
2 drops	Green food coloring
	Crushed ice

Place the limeade into an electric blender. Add a can of bourbon and a couple of drops of green food coloring. Add enough crushed ice to finish filling the blender. Cover and pulse until the ingredients are the consistency of a slushy.

HOLIDAY PUNCH

Ingredients for 15 servings

2 qts	Eggnog [in the dairy case]
28 oz	Ginger ale [bottle]
6 oz	Frozen orange juice, undiluted and slightly thawed

Mix all of the chilled ingredients together in a medium-size punch bowl.

LEMONADE

Ingredients for 4 servings

2 cups	Water
1 cup	Sugar
3 cups	Ice [approximately 18 cubes]
1 cup	Lemon juice [approximately juice from 8 lemons]

Stir sugar and water in a saucepan over low heat. After sugar completely dissolved, remove from heat and stir in the ice. Stir in the lemon juice last. Serve in a tall glass over ice. Garnish with a lemon slice or a sprig of mint.

CHAMPAGNE LEMONADE

Ingredients for 8 servings

1 cup	Sugar
3 cups	Water
1 1/2 cups	Lemon juice, freshly squeezed
1 bottle	Champagne or sparkling wine
8 thin	Lemon slices or cherries with stems

Put the sugar and one cup of water into a small saucepan. Bring the mixture to a boil and continue to boil for 1 minute or until the sugar is dissolved. Remove from the heat and let the mixture cool. Mix the cooled mixture with the lemon juice and 2 cups of water in a pitcher. Mix well. Fill a champagne flute halfway with the lemonade and top with champagne. Garnish with a lemon slice or a stemmed cherry.

LIME SHERBET PUNCH

Ingredients for 20 servings

2 qts	Lime sherbet
2 liters	Ginger ale
46 oz	Pineapple juice [can]
	Maraschino cherries, optional

Place the ginger ale, pineapple juice, and sherbet in a punch bowl. Place a cherry in each punch cup for added color.

MARGARITAS

Ingredients for 6 servings

1/2 cup	Lime juice, fresh [approximately 5 limes]
1	Lime, halved
2 tbsp	Lemon juice, fresh
1 cup	Triple Sec
1 cup	Tequila, white
2 cups	Ice [extra for serving, if desired]
1 dish	Salt

Combine the lime juice, lemon juice, tequila, Triple Sec, and ice in a blender and puree. Pour over extra ice in a shaker. Shake well. Rub the cut lime around the rim of the serving glasses and dip them into the plate of salt. Strain the margarita mix into the glasses.

VANILLA MILKSHAKE

Ingredients for 4 servings

1 qt	Vanilla ice cream
8 tbsp	Sugar
2 tsp	Vanilla
2 cups	Milk

Mix all of the ingredients in a blender until smooth. Serve in tall glasses.

Variation: Put 1 quart coffee ice cream into a blender with 20 ice cubes and 2 cups of half and half. Blend the milk, ice cubes, and ice cream together and serve in a tall glass with a straw. Top the shake with a teaspoon of chocolate syrup.

When you drop a lemon slice in your tea, push a small clove into the peel for a wonderful flavor addition.

MINT JULEP

Ingredients for 40 servings

2 cups	Sugar
2 cups	Water
	Fresh mint springs
	Bourbon
	Crushed ice

Boil the water and sugar together for 5 minutes, making a simple syrup. Cool. Place the simple syrup in a glass jar with 6 or 8 mint sprigs and put the lid on the jar. Refrigerate overnight. To make the julep, fill a glass with crushed ice and add 1 tablespoon of mint syrup and 2 ounces of bourbon. Stir rapidly to frost the outside of the glass. Garnish with a sprig of mint.

PUNCH FOR 300

Ingredients for 300 servings

30 pks	Kool-Aid
27 cups	Sugar
3 lg	Frozen orange juice [12 oz each], undiluted
3 sm	Frozen lemonade, undiluted
3 qts	Pineapple juice
3 qts	Ginger ale
7 1/2 gal	Water

Mix all of the ingredients together. Chill for 12 hours before serving. Ice molds can be made a couple of days in advance with extra pineapple juice.

Helpful hint: NEVER put an ice mold into a glass punch bowl without first putting some of the punch in first. The glass bowl will crack from the cold ice.

MOCHA PUNCH

Ingredients for 45 cups

1 1/2 qts	Water
1/2 cup	Chocolate drink mix [powdered, any brand]
1/2 cup	Sugar
1/4 cup	Instant coffee granules
1/2 gal	Vanilla ice cream
1/2 gal	Chocolate ice cream
1 cup	Whipping cream, whipped and slightly sweetened
	Chocolate curls, optional

Bring the water to a boil in a large saucepan. Remove from the heat and add the drink mix, sugar, and coffee. Stir until dissolved. Cover and refrigerate for 4 hours or overnight. Pour into a punch bowl about 30 minutes before serving. Add the ice cream by scoopfuls. Stir until partially melted. Garnish individual servings with a dollop of whipped cream and chocolate curls.

INSTANT RUSSIAN TEA, CAIRO STYLE

Ingredients for 36 servings

2 cups	Tang
2 pkg	Lemonade mix [or orange Jell-O]
1/2 cup	Instant tea
2 1/2 cups	Sugar [2 cups if using sweetened lemonade]
2 tsp	Cinnamon, ground
1 tsp	Cloves, ground

Mix all of the ingredients together and store in an airtight container. Use 3 [or more] teaspoons per cup of boiling water.

Helpful hint: Try this on a cold day or if you have a scratchy throat.

WHISKEY SOURS

Ingredients for 4 servings

2/3 cup	Sugar
2/3 cup	Water
1/2 cup	Lemon juice, freshly squeezed and strained [4 lemons]
1/2 cup	Lime juice, freshly squeezed and strained [4 limes]
3/4 cup	Whiskey [Jack Daniel's]
	Maraschino cherries
	Ice cubes

In a small pan, bring the sugar and water to a boil. Cool. Combine the whiskey and juices. Add the cooled syrup. Fill a cocktail shaker half full with ice cubes. Pour the whiskey mixture over the ice until shaker is 2/3 full. Shake for about 15 seconds and pour into glasses. Add a maraschino cherry and serve cold.

Helpful hint: Equal amounts of sugar and water is called Simple syrup. Simple syrup is used in pharmacy as a base for liquid preparations.

Breads

BREAKFAST BISCUITS

Ingredients for 3 dozen

5 cups	Self-rising flour
1 pkg	Yeast
2 tsp	Sugar
1/4 cup	Warm water [110–115 degrees]
2 cups	Buttermilk
1 tsp	Soda
1 cup	Vegetable oil
	Melted butter

Dissolve the yeast and sugar in the warm water and set aside. Combine the flour, soda, yeast mixture, buttermilk, and oil in a large bowl and blend well. Roll on a floured surface to 1-inch or 1-1/2-inch thickness. Cut the dough with a 2-1/2- to 3-inch biscuit cutter. Place the biscuits on an oiled cookie sheet. Brush the tops with melted butter. Bake in a 400-degree oven for 12 minutes or until lightly brown and done. Leftover dough may be stored in a tightly-covered bowl in the refrigerator for a few days.

ROSALIND'S BUTTERMILK BISCUITS

Ingredients for 10 biscuits

2 cups	Self-rising flour
1 1/2 cups	Buttermilk
1 tbsp	Cooking oil
1 stick	Butter

Heat a large black skillet in a 375-degree oven. Mix the flour, buttermilk, and oil together. Melt the stick of butter in the hot skillet and drop the batter into the hot skillet immediately with a tablespoon or an ice cream scoop. Bake in a 375-degree oven until done.

EASY CHEESE BISCUITS

Ingredients for 12 biscuits

1 cup	Self-rising flour
2 tbsp	Mayonnaise
1/2 cup	Buttermilk
3/4 cup	Cheddar cheese, grated

Mix of all the ingredients together. Drop by spoonfuls onto an oiled pan [I use a black iron skillet]. Bake in a 350-degree oven for 20–25 minutes, or until lightly brown.

ROSEMARY AND WHITE CHEDDAR WAFERS

Ingredients for 2 dozens

8 oz	White cheddar cheese [Cabot], grated
1 stick	Butter, room temperature
2 cups	Flour, all-purpose
2 tsp	Rosemary [fresh], chopped fine
1/4 tsp	Salt
1/4 tsp	Pepper, freshly ground

Cream the butter and cheese together until smooth. Whisk the dry ingredients together. Gradually add the dry ingredients to the butter and cheese, beating until the mixture is smooth. Halve the mixture and roll into 2 logs. Wrap in plastic wrap. At this point, cut an empty paper towel cardboard roll up one side. Place the wrapped dough inside and secure with a heavy rubber band. Freeze. Slice 1/4 rounds, place on a baking sheet, and bake in a 350-degree oven for 20–25 minutes [or until golden brown]. For a biscuit-like wafer, add 1/2 teaspoon of baking powder to the flour mixture.

CHEESE WAFERS

Ingredients for 3 dozens

2 cups	Flour, all-purpose
2 cups	Sharp cheddar cheese [grated]
2 sticks	Butter, room temperature
2 cups	Rice Krispies
1/2 tsp	Salt
1/2 tsp	Red pepper [ground]
1/2 tsp	Paprika

Whisk the dry ingredients together. Mix all of the ingredients together. Roll the dough out into logs and wrap in plastic wrap. Chill until firm. Slice into disks, place them onto ungreased cookie sheets, and bake in a 325-degree oven about 30 minutes [or until the wafers can be removed with a spatula easily]. The dough can be rolled into small balls and pressed onto cookie sheets and baked, also. This wafer is great served with a salad or as an appetizer with wine.

CHIVE BISCUITS

Ingredients for 8 biscuits

2 cups	Flour, all-purpose
1 tbsp	Baking powder
1 stick	Cold butter, cubed small
3/4 cup	Half and half
1 tsp	Sugar
1 tsp	Salt
1/2 cup	Chopped chives [fresh]
1	Egg
1 tbsp	Water

Whisk together the flour, baking powder, salt, and sugar. Mix the butter and flour mixture together with the paddle attachment. Mix on low speed until the butter is the size of small peas. While mixing on low speed, add the half and half. Beat until just mixed. Add the chives and fold in until just combined. Knead the dough on a well-floured surface. Roll out into a rectangle until 3/4 inch thick. Cut with a 2-inch or 2-1/2-inch biscuit cutter. Place on a cookie sheet lined with parchment paper. Beat the egg and water lightly and brush each biscuit with the wash. Bake in a 350-degree oven for 20 minutes or until lightly browned on top. Serve warm.

Helpful hint: Chopped fresh parsley leaves or Parmesan cheese may be substituted for the chives.

BUTTERED BISCUITS

Ingredients for 36

2 cups	Self-rising flour
2 sticks	Butter
8 oz	Sour cream

Melt the butter and mix it with the flour. Add the sour cream and mix. Drop the batter into very lightly greased miniature muffin tins. Bake for 20 minutes at 375 degrees.

CHEESE BISCUITS

Ingredients for 4 dozen

Ingredients are the same as CHEESE STRAWS

Make according to CHEESE STRAWS recipe. Roll 1/3 of mixture in a piece of plastic wrap. Lightly roll plastic wrap on a hard surface until evenly distributed. Twist ends of plastic wrap and place in refrigerator. Repeat the procedure. Chill overnight or for several days. Remove when ready to bake and slice in desired thickness. Bake on a cookie sheet at 325 degrees for approximately 20 minutes. These are good as a snack or served with a salad. Before slicing, the chilled dough can be rolled in finely-chopped pecans or sesame seeds for an added touch.

Helpful hint: Save empty paper towel rolls, cut down one side, and place rolls of wrapped dough inside. This prevents the rolls from having a flat side.

For variation, add 1 cup of finely chopped nuts to the batter or 1/4 cup of sesame seeds.

MAYONNAISE DROP BISCUITS

Ingredients for 12

2 cups	Self-rising flour
1 cup	Milk
1/2 cup	Mayonnaise [or 4 heaping tablespoons]

Combine all of the ingredients, mixing well. Drop into greased muffin pans. Bake in a preheated 400-degree oven for 12–15 minutes. Optional: May add 1 teaspoon of sugar.

SOUR CREAM BISCUITS

Ingredients for 36

2 cups	Bisquick
1 stick	Butter
8 oz	Sour cream

Mix Bisquick and sour cream. Melt the butter and add it to the batter. Fill greased miniature muffin tins 3/4 full. Bake in a 400-degree oven for 10 minutes.

SWEET POTATO BISCUITS

Ingredients for 2 dozen

5 cups	Flour, all-purpose
1 cup	Brown sugar, packed
2 tbsp	Baking powder
1 1/2 tsp	Cinnamon, ground
1 tsp	Salt
1 tsp	Ginger, ground
1/2 tsp	Allspice, ground
1 cup	Vegetable shortening
1 cup	Cream, whipping
1/2 cup	Pecans, chopped
1 can	Sweet potatoes, mashed or strained

Stir together the flour, brown sugar, baking powder, cinnamon, salt, ginger, and allspice. Add the shortening and cut with a pastry cutter until crumbly. Add the sweet potatoes and mix well with a large spoon. Add the cream and the pecans. Stir until just moistened. Turn the dough out onto a lightly-floured surface and roll to 1 1/2 inches thick. Cut out biscuits with a 2-inch biscuit cutter. Place biscuits 1 inch apart on a baking sheet. Bake in a 350-degree oven for 25–30 minutes or until golden brown. Serve warm or at room temperature.

Helpful hint: The unbaked biscuits can be frozen between layers of wax paper for two or three months. Thaw and bake.

Two knives can be used instead of a pastry cutter.

BISCUIT BREAD

Ingredients for 8 servings

1 cup	Flour, self-rising
1 cup	Buttermilk
1/2 stick	Butter

Put the butter into a black iron skillet. Place the skillet into a 375-degree oven and let the skillet get hot while the butter melts. [The temperature may vary in different ovens.] Whisk the flour and milk together until blended. Pour the mixture into the hot skillet. [The batter should sizzle a little when poured into the skillet.] Bake until the bread is golden brown on top.

Helpful hint: This recipe is easily doubled.

BLEU CHEESE CRACKERS

Ingredients for 2 dozen

1 stick	Butter, room temperature
8 oz	Bleu cheese
1 1/2 cups	Flour, all-purpose
1 tbsp	Water
1 tsp	Ground peppercorns
1 tsp	Salt
1/2 cup	Chopped walnuts
1 lg	Egg mixed with 2 teaspoons of water

Whisk the flour, salt, and pepper together in a small bowl. Mix the butter and bleu cheese together until smooth and creamy, about 1 minute with an electric mixer. Add the flour mixture, beating for about a minute on low speed. Add 1 tablespoon of water and mix until just combined. Using hands, shape and roll the dough into a long log, dusting with a little flour if needed. Brush the log with the egg wash, covering the log completely, and roll it in the chopped walnuts. Cut the log into 2 pieces and place them on plastic wrap. [I use empty paper towel rolls to hold the plastic-wrapped logs.] Cut the paper towel rolls lengthwise. Place the plastic-wrapped dough into the rolls and secure them with rubber bands. Chill the rolls in the refrigerator for several hours or for several days. Slice the logs into rounds with a thin, sharp knife. [The number of crackers depend on how thick they are sliced. Results may be 2 or 3 dozen.] Place the rounds on a parchment-lined baking sheet and bake in a 350-degree oven until lightly browned, about 22 minutes. Cool completely and keep in an airtight container. Serve with salads or as an appetizer.

BLUEBERRY BREAD

Ingredients for 12 servings

3 cups	Flour, all-purpose
1 tsp	Baking soda
1 tsp	Salt
2 tbsp	Cinnamon
1 1/4 cups	Sugar
1 1/2 cups	Vegetable oil
4	Eggs, beaten
1/4 cup	Water
2 cups	Blueberries

Grease 2 loaf pans. Set aside. Combine the first five ingredients and mix well. Add the remaining ingredients to the flour mixture and stir until moist. Pour half of the batter into each pan. Bake in a 350-degree oven for 60 minutes or until done. Cool in the pans. Slice and serve.

CHEW BREAD

Ingredients for 24 bars

3/4 cup	Butter, melted [1 1/2 sticks]
1 box	Light brown sugar
3 lg	Eggs
2 cups	Flour, self-rising
1 tsp	Vanilla
2 cups	Pecans, chopped

Mix the butter, sugar, and eggs [adding the eggs one at a time]. Add the flour and vanilla, mix. Add the nuts last and mix. Pour into an oiled 9x13-inch pan or baking dish. Bake in a 325-degree oven until brown, about 45 minutes. Cut into squares.

ROSALIND'S TOASTED BREAD

Ingredients for 10 servings

1 loaf	Italian bread
1/2 stick	Butter, softened
	Garlic salt with parsley
	Shredded Parmesan cheese

Slice the Italian bread into 3/4-inch sections. Spread softened butter evenly over the bread slices. Sprinkle a little of the garlic salt over the butter. Sprinkle shredded Parmesan cheese over the salt. Place the bread into a 350-degree oven and immediately turn the oven to broil. Toast the bread until the edges turn a golden brown. Serve while hot.

Helpful hint: This bread is great served with steaks.

EASY CORN BREAD

Ingredients for 8 servings

1 1/4 cups	Cornmeal, self-rising
1 lg	Egg
1 cup	Buttermilk
3 tbsp	Oil
1 tbsp	Sugar [optional]
	Oil for black skillet

Lightly beat the egg with a fork. Mix the egg with the cornmeal, buttermilk, and 3 tablespoons of oil. Place 2 or 3 tablespoons of additional oil in a black skillet. Place the skillet in the oven and preheat the oven to 400 degrees. Pour the batter into the hot skillet. Bake for 30 minutes or until done and is golden brown on top.

FRIED CORN BREAD

Ingredients for 8 servings

1 1/2 cups	Meal, all-purpose
4 tbsp	Flour, self-rising
1 tsp	Salt
1 tbsp	Sugar
1 1/4 cups	Water
3 tbsp	Crisco
	Extra water and oil, if necessary

Mix the first 5 ingredients together, adding enough water to make the batter soupy. Put 2 tablespoons of oil into a hot skillet. Add a small amount of batter to the very hot oil. Turn the bread once when it has browned [air bubbles will appear throughout the bread when ready to turn]. Repeat the procedure, adding more water or oil if needed. Drain on paper towels.

SOUR CREAM CORN BREAD

Ingredients for 1

1 cup	Self-rising cornmeal
2	Eggs, slightly beaten
1/2 cup	Cooking oil [or 1 stick of butter]
1/2 cup	Cream-style corn [or 4 oz can]
1 cup	Sour cream
1/2	Medium onion, grated [optional]

Mix all ingredients together except for the sour cream. Fold sour cream into the mixture and mix well. Heat a well-oiled 10-inch iron skillet in the oven while mixing the ingredients. Pour mixture into the hot skillet. It should sizzle when it is poured into the skillet. This helps to form a crust. Bake in a preheated 450-degree oven for 15 or 20 minutes. [If that is too hot, reduce heat to 375 degrees.]

CRACKLIN' BREAD [OLD SOUTH]

Ingredients for 8 servings

1 cup	Cornmeal
1/2 cup	Flour
1/4 cup	Sugar
2 tsp	Baking powder
1/4 cup	Salt
3/4 cup	Milk
1 lg	Egg, beaten with a fork
1/2 cup	Cracklings
1/4 cup	Shortening [solid], melted

Combine the cornmeal, flour, sugar, baking powder, and salt in a bowl. Add the egg to the milk and gradually incorporate with the dry ingredients, mixing well. Stir in the melted shortening. Fold in the cracklings. Spread an 8-inch square baking pan with some solid shortening. Pour the mixture into the pan and bake in a 400-degree oven for 25–30 minutes.

Helpful hint: This recipe is not for everyone. Cracklings are like collards. You either like them or hate them.

PARMESAN CRACKERS

Ingredients for 2 dozens

3 oz	Parmesan cheese, grated
1 stick	Butter, softened
1 1/4 cups	Flour, all purpose
3/4 tsp	Freshly ground black pepper [more or less, according to taste]
1 tsp	Fresh thyme leaves, chopped

Mix the butter until creamy. Add the grated cheese and mix. Add the remaining ingredients and mix well. Form the dough into a log. Roll the mixture on a smooth surface. Press and roll until the log is about 12 inches long. Wrap in plastic wrap and place in the refrigerator for several hours or overnight. Cut the log into 1/4- to 1/2-inch slices and place on a baking sheet. Bake in a 350-degree oven for 22 minutes. To make the crackers more crisp, turn the heat off and let them remain in the oven for another 45 minutes.

Helpful hint: If unsalted butter is used, add 1/4 teaspoon of salt.

HUSH PUPPIES

Ingredients for 1 dozen

1/2 cup	Cornmeal, not self-rising
1/2 cup	Flour, all-purpose
1 tsp	Baking powder
1 pinch	Baking soda
1/4 tsp	Salt
1 tbsp	Sugar
1 lg	Egg, lightly beaten with a fork
1/2 cup	Buttermilk
1 1/2 tsp	Vegetable oil
1 med	Yellow onion, chopped
	Oil for frying

Dissolve the baking soda in the buttermilk. Whisk or mix the remaining dry ingredients together in a mixing bowl. Mix in the buttermilk, egg, and vegetable oil. Add the chopped onion. Drop small spoonfuls of the batter in hot oil deep enough for them to float when they are brown and done.

Helpful hint: Truman likes to fry hush puppies in logs rather than rounds. This method seems to cook them more evenly.

QUICKY STICKY BUNS

Ingredients for 9 portions

3 tbsp	Brown sugar, divided
1/4 cup	Karo syrup, light or dark
1/4 cup	Coarsely chopped pecans
2 tbsp	Butter, divided in half and softened
1 tsp	Cinnamon
1 can	Crescent dinner rolls [from the dairy case]

In a small bowl, combine 2 tablespoons of brown sugar, the corn syrup, the pecans, and 1 tablespoon of the butter. Spoon about 2 teaspoons of the mixture into each 2-1/2-inch muffin pan cups [9] which have been sprayed with Pam. Unroll entire crescent roll dough and pinch all seams together to form 1 rectangle. Combine remaining 1 tablespoon of sugar and the cinnamon. Spread dough with the remaining 1 tablespoon of butter and then sprinkle the cinnamon/sugar mixture over all. Roll up from the short end. Cut into 9 slices and place a slice into each cup. Bake in a preheated 350-degree oven for 25 minutes or until golden brown. Immediately invert onto a cookie sheet or tray. When cool, they will not turn out of cups. Cool 10 minutes.

APPLE MUFFINS

Ingredients for 3 dozen

2 lg	Apples [Granny Smith or apples of choice], peeled and grated
2 sticks	Butter
1 1/2 cups	Raisins
1 cup	Water
2 tsp	Cinnamon
2 tsp	Nutmeg
1/2 tsp	Cloves
2 cups	Sugar
3 1/2 cups	Flour, all-purpose
1 pinch	Salt
2 tsp	Baking soda
1 cup	Chopped walnuts

Boil the first 8 ingredients together in a heavy saucepan for 15 minutes. Cool. Whisk the flour, baking soda, and salt together. Combine the two mixtures, add the walnuts, and mix. Spray or oil miniature muffin pans. Fill the muffin cups almost to the top [using a small ice cream scoop]. Bake in a 350-degree oven for 15 minutes or until brown.

POPPY SEED MUFFINS

Ingredients for 1 dozen

1 1/2 cups	Bisquick
1/2 cup	Sugar
1 tbsp	Poppy seed
3/4 cup	Sour cream
1 lg	Egg, beaten
1 tsp	Vanilla

In a bowl, whisk together the Bisquick, sugar, and poppy seed. Add the egg, sour cream, and vanilla. Stir. Drop the batter into oiled muffin tins. Bake in a 375-degree oven for 15–20 minutes, or until golden brown.

SOUR CREAM MUFFINS

Ingredients for 10 servings

Stick	Butter, melted
8 oz	Sour cream
1 cup	Self-rising flour

Mix all ingredients well. Fill oiled muffin tins 2/3 full. Bake in a 400-degree oven for 20–25 minutes. Let muffins rest for 2 or 3 minutes and remove from tins.

EASY HERB AND BUTTERED ROLLS

Ingredients for 2 dozen

12	Frozen rolls, halved
2 tbsp	Onion flakes [in spice section]
2 tbsp	Garlic salt with parsley
1/3 cup	Butter, melted

Mix the melted butter and onion flakes. Dip each roll in the mixture and place in a baking pan. Sprinkle well with the garlic and parsley salt. Cover loosely with plastic wrap and let rise until at least doubled in size. Bake in a 350-degree oven for 25–30 minutes or until golden brown.

HERB ROLLS

Ingredients for 40 rolls

1 pkg	Buttermilk biscuits [in the dairy case]
1/4 cup	Butter [1/2 stick], melted
1/2 tsp	Dill weed
1/2 tsp	Minced onion [bottled in the spice section]
1 1/2 tsp	Parsley flakes

Blend the melted butter, parsley, dill, and onion together and pour into a 9-inch pie pan. Cut the biscuits into quarters and swish each one in the melted mixture. Arrange the pieces in the pie pan [they will be touching]. Bake in a 400-degree oven for 12–15 minutes or until brown. After removing from the oven, let stand for a few minutes to absorb the seasonings. Pretty and nice for luncheons or buffet dinners.

SAUSAGE AND CHEESE MUFFINS

Ingredients for 2 dozen

1 lb	Hot sausage [bulk]
10 1/2 oz	Campbell's cheddar cheese soup [can]
3/4 can	Water
3 cups	Bisquick

Cook sausage until brown, drain, and set aside. In a bowl, whisk the soup and water until blended. Add the Bisquick and mix well. Stir in the sausage. Drop the batter [should be a sticky consistency] into sprayed or greased muffin pans. Bake in a 350-degree oven for 25 minutes or until lightly browned on top. These muffins freeze well. Reheat in the microwave or foil wrapped in an oven. These are great served as an appetizer [small muffin pans] or served at a morning party.

Helpful hint: Use only the recommended brands for best results.

STIR AND DROP ROLLS

Ingredients for 48 rolls

1 pkg	Yeast
1 cup	Warm water
4 tbsp	Sugar
1 tsp	Salt
1	Egg, room temperature
3 cups	Flour [all-purpose], sifted
4 tbsp	Salad oil

In a bowl, dissolve the yeast in warm water. Add the next 3 ingredients and stir to mix well. Add the oil and half of the flour to the mixture and stir. Add the remaining flour and blend. Set the dough in a warm place, cover, and let rise for 30 minutes. Stir down. Using a spoon, drop dough into greased, small muffin tins. Tins should be half full. Let rise again until doubled in size. Bake in a 400-degree oven for 10–15 minutes or until light brown.

YEAST ROLLS

Ingredients for 4 dozen

1 cup	Milk, scalded
1 cup	Water
1/2 cup	Pure vegetable oil
1/2 cup	Sugar
1 tsp	Salt
2 pkgs	Yeast
1 lg	Egg
7 1/2 cups	Flour, all-purpose

Scald the milk [heat until steam rises, but don't boil]. Add the sugar, salt, oil, and water. Beat in the egg. Add the yeast and let dissolve. Add enough flour to make a stiff dough. Cover the dough and let rise a couple of hours. Roll out the dough and cut into desired size. Place the rolls on a baking sheet and let rise again for another hour. Bake in a 350-degree oven for 20 minutes or until done.

Helpful hint for variations:
CHEESE ROLLS: Add 1 cup of grated cheese while mixing. Optional: When done, brush with 1/4 cup of melted butter mixed with 1/2 teaspoon of garlic powder.

GARLIC BREAD: Add 1 1/2 teaspoon [or to taste] of garlic powder to the flour.

OLIVE BREAD: Add 1 cup of chopped olives of your choice while mixing.

Extras

ROSALIND'S MOCK APPLE RINGS

Ingredients for 7 quarts

7 lbs	Large cucumbers, weighed before peeling and coring
1 cup	Lime
3 cups	White vinegar
1 tbsp	Alum
1 oz	Red food coloring [bottle]
2 cups	Water
5 lbs	Sugar
8	Cinnamon sticks
2 1/4 oz	Red hot candies

Peel, core, and cut the cucumbers into 1/4-inch slices [or rounds]. Mix 1 cup of lime to a gallon of water and pour over the cucumbers. Soak for 24 hours. Wash the cucumbers and rinse until the water is clear. Soak [covered] in ice water for 3 hours. Drain off the water. Mix 1 cup vinegar with 1 tablespoon of alum, bottle of red food coloring, and 1 cup of water. Pour mixture over the cucumbers and finish covering with water. Simmer for 2 hours. Pour off and throw away the liquid. Rinse the cucumbers. Mix 2 cups of vinegar, 2 cups of water, 5 pounds of sugar, cinnamon sticks, and red hot candy. Bring to a boil, boiling until the candy completely melts. Pour the liquid over the cucumber rounds. Cover and soak for 24 hours. Drain off the liquid and save. Pack the rounds in sterilized jars. Bring the saved liquid to a boil and pour over the rounds. Seal. Do not double. However, a little extra liquid may be needed.

BISCOTTI
[THANKS, GRANDDAUGHTER LAURA]

Ingredients for 1 batch

2 1/4 cups	Flour, all-purpose
1 1/2 tsp	Baking powder
3/4 tsp	Salt
3/4 stick	Unsalted butter, room temperature
3/4 cup	Sugar
2 lg	Eggs
1 tbsp	Lemon zest
1 1/2 tsp	Vanilla
1 tsp	Whole aniseed
1 cup	Dried, sweetened cranberries
3/4 cup	Pistachios [shelled, natural, and unsalted]

Line 3 large baking sheets with parchment paper. Sift the first 3 ingredients into a medium bowl. Beat the butter and sugar in a large bowl with a mixer. Beat in the eggs one at a time. Mix in the lemon zest, vanilla, and aniseed. Beat in the flour mixture until blended. Stir in the cranberries and pistachios [the dough will be sticky]. Turn the dough out onto a lightly-floured surface, gather the dough together, and divide in half. Roll each half into 15-inch-long log about 1 1/4 inches wide. Carefully transfer the logs to one prepared baking sheet, spacing 3 inches apart. Bake the logs in a 325-degree oven until almost firm to the touch but still pale, about 28 minutes. Cool logs on the baking sheet for 10 minutes. [Maintain the oven temperature.] Carefully transfer the parchment paper with the logs on it to a cutting board. Using a serrated knife and a gentle sawing motion, cut the logs crosswise into generous 1/2-inch-thick slices. Place slices, one cut-side down, onto the remaining prepared sheets. Bake until firm and pale golden, about 9 minutes per side. Transfer the cookies to racks and cool.

GRANDDAUGHTER LAURA'S CHIVE BUTTER

Ingredients for 5 ounces

1 stick	Butter, softened
4 tbsp	Chopped chives
1 tbsp	Lemon juice
	Salt
	Pepper

Cream the softened butter together until blended. Mix in the lemon juice. Season to taste. Cover and store in the refrigerator for several days. Serve on baked potatoes, cooked vegetables, lamb, fish, or cooked eggs.

FRUITY BUTTER

Ingredients for 1 cup

1 stick	Butter, softened
1/3 cup	Powdered sugar
1 tbsp	Fruit preserves

Combine all of the ingredients in a small bowl and beat until smooth. Store in an airtight container in the refrigerator for 2 weeks. Any sweet preserves can be used [strawberry, blackberry, raspberry, pineapple, or your choice]. A candy mold can be used to make pretty pats of butter. If necessary, freeze them and pop the butter out of the molds and store in an airtight container in the refrigerator until ready to use.

ROSALIND'S CROUTONS

Ingredients for 8 servings

8 slices	Bread [several days old]
1 stick	Butter
	Garlic bread sprinkle
	Garlic salt
	Herbs de Provence, optional

Melt the butter in a small saucepan or in the oven. Cut the bread slices into 16 cubes each [cutting four times each way] and spread onto a baking tray. Drizzle with the melted butter, trying to coat each cube. Sprinkle with the garlic salt, garlic bread sprinkle, and herbs. Bake in a 250-degree oven for 1 1/2 hours, turning the cubes occasionally. When the cubes are crusty, turn the oven off and let the croutons sit in the oven for another 30–40 minutes. Serve on salads or store in an airtight container and save for snacking.

Helpful hint: Hot dog buns make good croutons. Slice lengthwise and cube. Coat the cubes with a melted stick of butter, garlic salt, Parmesan cheese, and bake until crusty. This is a great recipe to use leftover buns or bread.

FLOUR FOR FRYING

Ingredients for 4 1/2 cups

2 1/2 lbs	Flour, all-purpose
1 tbsp	Cayenne pepper
1 1/2 tbsp	Lawry's seasoned salt
1 1/2 tbsp	White pepper
1 1/2 tbsp	Black pepper

Mix all ingredients together and store in an airtight container.

POTATOES: Cut potatoes and boil until nearly tender. Chill in ice water. Flour and fry.

SHRIMP: Dip shrimp in eggs and lemon juice mixture. Flour and dip again. Flour again and fry.

CHICKEN: Dip chicken in Crystal Hot Sauce. Flour and fry.

HAM GLAZE

Ingredients for 2 cups

18 oz	Orange marmalade
6 oz	Coke Classic [1/2 can]

Combine the marmalade and Coke in a saucepan and boil for 20 minutes or until liquid is reduced. Baste the ham with sauce for the last 20 minutes of cooking.

HONEY BUTTER

Ingredients for 1 cup

1/2 cup	Butter
1/4 cup	Honey

Let the butter soften to room temperature. Whip the butter and honey together until light and fluffy. Spread while soft or put into mint molds and chill or freeze slightly. Pop the molded butter out and store in an airtight container in the refrigerator until ready to use.

PAN PREP

Ingredients for 14 ounces

1/4 cup	Oil
1/4 cup	Flour
1 1/4 cups	Crisco

Mix ingredients thoroughly. Store in an airtight container in the refrigerator [keeps indefinitely]. Spread in baking tins and pans when needed.

ROSALIND'S CRYSTALIZED PICKLES

Ingredients for 6 quarts

7 lbs	Cucumbers [fresh, medium size]
	Lime
	White vinegar
	Ginger
3 tbsp	Pickling spices
	Sugar

Wash cucumbers until they are free of dirt and cut into 1/4-inch rounds. Place into a glass or stoneware container and cover well with lime water [1 cup of lime per 1 gallon of water]. Soak for 24 hours, stirring the solution occasionally since the lime will settle to the bottom. Pour off the lime water and wash well. Change the water every hour for 4 hours. Put the cucumber rounds back into the container and cover well with ginger water [1 tablespoon of ginger per 1 gallon of water]. Soak for 4–6 hours or overnight. Drain and rinse. Mix enough sugar and white vinegar to cover the rounds [2 cups of sugar to 1 cup of vinegar]. Bring the liquid mixture and the spices to a boil [note the helpful hint below]. Put the cucumber rounds into the boiling liquid and cook until they become a dark green and the liquid becomes syrupy [about 2 hours]. Remove the spices and put the rounds and syrup into clean and sterilized [put into boiling water for a couple of minutes] jars and seal.

Helpful hint: To avoid the spices from floating in the liquid, it is best to tie [with cotton twine] the spices in a clean white cloth or cheesecloth. They can be easily removed from the syrup after cooking. Also, coffee filters with NO SEAMS can be used instead of cheesecloth. Unwaxed dental floss may be used to tie the spices in the wrapper instead of kitchen twine.

PEACH PICKLES

Ingredients for 1 quart

2 cans	Peach halves [15 oz]
1 1/2 cup	Sugar
1 cup	Apple cider vinegar
4	Cinnamon sticks
2 tsp	Whole cloves

Drain the peaches, reserving the syrup. Combine the syrup, vinegar, and spices. Bring to a boil. Lower the heat and simmer for 10 minutes. Put the peach halves into a quart jar. Place a strainer on top of the jar and pour the hot syrup over the peaches. Cover, cool, and keep in the refrigerator.

Helpful hint: A can of pineapple slices or chunks can be opened and drained into any extra liquid. Bring to a boil and pour over pineapple placed in another quart jar. Cover, cool, and store in the refrigerator.

PEAR PICKLES

Ingredients for 8 quarts

7 lbs	Pears	2 tbsp	Whole cloves
2 1/2 cups	Sugar	3 tsp	Cinnamon
1 1/2 cups	Vinegar		Fruit-Fresh
2 tbsp	Pickling spice		[optional]

Wash, peel, and quarter the pears. Place the pear quarters in water with the Fruit-Fresh to prevent browning. Tie the spices in cheesecloth. Mix the vinegar and sugar in a stainless steel or enamel pan. Drop in the spice bag. Bring to a boil and add the drained pears. Do not cover. Cook until tender when pierced with a fork. Sterilize the jars and lids. Pack the pears in the jars. Cover with the hot syrup and discard the spices. Wipe the top of the jars with a paper towel if any syrup gets on the jars. Seal.

Helpful hint: If the pears are very firm, they may need to be pre-cooked for a few minutes.

ROSALIND'S SEASONED SALT

Ingredients for 32 ounces

26 oz	Salt	2 tbsp	Garlic powder
3 tbsp	Pepper	2 tbsp	Chili powder
4 tbsp	Cayenne	2 tbsp	Accent
	[red pepper]		

Mix all ingredients together. Keep a shaker full ready to use on steaks, ribs, roasts, or anything that needs seasoning. This makes a nice gift when put in a pretty shaker and tied with a festive ribbon. Also, it is a nice addition to a gift basket.

Truman's

Grill

GRILLED ASPARAGUS

Ingredients for 4 servings

1 lb	Asparagus, fresh
	Olive oil
1	Lemon
	Sea salt
	Fresh cracked pepper

Trim the tough ends off of the asparagus. This can be done by snapping the ends where they break naturally, or they may be cut for even lengths. Drizzle with a good olive oil. Squeeze the juice of a lemon over the spears. Shake the sea salt and grate the pepper over the asparagus. Cook on a hot grill for 10 minutes or until crisp-tender.

TRUMAN'S ASPARAGUS

Ingredients for 4 servings

24	Asparagus spears, fresh
	Olive oil
	Rosalind's Seasoned Salt

Wash asparagus and break tough ends off. Hold the tough ends with one hand and slide other hand up the spears, bending gently until the spears break naturally. Drizzle with the olive oil. Sprinkle with seasoned salt. Lay spears across the grill and cook at 350 degrees for 5 minutes or until crisp-tender. Do not turn.

ROSALIND'S BANANA FOSTER

Ingredients for 1 serving

1	Banana, ripe
2 tbsp	Brown sugar
1 tbsp	Kahlúa
2 tbsp	Butter, cut into 2 or 3 pieces
	Parchment paper
	Aluminum foil

Make a pouch the length of the banana with aluminum foil, lined with parchment paper. Peel the banana and slice lengthwise. Place the banana into the pouch. Place the sugar, Kahlúa, and the butter inside the cut banana. Sprinkle with the cinnamon. Seal the pouch and cook over direct heat at 250–300 degrees for 5–7 minutes. Serve hot with a scoop of vanilla ice cream or non-fat yogurt.

GRILLED BREAD

Ingredients for 12 slices

1	Loaf Italian bread [or bread of choice]
	Butter, room temperature
	Garlic salt with parsley
	Grated Parmesan cheese

Slice the bread to desired thickness. Spread one side with butter. Sprinkle the butter with garlic salt. Sprinkle the garlic salt with Parmesan cheese. Heat the grill to 250 degrees. Place the bread on the grill with the buttered side up, being careful not to burn. Turn the bread over and brown the buttered side.

BEER CAN CHICKEN

Ingredients for 4 servings

2	Chickens [4–6 lbs each]
1 1/2 sticks	Butter
4	Lemons
1 1/2 oz	Soy sauce
1/2 oz	Tabasco sauce
	Salt
	Pepper
	Lemon pepper

Zest the lemons and squeeze the juice. Mix the butter, lemon juice, zest, soy sauce, hot sauce, and 4 lemon hulls [the squeezed lemon halves] together in a small saucepan over low heat on the stove. Heat the mixture until it reaches a low boil. Bring the grill heat up to 350–400 degrees. Wash the chickens and pat dry. Salt, pepper, and lemon pepper liberally. Place the chickens on 3/4-full beer cans in an upright position. Place the chickens [and beer] on the heated grill with a drip pan placed underneath to catch liquids. Cook for one hour over indirect heat. After one hour, begin to baste the chickens every 5 minutes until the chickens are done [the juices will be clear]. When the chicken temperature reaches 165–170 degrees, the chickens are done.

Helpful hint: The size of the chickens may vary.

Rice can be cooked ahead of time. Reheat rice in a boiler with a little water added.

BACON-WRAPPED CHICKEN BREASTS

Ingredients for 4 servings

4 small	Chicken breasts
12 oz	Coca-Cola
1 med	White onion, diced
2 cloves	Garlic, crushed
8 slices	Bacon
	Salt
	Pepper
	Rosalind's Seasoned Salt [to taste]

GLAZE	
2 tbsp	Orange marmalade
2 tbsp	Vegetable oil
1 tbsp	Water

Mix the glaze ingredients together and lightly whip. Set aside. Mix the cola, garlic, and onion together. Place the chicken breasts into a container and pour the mixture over them. Cover and refrigerate for 8 hours or more. Remove the chicken breasts from the marinade and pat dry. Salt and pepper to taste and rub with Rosalind's Seasoned Salt. Wrap the chicken breasts with bacon slices and secure with toothpicks. Place the chicken on a preheated 325-degree grill and cook over indirect heat for one hour [or until the chicken temperature reaches 170 degrees]. Brush with the glaze and heat until it is caramelized. Slice the breasts diagonally and serve.

GRILLED CITRUS CHICKEN

Ingredients for 6 servings

6	Boneless chicken breasts, halved
2/3 cup	Soy sauce
1/4 cup	Orange juice
2 tbsp	Lemon juice
2	Cloves garlic, pressed
	[or 2 teaspoon chopped garlic in a jar]

Place chicken breasts into a gallon ziplock bag. Mix rest of the ingredients and pour into the bag with the chicken. Gently press air out of the bag and close the top securely. Turn the bag over until the chicken is well coated. Marinate 1 hour or overnight. Remove the chicken and discard marinade. Grill the chicken in a 500-degree grill for 5 minutes on one side. Turn and grill for 6 minutes on the other side, or until it is done. Chicken can be cooked in the oven by broiling, skin-side down, 5 inches from the heat for 8 minutes. Turn over and cook 6 minutes longer, or until there is no pink in the center of the chicken.

Helpful hint: If your grill does not have a thermometer, you may want to test this on your grill to perfect the cooking before inviting guests.

BARBECUE CHICKEN WINGS

Ingredients for 6 servings

4 lbs	Chicken wings
6 oz	Hidden Valley Original Ranch Dressing
	Salt
	Pepper
8 oz	Barbecue sauce

Cut the wings into 3 pieces and discard the tips. Salt and pepper the wings liberally. Marinate the wings in the Hidden Valley Ranch Dressing for 2 hours or more. Discard the excess dressing and wrap the wings in heavy-duty foil, using 5 or 6 wrappings to seal well. Heat the grill to 300 degrees. Cook the wrapped wings over direct heat for 1 hour and 30 minutes, turning every 10–15 minutes. After removing from the grill, allow the wings to rest for 30 minutes before unwrapping. Open the foil carefully [it's hot] and place the wings on the grill over direct heat. Baste well with barbecue sauce, preferably Rosalind's sauce, until the desired char is achieved.

Helpful hint: These wings make delicious appetizers.

GRILLED CORNISH GAME HENS

Ingredients for 4 servings

2	Cornish game hens, split in half
1 pkg	Good Seasons dry Italian salad dressing mix
	Garlic powder, to taste
	ORANGE GLAZE
1/4 cup	Orange marmalade
1/4 cup	Heinz 57 sauce

Sprinkle the hen halves with garlic powder and dressing mix [keeping in mind that a little garlic powder goes a long way]. Cover and place in the refrigerator for 8 hours. Cook over medium gray coals until the thighs are tender. Mix the glaze ingredients. Baste the hens frequently the last 20 minutes of grilling.

Helpful hint: The hens may be cooked in a 350-degree oven for 1 hour or until the thighs are tender and loose.

LOBSTER

Ingredients for 1 serving

1 lg	Lobster [live]
4 tbsp	Butter
1 med	Lemon, juiced
	Salt
	Pepper

Kill the lobster by stabbing the tip of a sharp knife into the cross-shaped point behind the head. Split the lobster lengthwise down the middle and remove the intestines and other unwanted parts. Remove the claws from the lobster. Melt the butter with lemon juice to use as a sauce when serving. Salt and pepper the lobster and place on a 350-degree grill [cut-side up] for 10–15 minutes or until the meat turns opaque. Place the claws on the grill at the same time and leave on the grill for 15–20 minutes. Serve while still warm.

Helpful hint: Do not overcook.

PORK LOIN

Ingredients for 8 servings

4 1/2 pound	Pork loin
	Salt
	Pepper
	Rosalind's Seasoned Salt
	Aluminum foil

Preheat the grill to 350 degrees. Salt and pepper the meat liberally. Rub the meat liberally with Rosalind's Seasoned Salt.

Wrap the meat securely in foil [5 or 6 times, alternating the closures of the foil from top to bottom]. This procedure is necessary for tenderizing the meat. Cook the loin [turning every 30 minutes] for 30 minutes per pound or until done. Remove the loin from the grill and let rest in the foil for about 30 minutes before slicing.

Helpful hint: For a delicious barbecue add Rosalind's Barbecue Sauce, either slicing or pulling the pork. Also, the weight of the loin may vary according to need.

DRUNKEN PORK LOIN

Ingredients for 8 servings

4 lbs	Pork loin, boneless
1/4 cup	Apricot jam, or other fruit jams
1/4 cup	Honey mustard
2 tbsp	Whiskey
1 tbsp	Fresh thyme, or a couple of whole sprigs

Pierce pork over the surface with a fork. Combine the next 4 ingredients in a bowl. Place the pork loin and half of the mixture in a large ziplock plastic bag. Chill in the refrigerator overnight, or for several hours. Turn the plastic bag several times. Grill the pork over indirect heat for 1 hour and 20 minutes. The coals can be placed around the sides of the grill and a disposable drip pan [approximately 8x12 inches] placed in the center. The pork loin should be placed over the drip pan, close lid, and cook. Baste the loin with the remaining jam mixture the last 10 minutes of cooking. The thermometer should register 175–180 degrees for well done, 160–165 degrees for medium, and 155 degrees for rare.

GLAZED PORK TENDERLOINS

Ingredients for 8 servings

4 lbs	Pork tenderloin
2 med	Onions [cut into wedges or 1/4-inch slices]
2 cups	Molasses
1/4 cup	Canola oil
1/4 cup	Lemon juice
1/4 cup	Worcestershire sauce
1/4 cup	Soy sauce
2 tbsp	Garlic, minced
3 tbsp	Ginger, grated

Place all of the ingredients into a gallon ziplock bag. Marinate for several hours or overnight, turning occasionally. Grill the tenderloins for 10–12 minutes on each side or until the temperature reaches 160 degrees. Strain the marinade and boil for 45 minutes in a saucepan or until it thickens slightly. Serve the marinade over the meat or as a dipping sauce.

QUESADILLAS

Ingredients for 8 servings

8	Flour tortillas, 10-inch size
6 oz	Cheese, sliced thin [cheddar or mozzarella]
4	Roma tomatoes, chopped and blotted
8 oz	Ham, turkey, or chicken [cooked and chopped into small pieces]
2 oz	Diced jalapeno peppers
3 oz	Butter, melted

Divide the cheese slices and place them on half of each tortilla. Top the cheese with the meat, tomatoes, and jalapeno peppers. Fold the plain half of the tortillas over the vegetables, etc. [At this point, these may be tightly wrapped in plastic wrap and stored in the refrigerator.] Heat the grill to 200–250 degrees. Place the quesadillas on the grill and cook to a golden brown stage and the cheese is slightly melted, approximately 1–2 minutes on each side. Brush the outsides with the butter as they are grilling. [Watch closely, they will burn easily.] Serve whole or cut into wedges.

Helpful hint: Mix and match your ingredients. Veggie quesadillas are good prepared this way.

PRIME RIB

Ingredients for 8 servings

6 lbs	Beef tenderloin
	Salt
	Pepper
	Rosalind's Seasoned Salt

Salt and pepper the meat and rub with the seasoned salt. Preheat the grill to 350 degrees. Place the tenderloin into a roasting rack over a pan of water [to prevent drying]. Grill the meat for 12 minutes per pound or until meat thermometer registers 120 degrees in the center. Remove the meat from the grill, cover with aluminum foil, and let rest for 25 minutes before slicing.

Helpful hint: Warming the plates helps to keep the meat from cooling too quickly.

SALMON STEAKS

Ingredients for 4 servings

4 med	Salmon steaks
1 tsp	Cooking oil
2 tsp	Lemon juice, divided
2 tbsp	Butter
1/2 tsp	Chopped parsley [dried]
	Salt
	Pepper

Melt the butter with one teaspoon of the lemon juice. Add the chopped parsley, salt, and pepper. Season the salmon steaks with the other teaspoon of lemon juice. Brush the salmon with the cooking oil. Grill over high heat [350 degrees] with the skin-side down for 10–12 minutes or until the salmon begins to flake. Serve with the lemon butter on the side.

SALMON AND MAPLE-CHERRY GLAZE

Ingredients for 4 servings

2 lbs	Fresh salmon
	Salt
	Pepper
2/3 cup	Maple syrup [real maple syrup]
1/2 cup	Water
3 tbsp	Dried cherries, minced
1 tbsp	Sugar
2 tsp	Lemon juice [may use bottled]
2 tsp	Soy sauce

Combine the last six ingredients [sauce ingredients] together in a small saucepan. Simmer over medium heat until the mixture is reduced. [The liquid drops should hang from a stirring spoon.] Cut the salmon into four steaks. Salt and pepper the steaks. Baste with the sauce. Place on a 350-degree grill, skin-side down. After 4 minutes, baste again. After another 4 minutes, baste again and turn. Repeat the process of basting and remove from the grill. [The salmon will be well-done.] Bring the sauce to a quick boil and serve with the salmon, rice pilaf, and a salad.

Helpful hint: Spray the grill with a non-stick spray. The salmon is prone to stick to the grill. Also, this could be cooked in a conventional oven.

SALMON WITH ORANGE GLAZE

Ingredients for 4 servings

2 lbs	Salmon [fresh]
2 oz	Sweet orange marmalade
1 oz	Olive oil [light]
1 oz	Water
	Salt [to taste]
	Pepper [to taste]

Salt and pepper the salmon. Mix the olive oil, marmalade, and water together for the glaze. Heat the grill to 350 degrees. Place the salmon on the grill with the skin-side down and brush with the glaze. Cook for 6–8 minutes, applying the glaze every 2–3 minutes. Turn the salmon with a spatula. Apply the glaze until the salmon is done [the total cooking time is 12–15 minutes].

Helpful hint: The salmon will begin to flake when it is done.

GRILLED SHRIMP

Ingredients for 2 dozen

1 lb	Medium shrimp [20–26 count], cleaned with tails left on

BASTING SAUCE

1/3 stick	Butter
1	Lemon [zest and juice]
3/4 oz	Soy sauce
1/3 oz	Hot sauce
	Salt
	Pepper
1 tsp	Herbes de Provence [optional]

Combine the sauce ingredients in a small saucepan. Place the pan on low heat and warm [do not boil]. Wash, salt, and pepper the shrimp, and place on skewers. Heat the grill to 250–300 degrees. Place the skewered shrimp on the grate over direct heat. Cook for 4–5 minutes on each side while basting with the sauce. The shrimp will turn white and the tails will turn a pinkish red when done.

Helpful hint: Do not overcook.

SKEWERED SHRIMP

Ingredients for 4 servings

1 lb	Shrimp [after peeled and deveined]
1 stick	Butter, melted
	Salt, to taste
	Lemon pepper, to taste

Place the shrimp on skewers. Brush with melted butter. Season with salt and lemon pepper. Heat the grill to 250 degrees. Place the skewered shrimp on the grill grate and cook for 3 or 4 minutes on each side or until the shrimp turn pink and are tender. Do not overcook.

TRAVIS' BABY LUV RIBS

Ingredients for 4 servings

2 full	Racks of baby back ribs
1 roll	Heavy-duty aluminum foil
1 bottle	Barbecue sauce [your favorite]

	RUB INGREDIENTS
1 tbsp	Paprika
3/4 tsp	Onion powder
1 tsp	Cayenne pepper
1/2 tsp	Garlic powder
1 tsp	Mustard, ground
3/4 tsp	Cumin, ground
1/4 tsp	Allspice, ground
2 tbsp	Light brown sugar
2 tsp	Salt
2 tsp	Pepper

Combine the rub ingredients in a bowl and mix. Rinse the ribs in cold water and place each rack [or half rack] on a separate piece of heavy-duty aluminum foil. [The ribs may be easier to handle or may fit on a grill better if cut into half racks.] Apply half of the rub evenly to one side of the ribs. Turn the ribs over and apply the remaining rub to the other sides of the racks. Seal each rack [or half rack] separately in aluminum foil. Wrap each rack [or half rack] in two more layers of aluminum foil, sealing each layer well to keep the steam in the foil. Grill the ribs, turning every 30 minutes, at 275–300 degrees for 2 hours or until done. Uncover the ribs and baste with barbecue sauce. Grill for another 15 minutes or until they reach the desired appearance.

Travis' tip: Grill your favorite vegetable kabob or corn on the cob while finishing the ribs for an immediate feast when done!

TRUMAN'S BABY BACK RIBS

Ingredients for 2 servings

1 rack	Baby back ribs [about 3 pounds]
1 oz	Rosalind's Seasoned Salt
	Salt
	Pepper
4 oz	Rosalind's Barbecue Sauce
1 1/2 tbsp	Jack Daniel's whiskey [optional]
	Lots of heavy-duty foil

Clean the rack of ribs and peel the membrane from the underside. Salt and pepper liberally. Rub the ribs well with Rosalind's Seasoned Salt. Wrap the meat thoroughly with aluminum foil. Cook on the grill at 300 degrees for 2 hours. Mix the Jack Daniel's with Rosalind's Barbecue Sauce. Remove the ribs from the foil and baste liberally with sauce. Lower the heat and continue cooking for 15 additional minutes while turning and applying more sauce. [The meat should be pulling away from the bones, but not quite falling off the bones.]

Helpful hint: Place a roll of paper towels on the table and enjoy!

VEGGIE KABOBS

Ingredients for 2 servings

1 lg	Bell pepper
2 small	Squash [baby squash]
2 med	Onions [sweet or white]
	Oil [canola or olive]
	Seasoning salt [Rosalind's or your choice]

Slice the bell pepper lengthwise into fourths and cuts the fourths into halves. Slice the squash into halves and cut the halves across the center, making 4 pieces. Cut the 2 onions into fourths, keeping the center of the onions intact. Skewer the vegetables starting with the bell pepper, next squash, next onion, and then repeat [try to skewer the onion in the direct center]. It is good to begin and end with a bell pepper slice with the skins turned outward to hold the other veggies. Brush with the oil and sprinkle with the seasoning salt. Place the kabobs on a 300-degree grill. Rotate them every 3–4 minutes until they are done [about 12–15 minutes].

BARBECUE VENISON

Ingredients for 8 servings

1/4	Deer [either shoulder or ham]
2	Apples
2	Onions
4	Irish potatoes
	Rosalind's Barbecue Sauce
	[or sauce of your choice]
	Salt
	Pepper

Salt and pepper the meat. Slice the apples, potatoes, and onions. Wrap the meat in heavy foil, placing the apples, potatoes, and onions around the meat. Wrap again five more times with the foil [poor man's pressure cooker]. Cook over direct heat, turning every 30 minutes. Cook the meat 20 minutes per pound or until it is done. Unwrap the meat and discard the apples, onions, and potatoes. Slice the meat and place it into a boiler. Add the barbecue sauce and heat.

Grits

GRITS CAKES AND GRAVY

Ingredients for 1 serving

1 cup	Grits [quick cooking]
1 cup	Water
1 cup	Milk
	Salt [to taste]
	Pepper [to taste]

Cook the grits, water, milk, and seasonings together in a heavy-bottom pan, stirring often. Oil a heatproof dish. Pour the grits into the dish and smooth the top. Chill. Cut with a round, 3-inch cookie cutter and fry in oil.

GRAVY: Cook about 4 tablespoons of flour in 2 tablespoons of bacon grease, stirring until brown [do not scorch]. Add equal amounts of milk and chicken broth until the flour is smooth.

GRITS CASSEROLE

Ingredients for 6 servings

1 1/2 cups	Grits
6 cups	Boiling water
	Salt, according to taste
3 sticks	Butter, melted
3 lg	Egg, lightly beaten
1 lb	Cheese, shredded
1 dash	Tabasco sauce
1 pinch	Red pepper

Cook the grits in the boiling water with a little salt, keeping in mind that the cheese will also add some flavor. Cool the hot grits until just warm. Add a little warm grits to the eggs to temper them. Add all of the ingredients together and pour the mixture into an oiled casserole dish. Bake in a 250-degree oven for 1 hour or until cooked through.

Helpful hint: A little paprika may be sprinkled over the top before baking to add a little color. This recipe is good to serve at a fish fry with my hush puppies.

To prevent your salt from lumping, put a few grains of rice in it to absorb excess moisture.

EGG AND GRITS CASSEROLE

Ingredients for 8 servings

3 cups	Cooked grits
1 lb	Sausage, bulk not links
2 1/2 cups	Cheddar cheese, shredded
3 tbsp	Butter
3	Eggs
1 1/2 cup	Milk
1 tsp	Garlic salt
	Pepper, to taste

Brown the sausage and drain well. Mix the sausage with the grits, cheese, butter, garlic salt, and pepper. In another bowl, mix the eggs and milk. Combine the two mixtures and pour into a 9x13-inch dish which has been slightly oiled. Bake in a 350-degree oven for one hour or until set [won't jiggle in the center].

CHEESE GRITS

Ingredients for 8 servings

1 cup	Grits, quick cooking
4 cups	Water
1/3 cup	Butter
6 oz	Velveeta cheese
	Salt, to taste

Cook the grits in boiling water, stirring often. When smooth, add the butter. Stir well. Add the cheese, stirring well on low heat. Cover and keep warm.

GRITS FLORENTINE WITH ALFREDO SAUCE
[THANKS, MARLON]

Ingredients for 8 servings

1 cup	Grits [quick]
4 cups	Boiling water
1/2 stick	Butter
1/2 tsp	Salt
10 oz	Frozen chopped spinach [thawed and drained well]
2 tsp	Dry mustard
4 lg	Eggs, beaten
1 cup	Alfredo sauce [5 Brothers]
1/2 cup	Ragu Roasted Garlic and Parmesan Cheese Sauce
2 1/2 cups	Mozzarella cheese, shredded [divided]
2/3 cup	Parmesan cheese, shredded

Cook the grits in boiling water, salt, and butter. Reduce the heat and cook for 5–7 minutes, stirring constantly until the grits are done and thickened. Mix all of the remaining ingredients, except for 1/2 cup of mozzarella cheese, and add to the hot grits. Pour the mixture into an oiled 8x8-inch baking dish [for a thinner casserole, this can be baked in a 9x9 baking dish]. Bake in a 350-degree oven for 30–35 minutes. Top with 1/2 cup of shredded mozzarella cheese and bake another 10 minutes, or until the top begins to brown. Let rest for 10 minutes before serving.

GARLIC AND CHEESE GRITS CASSEROLE

Ingredients for 6 servings

1 cup	Grits
4 cups	Water
1 tsp	Salt
8 oz	Garlic cheese
1 stick	Butter
2/3 cup	Milk [approximately]
2	Eggs

Cook grits as directed on package. While still hot, add stick of butter and log of garlic cheese. Cool slightly. Place 2 eggs into a measuring cup and add enough milk to make a full cup. Beat well and add to grits mixture. [Temper the egg mixture by adding a little of the warm grits to it and then add it to the grits mixture.] Pour into a 2-quart baking dish. Bake in 350-degree oven for 30 minutes. [The grits should be a golden brown on top.] Optional: Sprinkle with paprika before baking.

Helpful hint: May add a little bit of cayenne pepper to hot grits for a little kick. Also, Velveeta cheese may be used instead of garlic cheese. Add 1/4 teaspoon of garlic powder [or to your taste].

GRITS PIE [WHY NOT]

Ingredients for 8 servings

1/4 cup	Grits, quick cooking	3 lg	Eggs, slightly beaten
1 cup	Water	1/4 cup	Buttermilk
1/8 tsp	Salt	1 tsp	Vanilla
3/4 cup	Sugar	9 inch	Pie shell, pre-baked
1 stick	Butter		for 2 or 3 minutes
2 tbsp	Flour, all-purpose		

Put the grits, water, and salt into a saucepan and boil [stirring constantly] for 4 or 5 minutes or until the grits are creamy. Add the stick of butter and cook a minute more or until the butter melts. Set aside and let cool slightly. In a bowl, whisk the eggs lightly and add the sugar, flour, buttermilk, and vanilla. Mix well. Slowly add the cooled grits to the egg mixture. Pour into the pie shell. Bake in a 325-degree oven until set, about 35–40 minutes. Serve warm or cold. May be served with sweetened whip cream or by itself.

GRITS PUDDING

Ingredients for 4 servings

1/4 cup	Grits	2 tbsp	Butter
	[quick-cooking grits]	2 lg	Eggs
1 cup	Water	1/4 cup	Sugar
1/4 tsp	Salt	1/3 cup	Raisins
2 cups	Milk		Ground nutmeg

Bring the water and the salt to a boil in a heavy saucepan. Stir in the grits and cook for 4 or 5 minutes. Gradually stir in the milk and bring the mixture back up to a boil. Keep stirring to avoid scorching. Remove from the heat and stir in the butter. In a bowl, beat the eggs and sugar together until frothy. Add 1/4 cup of the hot mixture while beating. Add another 1/4 cup of the mixture while beating. Repeat the procedure until all of the mixture has been added. Stir in the raisins. Pour the mixture into a buttered 1-1/2-quart casserole dish. Place the casserole dish into a larger baking pan. Add 1 inch of hot water to the pan. Bake in a 350-degree oven for 1 hour. Stir after 15 minutes of baking and again after another 10 minutes of baking. Sprinkle with nutmeg.

SAUSAGE AND GRITS CASSEROLE

Ingredients for 8 servings

1 lb	Hot sausage, browned and drained
1 lb	Mild sausage, browned and drained
1 1/2 cups	Grits
6 lg	Eggs
6 cups	Cheese, shredded
1 cup	Milk
	Salt
	Pepper

Cook the grits in salted water according to the directions on the package. Beat the eggs and milk with a whisk. Mix the drained sausage, cooked [slightly cooled] grits, milk, and eggs together, while stirring. Add the cheese. Add salt and pepper to taste. Pour into a casserole dish, cover, and refrigerate overnight. Bake in a 350-degree oven for 1 hour.

Helpful hint: Use a good brand of sausage, such as Jimmy Dean. It is also good to use the same brand for the hot and mild sausage.

Pork

MOZZARELLA-HAM CASSEROLE

Ingredients for 6 servings

6 slices	White bread [crust trimmed off]
2 cups	Cooked ham [diced]
3	Eggs [slightly beaten]
1 tsp	Mustard
1 tsp	Worcestershire sauce
1 cup	Milk
1 cup	Half and half
1 cup	Mozzarella cheese [shredded]
1/2 tsp	Salt
	Pepper

Trim bread and place in a 9x13-inch casserole dish. Dice the cooked ham and spread over the slices of bread. Top with the grated cheese. Mix the milk, eggs, salt, pepper, mustard, and Worcestershire sauce together. Pour over the layers and let rest for 10 minutes. Bake in a 350-degree oven for 30 minutes or until firm.

Helpful hint: A pound of sausage can be used instead of the ham. Brown the sausage and drain. Spread sausage over the slices of bread. Grate 1 cup of sharp [or medium] cheddar cheese, instead of mozzarella, and sprinkle over the sausage. Follow the milk, eggs, etc. recipe and bake as stated above.

PLUM-GOOD PORK LOIN

Ingredients for 8 servings

6 lbs	Boneless pork loin or pork tenderloin
2 tbsp	Butter
1 med	White onion, chopped
1/4 cup	Brown sugar, packed
1/2 cup	Water
2 tbsp	Lemon juice
1/4 cup	Soy sauce
1/3 cup	Chili sauce
2 tsp	Prepared mustard
3 drops	Hot sauce
16 oz	Plum preserves
	[or plum jam if preserves aren't available]
	Garlic salt
	Onion salt [optional]

Sprinkle the pork generously with garlic [and onion] salt. Place the fat-side up on the rack of a roasting pan. Pour 2 cups of water into the pan. Cook 25 minutes per pound in a 325-degree oven. Sauté the chopped onion in butter and add the other ingredients. Simmer for another 15 minutes and set aside. When the pork has cooked, pour off the fat and place the loin in the pan or in another baking dish. Cover with the glaze and return to the oven for an additional 30 minutes. Baste often. Some of the glaze can be reserved to serve with rice or dressing.

Helpful hint: Whole cranberry sauce can be substituted for the plum preserves for a different flavor.

PORK LOIN WITH GRAVY

Ingredients for 8 servings

3 1/2 lb	Pork loin
2 tbsp	Lawry's seasoned salt [or Rosalind's Seasoned Salt]
2 tbsp	Garlic pepper blend
1 tbsp	Garlic powder [or less, to taste]
1 med	Onion, chopped
1 tbsp	Kitchen Bouquet sauce
1 tbsp	Flour
	Salt
	Pepper

Wash, pat dry, and coat the pork loin with the first 3 seasonings. Place the onions in the bottom of a roasting pan and place the pork loin on the top of the pan. Bake uncovered in a 350-degree oven for 1 1/2 hours or until a meat thermometer reaches 160 degrees. When reaching the desired doneness, remove the loin and add enough water to the drippings to make about 4 cups of liquid. In a cup, mix the flour with a small amount of water to make a paste. Slowly add enough water to dilute the flour mixture, but not lump. Add to the dripping liquids and reduce. This can be done in a boiler on top of the stove. Adjust the seasoning with salt and pepper. When the onion gravy is the desired thickness, pour it over the sliced loin.

PORK SCALOPPINE AND MUSHROOMS

Ingredients for 6 servings

1	Pork tenderloin
10 oz	Mushrooms [fresh], cleaned and sliced
2	Celery stalks, sliced
5 tbsp	Butter, divided
1 cup	Chicken broth
1/2 cup	Cream
2 tbsp	Parsley, fresh
	Salt
	Pepper
1 lb	Egg noodles, bag

Cook egg noodles, drain, cool, and stir in 2 tablespoons of butter. Set aside. Slice pork tenderloin into 1-inch medallions. Salt, pepper, and brown in 1 tablespoon of butter. Place the meat in a casserole dish and place in a 200-degree oven. Put remaining butter [2 tablespoons] in fry pan, add the mushrooms and celery, and brown. Add 1 cup of chicken stock and reduce till almost level in the pan. Add 1/2 cup cream and cook another minute or two. Pour over the meat. Serve over the noodles.

If a guest drops sauces or gravy on an upholstered chair, dust the fabric with cornstarch and vacuum. This may take two or three times.

ROSALIND'S PORK LOIN

Ingredients for 8 servings

6 lbs	Pork tenderloin
1 med	White onion, chopped
2 tbsp	Butter
1 tbsp	Tomato paste
2 cloves	Garlic, minced
1/4 cup	Dark brown sugar, packed
1/2 cup	Water
2 tbsp	Lemon-juice
1/8 cup	Soy sauce
2 tsp	Yellow mustard
2 drops	Hot sauce [optional, for extra spice]
8 oz	Red pepper jelly
	Salt
	Pepper

Sprinkle all sides of the pork loin with salt and pepper. Place the fat-side up in a baking dish. Cook for 30 minutes per pound in a 325-degree oven. [When well done, the juices will be clear when knife or fork is inserted.] Sauté the onion in the butter until the onion is translucent. Add the garlic and cook 5 minutes more. Add the other ingredients and simmer for 30 minutes. Add the sauce to the cooked tenderloin and bake another 30 minutes. Baste often. Remove from the oven and let the loin rest for 15 minutes before slicing. Serve with white rice and spoon the sauce over all.

Helpful hint: Never cook pork or chicken if it has an odor.

ROSALIND'S STUFFED PORK ROAST

Ingredients for 8 servings

3 lb	Boneless pork loin
2 tart	Apples, peeled, cored, and chopped
3 tbsp	Butter
4 tbsp	Brown sugar
1 cup	Apple juice, or cider
6 oz	Stove top stuffing mix for chicken [box]
	Salt
	Pepper
	Garlic salt

With a very sharp filet knife, start cutting the pork loin [under the fat side] all the way down, being careful not to cut through the loin. Lay the cut part of the roast open and start cutting where it joins the main part of the roast. Cut in the opposite direction all the way down, being careful not to cut all the way through the meat. When finished, the roast should lie flat with the two folds still adjoining the center part of the meat. Heat the apple juice, butter, and brown sugar. Add the stuffing and apples. Mix well. Spoon the mixture down the center of the meat. Fold the bottom of the roast over the stuffing. Fold the top [fat side] of the roast over the first flap. Tie with an all-cotton cord or twine [butchers' cord or twine] all the way down the roast. This can be secured with large toothpicks, but not as effectively. Sprinkle liberally with salt, pepper, and a little garlic salt. Place fat-side up in a roasting pan which has the tray over water. The water in the bottom keeps the meat from drying out. Bake in a 350-degree oven until well done, about 2 1/2 hours. After removing the meat from the oven, cut the string away, and let it rest a few minutes before slicing.

PORK TENDERLOIN

Ingredients for 6 servings

3 lbs	Pork tenderloin
3 tbsp	Dijon mustard
2 tbsp	Olive oil
2 sprigs	Rosemary
	Cracked black pepper

Mix the olive oil and mustard together and place in a large ziplock plastic bag. Add the rosemary. Place the tenderloin in the bag, zip closed, and rotate the bag several time on a flat surface. Place the bag in the refrigerator for an hour or more, rotating it several times while it is marinating. Remove from the bag and cover with cracked black pepper. Bake in a 350-degree oven until the juices from the tenderloin are clear, 15–20 minutes per pound.

SAUSAGE CASSEROLE

Ingredients for 8 servings

16 oz	Sausage, hot or mild
8 oz	Crescent rolls, in the dairy case
3 oz	Cream cheese
8 oz	Cheddar cheese, sharp or mild
1	Small onion, chopped

Brown sausage and chopped onion. Drain excess grease and blot. Press half of crescent roll into bottom of 8x11-inch Pyrex dish, pinching the seams together. [For a thicker crust use 2 cans of crescent rolls.] Mix cream cheese with the meat and onion while meat is still hot. Spread mixture over the dough.

Cover the mixture with shredded cheese. Cover with the remainder of the crescent roll and stretch to seal. Bake in a 350-degree oven for 20–25 minutes or until the top is a golden brown. This can be made ahead and refrigerated after baking. Reheat and cut.

Variation: Use English muffins instead of crescent rolls. Divide the muffins, making 12 halves. Spoon sausage mixture over the muffins and bake in a 350-degree oven 10–15 minutes or until the cheese is bubbly. Velveeta cheese can be used instead of cheddar cheese. Melt the Velveeta in the sausage while the sausage is hot. Can be frozen until ready to bake and serve.

Poultry

CHICKEN A LA KING

Ingredients for 8 servings

5	Chicken breasts, or equal amount of chicken tenders
3 tbsp	Butter
1/2 cup	Green pepper, minced [optional]
4 oz	Sliced mushrooms, drained
3 tbsp	Flour
1 1/2 cup	Chicken broth
1 1/2 cup	Heavy cream
2	Egg yolks, beaten
2 oz	Pimiento [small jar or can] drained
	Salt and pepper to taste

Boil the chicken until it is tender, drain [reserving the broth], cool, and cut into cubes. Melt butter, add green pepper, and mushrooms. Cook 5 minutes. Add flour and stir until smooth. Gradually add the broth and cream, stirring constantly until mixture thickens and comes to a boil. Remove from heat and add the egg yolks, chicken, and chopped pimiento. Check the seasoning. If salt and pepper were used to season chicken, more may not be needed. Return to heat, but do not boil. Serve over rice, toast points, or in patty shells.

BAKED CHICKEN

Ingredients for 10

10	Boneless and skinless chicken thighs
2 cups	Corn Flakes, crushed
2 tsp	Salt
1/2 cup	Parmesan cheese, shredded
1/2 tsp	Cayenne pepper
3 lg	Eggs, slightly beaten
	Pam

Line a 9x13-inch baking pan with foil. Mix the Corn Flake crumbs, Parmesan cheese, salt, and cayenne pepper in a bowl. Whisk the eggs in another bowl. Dip each piece of chicken in the eggs and then roll in the crumb mixture, coating well. Place the chicken on the baking pan, side by side. Spray lightly with Pam. Bake in a 350-degree oven for 1 hour or until well done.

BRIDGE CLUB CHICKEN

Ingredients for 10 servings

10	Chicken breasts, skinned and deboned
2 1/2 oz	Jar of dried beef
8 oz	Sour cream
1 can	Cream of mushroom soup, undiluted
10	Bacon slices, uncooked
1 tbsp	Cornstarch
1/2 cup	White wine
	Black pepper

Flatten chicken breasts. [This can be done by placing chicken between pieces of plastic wrap and pounding them with a blunt object.] Place a slice of beef inside each piece of chicken and roll. Wrap a slice of bacon around each chicken roll and fasten with a toothpick. Place remaining beef in the bottom of a large casserole dish and put the chicken rolls on top of the beef in a single layer. Grind black pepper over the chicken. Mix the soup and sour cream. Mix the cornstarch and wine together. Combine the two mixtures and spoon it over the chicken, covering all of it. Cover with foil and bake at 350 degrees for 2 hours. This is good with slivered almonds sprinkled on top, or you may want to add a little pimiento when almost done for a little festive color. Serve with white rice.

Helpful hint: For more sauce, increase the liquid mixture by half or double the ingredients.

QUICK CHICKEN AND DRESSING

Ingredients for 8 servings

1 lg	Fryer [or 6 chicken breasts]
1 can	Cream of celery soup, undiluted
1 can	Cream of mushroom soup, undiluted
8 oz	Herbed or corn bread stuffing mix [package]
4 cups	Chicken broth
	Salt
	Pepper
3 tbsp	Butter

Boil the chicken in seasoned water until tender. Cool, debone, and cut the chicken into pieces. Spread the chicken into a 9x13-inch casserole dish. Mix the soups and pour over the chicken. [If using corn bread mix, pepper and onion or garlic salt may be sprinkled over the soups, but it is not necessary.] Dot with the butter. Spread the stuffing mix over the top. Pour the chicken broth over all. Bake in a 350-degree oven for 45 minutes or until bubbly and brown.

Helpful hint: When boiling chicken, add an onion, 2 or 3 stalks of celery, and a couple of carrots to the water to enhance the flavor of the chicken. Several sprigs of thyme, rosemary, and bay leaves are good, also. Remember to strain the chicken broth before using it.

CHICKEN CASSEROLE

Ingredients for 8 servings

6	Chicken breasts
1 1/2 tsp	Salt
1 cup	Water
1/2 cup	Celery, chopped
1	Onion [small], chopped
1 cup	White wine
1 lb	Mushrooms [or 8 oz can], sliced
6 oz	Wild rice, long grain
1/2 cup	Butter
1 cup	Sour cream
1 can	Cream of mushroom soup
	Slivered almonds

Bring chicken and the first 5 ingredients to a boil and simmer for 1 hour. Skin and bone chicken and cut into bite-size pieces. Strain liquid and use it to cook the rice according to the directions on the rice package. Sauté the mushrooms in the butter and mix with the soup and sour cream. Add the cooked rice and chicken. Pour into a 2-1/2- or 3-quart casserole dish and sprinkle with almonds. Bake for 1 hour in a 350-degree oven.

CHICKEN OR TURKEY CASSEROLE

Ingredients for 10 servings

4 cups	Chicken or turkey, stewed and cut into large bite-size pieces
2 cans	Cream of chicken soup
2 cups	Rice, cooked until just tender in chicken broth
1/2 cup	Mayonnaise
4 lg	Hard-boiled eggs, diced
4 tsp	Lemon juice
	Chicken broth [reserved]

TOPPING

1 small	Package of Pepperidge Farm corn bread dressing
2 tbsp	Butter, melted
1 small	Package slivered almonds

Mix the soup, lemon juice, and mayonnaise. Add the chicken. Fold in the rice and eggs. Add enough chicken broth until the mixture is soft. Pour into a buttered 9x13-inch casserole dish. Crush the dressing crumbs and add the butter and almonds. Spread over the top of the chicken mixture. Bake in a 325-degree oven for 60 minutes or until bubbly and lightly browned.

Helpful hint: If browning too quickly, cover loosely with foil.

WILD RICE AND CHICKEN CASSEROLE FOR A CROWD

Ingredients for 24 servings

2 sticks	Butter
1 cup	Flour, all-purpose [or Wondra]
1 tbsp	Salt [or a little more]
1/2 tsp	Pepper
3 cups	Chicken broth
4 1/2 cups	Milk
4 1/2 cups	Wild rice, cooked
6 cups	Chicken, cooked [or turkey]
18 oz	Sliced mushrooms, drained [3 cans, 6 oz each]
1 cup	Green bell pepper, chopped small
4 oz	Pimiento [chopped], drained
2/3 cup	Slivered almonds

Melt the butter in a large saucepan. Blend in the flour, salt, and pepper. Cook over low heat, stirring, until the mixture is smooth and bubbly. Add the chicken broth and milk. Heat to boiling, while stirring. Boil for one minute. Add the remaining ingredients, mixing well. Pour into two lightly-oiled 13x9-inch baking dishes. Bake in a 350-degree oven for 40–45 minutes. May garnish with minced parsley before serving.

Sprinkle chopped pimientos on top of green vegetables for a Christmas garnish.

CHICKEN CRESCENTS

Ingredients for 4 servings

1 pkg	Crescent rolls [8 count]
1 1/2 cups	Cooked chicken, chopped
2 tbsp	Butter, melted and divided
1 tbsp	Onion, chopped
3 oz	Cream cheese, softened
1/4 tsp	Salt
1/8 tsp	Pepper
	Seasoned croutons, crushed

Mix 1 tablespoon of melted butter with onion, salt, pepper, and cream cheese. Add the chicken and mix until thoroughly combined. Take the crescent rolls and make into 4 squares, pressing the seams together. Put 1/4 of the chicken mixture into the middle of the pastry, pull up all 4 corners, and pinch in the middle. Brush the tops of the bundles with the other tablespoon of butter. Sprinkle with the crushed croutons. Bake in a 350-degree oven for about 20–25 minutes or until golden brown.

CHICKEN AND CHEESE CRESCENTS

Ingredients for 8 servings

2 cups	Cooked chicken, chopped
1 cup	Cheddar cheese, shredded
1 can	Cream of chicken soup or cream of celery, undiluted
1 can	Milk [soup can]
1 pkg	Crescent rolls [in the dairy case]
2 oz	Pimiento, chopped [jar]

Lightly oil a small casserole dish. Unroll and separate the dinner rolls. Combine the chicken and cheese. Place 3 spoonfuls on each large end of the crescent triangles. Roll up the crescent rolls and place them seam-side down in the dish. Mix the soup and the milk together, adding the drained pimiento and any extra chicken and cheese to mixture. Pour the mixture over the roll-ups. Bake in a 350-degree oven for 45 minutes or until the roll-ups are golden brown on top.

CRAB-STUFFED CHICKEN BREASTS

Ingredients for 8 servings

8	Chicken breasts
1	Egg, well beaten
1 cup	Herb-seasoned stuffing
1 can	Cream of mushroom soup, divided
6 1/2 oz	Crabmeat [can, drained and flaked]
1/4 cup	Bell pepper, chopped
1 tbsp	Lemon juice
2 tsp	Worcestershire sauce
1 tbsp	Mustard
1/4 tbsp	Salt
1/4 cup	Oil
1 tsp	Onion juice
1/2 tsp	Pepper

Flatten the chicken breasts between two pieces of plastic wrap and sprinkle with salt. Combine beaten egg, stuffing, 1/2 can of undiluted soup, crabmeat, green pepper, lemon juice, Worcestershire sauce, and 1/4 teaspoon of salt. Mix well. Divide among the chicken and roll up. These can be secured with toothpicks. Combine remaining soup with the oil, onion juice, and pepper. Whisk together and use as a baste while baking. [A little Kitchen Bouquet can be added if desired.] Bake in a 350-degree oven until tender, basting every 10–15 minutes. The chicken breasts can be cooked over hot coals on the grill. Keep basting with sauce while grilling.

SWISS CHICKEN BREASTS

Ingredients for 6 servings

6	Chicken breast halves
6 oz	Swiss cheese slices
1 can	Cream of chicken soup [undiluted]
1/4 cup	White wine
1 cup	Herb-seasoned stuffing mix
1/4 cup	Butter [1/2 stick] melted

Salt and pepper the washed and blotted chicken halves. Place in an oiled 9x9-inch casserole dish. Place Swiss cheese on top of chicken. Mix the soup and wine. Pour over the chicken and cheese. Melt the butter and mix with the stuffing. Sprinkle over the top. Bake in a 350-degree oven for 45 minutes or until chicken is tender.

EASY CHICKEN CORDON BLEU

Ingredients for 6 servings

6	Chicken breasts [boneless]
6 slices	Swiss cheese
6 slices	Ham [a good sandwich brand]
3/4 stick	Butter, melted
3/4 cup	Italian bread crumbs [Progresso]

Flatten the chicken breasts by pounding or rolling with the skin-side down. Place 1 slice of cheese and 1 slice of ham on each chicken breast [skin-side down] and roll up. Secure each chicken breast with a toothpick. Roll each chicken roll-up in the melted butter and then roll in the crumbs. Place the chicken in a casserole dish, cover, and bake in a 350-degree oven for 45 minutes or until tender.

CHICKEN ENCHILADA CASSEROLE

Ingredients for 6 servings

3 cups	Chicken, cooked and diced
1 1/2 cups	Chicken broth
1 can	Cream of chicken soup
1 can	Cream of mushroom soup
4 oz	Green chiles [can], undrained and chopped
2 tbsp	Sherry, optional
6 cups	Slightly-crushed toasted corn tortilla chips [Doritos brand]
1 lb	Cheddar cheese, shredded
4 oz	Pimiento [jar], drained

Mix all of the ingredients together except for the cheese and chips. Cover the bottom of a buttered or oiled 9x13-inch baking dish with about 1/3 of the chips. Layer half of the chicken mixture over the chips. Then spread 1/3 of the grated cheese over the chicken mixture. Repeat the procedure, ending with the chips. Top with the remaining cheese, cover, and refrigerate for 1 hour or overnight. Or, the casserole may be frozen and baked later. Bake in a 350-degree oven for 45 minutes or until bubbly.

CHICKEN WITH CRANBERRY SAUCE

Ingredients for 6 servings

6	Chicken breasts, boned and skinned [or chicken tenders]
1 can	Whole cranberry sauce
1 tbsp	Lipton dry onion soup [or 1 pack if more chicken is used]
3/4 cup	French dressing

Mix cranberry sauce, onion soup mix, and French dressing. Marinate chicken in the mixture for 2 hours. Leave the chicken in the marinade and bake in a 325-degree oven for 1 1/2 hours. Serve over white rice.

CHICKEN DELIGHT

Ingredients for 8 servings

1	Fryer
1 can	Cream of chicken soup, undiluted
1 cup	Rice [not instant]
2 tbsp	Lemon juice
3/4 cup	Mayonnaise
2/3 cup	Sour cream
1 1/2 cups	Celery, chopped fine
1 small	Onion, chopped small
4 lg	Eggs, hard-boiled and chopped fine
1/2 cup	Cheese, shredded
3/4 cup	Ritz crackers, crushed very fine

Cook the fryer in seasoned water, adding an onion, 3 stalks of celery, and a carrot to add flavor. Cool chicken, debone, and cut into pieces. Cook the rice in some of the chicken broth until just tender. Except for the cracker crumbs, mix all of the ingredients together well until blended. Put into a casserole dish and cover with the cracker crumbs. Bake in a 350-degree oven for 25–35 minutes.

CHICKEN ITALIAN

Ingredients for 8 servings

8	Chicken breasts [or pieces of choice]
1 pkg	Dry onion soup mix
1 bottle	Italian dressing

Place the chicken, skin-side up, in a baking dish. Sprinkle with the dry onion soup mix. Pour the Italian dressing over all. Cover and marinate in the refrigerator overnight. Bake in a 350-degree oven for 1 1/2 hours. Uncover the last 15 minutes of baking to let brown.

Helpful hint: Remember to let refrigerated glass baking dishes return to almost room temperature before placing them in a hot oven.

To perk up wilted lettuce, soak it in cold water with a dash of lemon juice added. Cool it off in the refrigerator for about a half hour.

LEMON CHICKEN

Ingredients for 8 servings

8	Chicken breasts
	Salt
	Pepper
1 1/2 stick	Butter [divided]
1 tsp	Paprika
1/2 cup	Sherry [dry]
2 cans	Cream of chicken soup, undiluted
1/2 cup	Lemon juice, fresh
2 tbsp	Green capers
1 1/2 cup	Mozzarella cheese, shredded
2 tbsp	Parsley

Pound the chicken breasts between plastic wrap until thin. Salt and pepper to taste. Brown in 1 stick of butter. Melt the remaining 1/2 stick of butter and add the lemon juice and capers. Combine the paprika, sherry, and chicken soup, and mix well with the melted butter. Pour over the chicken in a baking dish. Cover with foil and bake in a 325-degree oven for 1 hour. Mix mozzarella cheese and parsley. Remove the foil and cover with the cheese. Bake until the cheese is melted.

CHICKEN MARSALA

Ingredients for 4 servings

2 lbs	Chicken breasts [cut into bite-size pieces] or chicken tenders
1/2 stick	Butter
1 clove	Garlic, minced
	Green onion tops [several]

1 pkg	Fresh mushrooms, sliced
1 pinch	Fresh rosemary
2 tsp	Fresh parsley
2 cans	Chicken broth
1/2 cup	Marsala [California Taylor Reserve]
	Wondra Quick Mixing Flour
	Salt
	Pepper [optional]

Cut chicken breasts into bite-size pieces. Brown in 1/2 stick butter until done. Add the minced garlic, green onion tops [cut], and chopped parsley. Add fresh rosemary, fresh mushrooms, and chicken broth. Let it reach a simmer and add 1/2 cup Marsala. Thicken with the Wondra Quick Mixing Flour and let simmer for about 20 minutes.

Helpful hint: Sheila adds a little of the Marsala while cooking the chicken to give it a deeper flavor.

MEXICAN CHICKEN

Ingredients for 6 servings

3 lb	Chicken, boiled and cut into pieces
1 med	Onion, chopped
3 tbsp	Butter
1 can	Cream of chicken soup
1 can	Cream of mushroom soup
1 cup	Chicken broth [reserved from cooked chicken]
1 can	Ro-Tel tomatoes and chiles
1 1/2 pkgs	Taco-flavored Doritos
1 1/2 cups	Cheddar cheese, shredded

Sauté the chopped onion in the butter until translucent. Combine the soups, chicken broth, tomatoes, and onions and mix well. Layer the tortillas, chicken, sauce, and cheese in a baking dish. Repeat the layers, ending with the cheese on top. Bake in a 350-degree oven for 30 minutes or until bubbly.

Helpful hint: Chicken breasts may be used instead of a whole chicken.

POPPY SEED CHICKEN

Ingredients for 8 servings

6 cups	Chicken, cooked and chopped small
10 oz	Cream of mushroom soup, undiluted
8 oz	Sour cream
1 cup	Chicken broth
1 stick	Butter, melted
2 tbsp	Poppy seed
	Ritz crackers [one stack, crushed]

Place the chopped chicken in a 9x13-inch casserole dish. Add salt and pepper if desired. Combine the soup, sour cream, and chicken broth and mix. Pour mixture over the chicken. Mix the crushed crackers with the butter and poppy seed. Sprinkle over the chicken mixture. Bake in a 350-degree oven until bubbly and the crackers are brown, about 30 minutes. Turkey can be substituted for chicken.

ROSALIND'S CHICKEN POT PIE

Ingredients for 6 servings

6	Chicken breasts
4 lg	Eggs
2 cups	Chicken broth
1 can	Cream of chicken soup [undiluted]
1 can	Cream of celery soup [undiluted]
2 cans	Veg-All [drained]
1/4 cup	Mayonnaise
	TOPPING
1 stick	Butter or margarine
2 cups	Self-rising flour
2 cups	Milk

Cook the chicken in seasoned water until done. Boil the eggs. Cut the chicken into bite-size pieces and place into an oiled 3-quart casserole dish. Slice the boiled eggs and place the slices over the chicken. Distribute the Veg-All over the eggs and chicken. Boil the chicken broth, condensed soups, and mayonnaise together and pour over the Veg-All.

TOPPING: Melt the butter and whisk it together with the flour and milk. Pour the mixture evenly over the chicken, trying to cover all of the areas. [Do not stir.] Bake in a 350-degree oven for 39–45 minutes or until bubbly around the edges. If it is bubbly and the top is not brown, turn the broiler on long enough to brown the top to a golden brown. Watch carefully when the broiler is on.

Helpful hint: This recipe is easily halved.

CHICKEN AND WILD RICE CASSEROLE

Ingredients for 6 servings

1 cup	Wild rice
1/2 cup	Onion, chopped
1 stick	Butter
1/4 cup	Flour
6 oz	Sliced mushrooms, jar
1 1/2 cups	Milk
	Chicken broth
3 cups	Chicken, cooked and chopped small
1/4 cup	Pimiento, diced
2 tbsp	Parsley, chopped small
1 1/2 tsp	Salt
1/4 tsp	Pepper
1/2 cup	Slivered almonds

Cook the wild rice according to the package directions. Cook the onion in the butter until translucent. Remove from the heat and stir in the flour. Drain the mushrooms and add enough chicken broth to the liquid to measure 1/2 cup. Stir the liquid into the flour mixture. Add the milk. Add the salt and pepper and cook over low heat, while stirring, until the mixture thickens. Add the chicken, rice, mushrooms, parsley, and pimientos. Mix and pour into a casserole dish. Sprinkle with the almonds. May cover with foil at this point and freeze or bake in a 350-degree oven for 30 minutes.

Helpful hint: Another rice may be used instead of wild rice, if desired.

EASY CHICKEN PIE

Ingredients for 8 servings

3 lb	Fryer, boiled and deboned
4	Eggs, hard-boiled
1 stick	Butter or oleo
1 cup	Flour, all-purpose
3 tsp	Baking powder
1 cup	Milk
1 can	Celery soup, undiluted
1 1/2 cup	Chicken stock

Place chicken pieces in a 3-quart casserole dish. Slice boiled eggs over chicken. Pour melted butter over the chicken and eggs. Mix the plain flour, baking powder, and milk together and pour over the above. Boil the celery soup and chicken stock together and pour over all. Bake in a 350-degree oven for 45 minutes or until the top is golden brown.

Helpful hint: This pot pie can boil over the sides of the dish. Placing a large baking pan under it can prevent the oven from becoming messy.

CHICKEN AND SHRIMP SUPREME

Ingredients for 12 servings

6	Chicken breasts
1 cup	Mushrooms, sliced
2 lbs	Shrimp
1/2 cup	White wine [or cooking sherry]
1/2 lb	Mild cheddar cheese, shredded
3	Egg yolks

1 stick	Butter
1 qt	Milk
1 cup	Flour
1 pinch	Salt
	Pepper

Steam the chicken in a small amount of water for 45 minutes or until tender. Bone and leave in large pieces. Make a sauce of the flour, butter, egg yolks, and milk. Salt and pepper to taste. Add the cheese and wine. Cover and keep in the refrigerator overnight. Cook the shrimp in lightly seasoned water about an hour before serving. About 30 minutes before serving, reheat the chicken and add the cooked and drained shrimp. Do not overcook the shrimp. They will cook a little more when added to the hot chicken mixture. Serve hot over cooked rice or pastry shells.

Perk up celery by placing the stalks in a
glass of cold water.

CHICKEN SPAGHETTI

Ingredients for 6 servings

16 oz	Angel hair pasta, cooked according to directions
3 cups	Chicken or turkey, cooked and cubed
1 med	Onion, chopped small
1/4 cup	Pimiento, diced

2 cans	Cream of mushroom soup, undiluted
1 cup	Chicken broth
1 tsp	Salt
1/2 tsp	Pepper
1 1/2 cups	Water chestnuts, sliced
4 oz	Mushrooms [sliced], drained
1/4 cup	Sherry
1/2 lb	Sharp cheddar cheese, shredded

Mix all of the ingredients together. Pour the mixture into a casserole dish and bake in a 350-degree oven for 50–60 minutes.

Helpful hint: This can be frozen, thawed, and baked later.

CHICKEN TETRAZZINI

Ingredients for 12 servings

16 oz	Angel hair pasta
1/2 cup	Chicken broth
4 cups	Cooked chicken, chopped
3 cans	Cream soup [chicken, mushroom, or celery]
8 oz	Sour cream
2 cups	Cheddar cheese, shredded
1/2 cup	Green pepper, chopped small
1/2 cup	Parmesan cheese
	Pimiento, chopped
1 tsp	Black pepper
1/2 tsp	Salt

Prepare the angel hair pasta according to directions on the package and drain. Return to the pot, add the chicken broth, and toss. Stir all of the remaining ingredients [except for the cheddar cheese] together in a large bowl, add the pasta, and toss well. Spoon the mixture into two lightly-oiled 7x11-inch baking dishes. Sprinkle the cheddar cheese evenly over the top. Cover and bake in a 350-degree oven for 30 minutes. Uncover and bake until the cheese is melted and bubbly [5 minutes or more].

Helpful hint: Unbaked casseroles may be frozen for 3–4 weeks. Thaw the casserole in the refrigerator overnight. Let it stand 30 minutes at room temperature before baking.

PARMESAN CHICKEN

Ingredients for 6 servings

6	Chicken breasts [boneless and skinless]
3/4 cup	Mayonnaise
1/2 cup	Parmesan, freshly grated [not in shaker]
	Italian bread crumbs
	Salt
	Pepper

Season the chicken breasts, keeping in mind that the mayonnaise and cheese are salty, also. Mix together the mayonnaise and cheese. Dip the chicken in the mixture and place into an oiled or sprayed baking dish, leaving a little space between them. Sprinkle bread crumbs over the chicken, covering well. Place a sheet of foil over the top, but do not seal. Bake in a 350-degree oven for 45 minutes or longer [until the chicken is tender when a fork is inserted and the juices are clear].

Helpful hint: Try this with rice pilaf and your favorite green salad.

CORNISH GAME HENS

Ingredients for 4 servings

2	Cornish game hens, halved
9 oz	Major Grey's Chutney
2	Lemons, juiced
	Salt
	Pepper
	Curry powder, medium
	Chopped fruit
	[1 red apple, 1 green apple, 2 oranges, 2 kiwis]

Shake the salt, pepper, and curry powder over the hen halves [these may be mixed together ahead of time]. Bake uncovered for 30 minutes in a 450-degree oven. Mix the chutney and the juice of 2 lemons. Baste the hens and bake for another 30 minutes in a 350-degree oven. Cover the hens with the mixed fruit and bake for another 30–45 minutes in a 350-degree oven.

Helpful hint: If kiwis are not available, pears or other fruit may be substituted.

CORNISH GAME HENS À L'ORANGE

Ingredients for 4 servings

2	Cornish game hens, halved and back bones removed
1 lg	Orange
8 oz	Sweet orange marmalade
1/3 cup	Orange juice
	Salt
	Pepper

Lightly salt and pepper the hen halves. Place fresh orange slices under the hens with their skin sides up on an oiled baking sheet. Bake in a 450-degree oven for 30 minutes. Mix the orange juice and marmalade together. Baste the hens with the mixture and bake in a 350-degree oven. Baste the hens every 10–15 minutes until the hens are tender.

ROASTED CORNISH GAME HENS

Ingredients for 4 servings

2	Cornish game hens, 2 1/2 lbs each [halved lengthwise and back bones removed]
1/3 cup	Soy sauce, regular or lite
2 2/3 tbsp	Dijon mustard
2 2/3 tbsp	Dark brown sugar, packed
1 1/3 tbsp	Fresh ginger, finely chopped or grated
1 1/3 tbsp	Sesame oil
2 tsp	Sesame seeds [optional or to taste]

Mix the 5 seasonings together in a Pyrex measuring cup. Pour half of the mixture into a small saucepan. Pour the other half into a 15x10x2-inch baking dish. Add the hens to the dish and turn to coat. Marinate for 30 minutes at room temperature or for up to 4 hours in the refrigerator, turning occasionally. Transfer the hens to a large rimmed baking dish with the skin sides up. Pour the marinade into the saucepan with the rest of the sauce. Sprinkle the hens with the sesame seeds. Roast them in a 425-degree oven for 40 minutes or until they are cooked through and are brown. Transfer the hens to a serving platter. While the hens are baking, bring the marinade to a boil, stirring often. Simmer until the sauce coats the back of a spoon, about 5 minutes. Serve the sauce over the hens or let everyone serve themselves.

Helpful hint: Some ovens cook faster than others. Reduce the heat, if needed.

DUCK CASSEROLE

Ingredients for 8 servings

3	Ducks
2 small	Onions
1	Apple, quartered
1 stalk	Celery
1 med	Potato, peeled and cut into wedges
3	Bay leaves
	Salt, to taste
	Pepper, to taste
	DRESSING
12 oz	Herb stuffing mix [I like Pepperidge Farm]
1 1/2 cup	Milk
1/2 cup	Celery, chopped
1 cup	Onion, chopped
1 1/3 cups	Butter, melted
1/2 cup	Mayonnaise
2 lg	Eggs, beaten
1 can	Cream of mushroom soup [10 3/4 oz], undiluted
3/4 cup	Cheddar cheese, shredded

Boil the ducks [in enough water to cover them] with the other 7 ingredients in a large pot until tender, about 2 hours. Cool and pick the meat off the bones [discard the skins, etc.]. Put the herb dressing in a large mixing bowl. Pour 1 1/2 cups of the duck broth over the dressing. Add the duck, milk, onion, celery, mayonnaise, eggs, and butter. Mix well. Cover and refrigerate overnight. Stir in the mushroom soup. Pour into a baking dish.

Bake in a 350-degree oven until set and brown, about 1 hour. Put the grated cheese over the top and continue baking until the cheese melts.

JOHN'S THANKSGIVING TURKEY

Ingredients for 8 servings

12 lb	Turkey
2 oz	Butter
2 tsp	Rosemary [fresh], chopped
2 tsp	Oregano [fresh], chopped
2 tsp	Thyme [fresh], chopped
3	White onions
7 oz	Beer
1 cup	Chicken broth
5 tsp	Salt, divided
1 tsp	Pepper
1	Baking bag
	Pam

Defrost the turkey, remove the giblets, wash and pat dry inside and out. Line a baking sheet with 2 layers of aluminum foil. Mix together the butter, rosemary, oregano, thyme, pepper, and 2 teaspoons of the salt. Put 3 teaspoons of salt, 1 tablespoon of the butter mixture, and a small onion into the cavity. Pull the neck skin over the cavity. Open the wings, twist them to the back of the turkey, and remove the tips to prevent puncturing the bag. Loosen skin on the breast with hand [from back of turkey] and spread 2 tablespoons of butter mixture between the skin and breast. Put remaining butter mixture into the turkey cavity. Loosely tie the legs [do not cross] with butcher string or unwaxed dental floss. Spray the inside of the turkey baking bag with Pam. Slice 2 onions, spread them in the bag, and set the turkey on top of the onions. Heat the chicken broth and beer until just boiling. To avoid the hot pan touching the bag, transfer the mixture to a glass measuring cup and pour over the turkey. Press out as much air as possible and seal the bag tightly. [All of this can be done the night before.] During cooking the bag will inflate, so place turkey in bag [on the foil lined baking sheet] on a lower rack and in the center of the oven, making sure that the bag will NOT touch the oven. Cook in a preheated 400-degree oven for 1 hour, plus 5 minutes for each pound over 12 pounds [20 lb turkey = 1 hour and 40 minutes]. Reduce the heat to 350 degrees, split the bag open, and peel back. Baste the turkey with the liquid in the bag. Cook for 1 hour, again adding 5 minutes for each pound over 12 [a meat thermometer inserted in the thickest part of the thigh and not touching the bone should read 170 degrees, and the leg should move easily]. If needed, continue to cook and check every 20 minutes until 170 degrees is reached. Baste with the liquid every time the turkey is checked. Lay aluminum foil over the legs and breast, if needed, to prevent over browning.

HOT TURKEY SOUFFLÉ

Ingredients for 6 servings

6 slices	White bread
2 cups	Turkey, cooked and diced
1/2 cup	Celery, chopped
1/2 cup	Green pepper, chopped
1 sm	Onion, chopped
1/2 cup	Mayonnaise
3/4 tsp	Salt
1 dash	Pepper
2 lg	Eggs, beaten
1 1/2 cups	Milk

1 can	Cream of mushroom soup
3 oz	Pimiento, drained and chopped [optional]
1/2 cup	Cheese, shredded [sharp or mild]

Cube 2 slices of bread and place in the bottom of 8x8-inch casserole dish. Combine the turkey, vegetables, mayonnaise, and seasonings. Spoon over the bread. Trim the crusts from the remaining slices of bread and arrange on top of the turkey mixture. Combine the eggs and milk and pour over the above. Cover and chill for 1 hour or overnight. When ready to bake, spoon the soup over the top. Bake in a 325-degree oven for 1 hour or until bubbly. Sprinkle the cheese on top the last few minutes of baking. If refrigerated overnight, let the casserole sit out for 2 or 3 hours before placing it into the oven.

TURKEY STROGANOFF

Ingredients for 8 servings

1 stick	Butter
1 clove	Garlic
1 cup	Onion, minced
1/2 cup	Water
2 cans	Cream of chicken soup, undiluted
8 oz	Sour cream [more, if desired]
2 cubes	Chicken bouillon
16 oz	Sliced mushrooms [can or jar], drained
	Salt
	Pepper
1	Turkey breast, roasted and sliced

Melt the butter and add the onion and garlic clove. Sauté. Remove the garlic clove. Add the water, soup, and bouillon cubes. Heat through. Just before serving, add the sour cream and mushrooms. Salt and pepper to taste, keeping in mind that sour cream will add more salt flavor to the sauce. Serve over the turkey slices and rice, or heat the turkey slices in the sauce and serve over rice.

Helpful hint: This is a good way to use leftover turkey or chicken. Adjust the sauce ingredients to fit a smaller amount of turkey.

Salads

ASPARAGUS SALAD

Ingredients for 8 servings

10 oz	Cream of celery or asparagus soup [can]
1 pkg	Unflavored gelatin
3 oz	Lemon Jell-O
8 oz	Cream cheese, softened
1/2 cup	Cold water
1/2 cup	Mayonnaise
3/4 cup	Celery, minced
1/2 cup	Bell pepper, minced
1/2 cup	Water chestnuts, sliced and diced
1 tbsp	Grated onion
1/2 cup	Pecans, chopped small
15 oz	Cut asparagus, drained

Heat the soup to boiling temperature. Remove from the heat and add the gelatin and Jell-O, stirring well. Add the cream cheese and blend, mixing well. Stir in the rest of the ingredients. Pour into a mold or dish. Chill and serve on a bed of lettuce.

Helpful hint: May take a can of asparagus spears, drain, and make a design by placing asparagus spears on the salad before it is completely congealed. Make the desired design and press slightly on spears. Chill until set.

AVOCADO SALAD

Ingredients for 9 servings

3 oz	Lime Jell-O [1 package]
1 cup	Boiling water
1 tbsp	Lemon juice
1 tbsp	Onion juice
1/2 cup	Celery, chopped
2 tbsp	Red pepper, chopped [or chopped pimiento]
1/2 cup	Mayonnaise [or salad dressing]
1/2 cup	Whipped cream
1	Avocado, cut into small pieces

Blend the Jell-O, boiling water, lemon juice, and onion juice together and cool. Add the remaining ingredients and pour into Pyrex container. Chill until firm and serve on a bed of lettuce.

Helpful hint: A dollop of mayonnaise and a smidgen of pimiento on top will dress up this salad.

BUTTER-BEAN SALAD

Ingredients for 8 servings

20 oz	Baby [petite] lima beans, frozen
12 oz	Shoepeg corn, can
	[or white whole kernel corn], drained
8	Green onions [bottoms and tops], chopped
1 cup	Mayonnaise [Hellman's]
3/4 cup	Red bell pepper, chopped
2 tbsp	Butter

Sauté the bell pepper in the butter until just tender. Drain on a paper towel and set aside. Cook the butter beans in seasoned water. [Season as though they are to be served as a side vegetable.] Boil for about 3 minutes and drain. Combine all of the ingredients and mix. Refrigerate leftovers.

Helpful hint: Diced pimientos can be substituted for the red bell pepper. Drain a 4 oz jar and add to salad.

BROCCOLI AND RAISIN SALAD

Ingredients for 8 servings

2	Bunches of broccoli
12	Bacon slices
1	Small red onion, chopped
1/2 cup	Raisins
1/2 cup	Pecan pieces, toasted
1 cup	Mayonnaise
1/2 cup	Sugar
2 tbsp	White vinegar

Cut broccoli into bite-size florets, wash, and blot. Fry bacon, blot, and crumble. Add raisins, onion, pecans, and bacon to broccoli and toss. In a separate bowl mix sugar, mayonnaise, and vinegar. Whisk until blended. Pour mayonnaise mixture over salad. Toss and refrigerate in a covered bowl. Refrigerate overnight or 24 hours for flavors to blend.

CAULIFLOWER AND BROCCOLI SALAD

Ingredients for 8 servings

1 lg	Cauliflower, cut up small
1 lg	Broccoli bunch, cut up small
1/2 cup	Golden raisins
1 lb	Bacon, fried and crumbled
1 cup	Mayonnaise
1 lg	Fuji apple, chopped fine
1/2 cup	Sugar
1/2 cup	Vinegar, apple cider

Mix the sugar and vinegar together in a boiler and heat until the sugar dissolves. Cool slightly and whisk the mayonnaise into the mixture. Toss all of the other ingredients together in a bowl and pour the vinegar, sugar, and mayonnaise mixture over all. Cover and refrigerate.

ALMOND CHICKEN SALAD

Ingredients for 6 servings

3 1/2 cups	Chicken, cooked and chopped small
1 cup	Celery, diced
1/2 cup	Mayonnaise
1 tsp	Salt
2 tbsp	Lemon juice
1/2 cup	Slivered almonds, lightly toasted

Mix the mayonnaise, lemon juice, and salt until well blended. Toss with the chicken, celery, and almonds. Serve on a bed of lettuce and top with a sprinkle of extra almonds.

Helpful hint: Canned chicken can be used if time is too short to cook and cool raw chicken.

ROSALIND'S CHICKEN SALAD

Ingredients for 6 servings

3 lb	Chicken
5	Eggs [hard-boiled]
2/3 cup	Sweet pickles [diced]
1 cup	Mayonnaise [Hellman's or Kraft]
1/2 cup	Diced celery
1 1/2 tbsp	Sweet pickle juice
1/2 tsp	Celery salt

Cook chicken in water which has been seasoned with salt and pepper. Cool chicken, discard all but the good meat. Cut chicken into bite-size pieces. Chop boiled eggs and add to chicken. Add pickles, celery, and mayonnaise. Add pickle juice and celery salt. Add more mayonnaise if too dry. Increase or decrease amount of ingredients according to taste. Cover and refrigerate.

Helpful hint: I like to add an onion, 2 carrots, and 2 celery stalks to the water to help flavor the chicken.

To perk up wilted lettuce, soak it in cold water with a dash of lemon juice added. Cool it off in the refrigerator for about a half hour.

ROSALIND'S CHINESE CHICKEN SALAD

Ingredients for 4 servings

10 oz	Classic romaine salad [bag] with carrots, etc.	1 tsp	Salt
		1/4 tsp	Black pepper, ground
1 cup	Rice noodles		Zest of 1 lemon
1 cup	Sliced almonds [toasted in a 250 degree oven for 15–20 minutes]		Olive oil
		12	Chicken tenders [or 4 thin chicken filets]
2 tsp	Cornstarch		
	Juice of 1/2 lemon		**DRESSING**
2	Egg whites	1/2 cup	Mayonnaise
1 cup	Bread crumbs [Japanese style]	1/4 cup	Sugar
		1 tbsp	White vinegar
1 tbsp	Parsley, chopped fine		

Blend egg whites, cornstarch, and lemon juice. Set aside. Combine bread crumbs, parsley, salt, pepper, and lemon zest in a second bowl. Dip the chicken in the egg and then roll in the crumb mixture. Place the chicken on a rack over a baking sheet to let dry for 20–30 minutes. Sauté the chicken in olive oil in a nonstick skillet over medium-low heat. Chicken should be golden on both sides. Place the chicken in a 400-degree oven for 10–15 minutes or until done. Remove and cool. Divide lettuce onto 4 plates. Sprinkle with almonds and noodles. Place the dressing ingredients in a bowl and whisk until well blended. Cover and place in the refrigerator until ready to serve. Drizzle dressing over the salad when ready to serve. Slice the chicken diagonally and place it on top of the salad.

HOT CHICKEN SALAD

Ingredients for 6 servings

2 cups	Cooked chicken, cut into desired pieces
10 1/2 oz	Cream of chicken soup, undiluted
3	Hard-boiled eggs, chopped
3/4 cup	Celery, diced
1/2 cup	Blanched almonds, lightly toasted
2/3 cup	Mayonnaise
2 tsp	Onions, minced
1/2	Lemon, juiced
1/2 cup	Shredded cheese [cheddar or Swiss], bread crumbs, potato chips, or crumbled Ritz crackers

Mix ingredients. Spoon into 8x12-inch baking dish. Top with cheese, crackers, crumbs, or crushed potato chips. Bake in a 350-degree oven for 20 minutes or until bubbly. A combination of crumbs and cheese is tasty.

RICH'S CHICKEN SALAD AMANDINE

Ingredients for 8 servings

3 1/2 lb	Chicken breasts, salt to taste
6	Celery ribs, diced
1/2 cup	Pickle relish
1 1/2 tsp	White pepper
2 cups	Mayonnaise
1/2 cup	Sliced almonds, toasted

Boil chicken breasts in lightly salted water until meat is tender. [Stock can be saved for future use.] Let chicken cool, remove bones, and leave chicken in medium-size strips. Fold mayonnaise, celery, pickle relish, and pepper together. Fold chicken into mayonnaise mixture. Cover and refrigerate until serving. Garnish with almond slices and serve on a bed of lettuce.

CHICKEN SALAD SUPREME

Ingredients for 6 servings

3 cups	Chicken breasts, cooked and cut into large pieces
1 cup	Celery, sliced
1 cup	Seedless grapes, halved
1 can	Mandarin oranges, drained
1 cup	Slivered almonds, lightly toasted
1 cup	Mayonnaise
1/2 cup	Sour cream
	Salt
	Pepper

Combine chicken, celery, grapes, oranges, and almonds. Mix the sour cream and mayonnaise. Lightly toss the two mixtures together and chill. Serve on lettuce, or a pastry shell, or on a slice of cantaloupe or honeydew melon. A little honey can be added if mixture is too dry.

HOT CHICKEN AND RICE SALAD

Ingredients for 8 servings

4 cups	Chicken, cooked and chopped
1 cup	Cooked rice
1/4 cup	Onion, diced
3/4 cup	Celery, chopped
1 can	Cream of chicken soup, undiluted
1 cup	Mayonnaise
3 lg	Eggs, boiled and chopped
2 oz	Diced pimientos [jar], drained
	Salt, to taste
	Pepper, to taste
1 sleeve	Ritz crackers, crushed
1 stick	Butter

Mix all of the ingredients together except for the Ritz crackers and the butter. Pour into a buttered 2-quart casserole dish. Cover with the crushed Ritz crackers. Melt the stick of butter and pour over the crumbs. Bake in a 350-degree oven until bubbly and lightly browned.

Helpful hint: May add 1/2 cup chopped water chestnuts or 1/2 cup chopped bell pepper.

CHICKEN-PECAN SALAD

Ingredients for 6 servings

2 1/2 cups	Cooked chicken, diced
1/2 cup	Celery, diced
1/4 cup	Sweet pickles, diced [or sweet pickle relish]
1/2 cup	Red apple, unpeeled and chopped

2 lg	Eggs, boiled and chopped
1 cup	Pecans, chopped [lightly toasted, optional]
1 cup	Mayonnaise

Mix all of the ingredients together. Serve on a bed of lettuce, in a tart shell, or in a fried flour tortilla.

Helpful hint: Flour tortillas can be deep fried until crisp. Hold them down in the oil with a dipper or a round utensil.

FROZEN FRUIT SALAD

Ingredients for 12 servings

20 oz	Crushed pineapple [can], drained well
15 oz	Royal Ann cherries [can], drained, blotted, and seeded
15 oz	Dark sweet cherries [can], drained and blotted
8 oz	Whipped cream cheese
1 cup	Heavy whipping cream
2 tsp	Powdered sugar
3/4 cup	Mayonnaise
3/4 cup	Slivered almonds, lightly toasted
1 pinch	Salt

Beat the mayonnaise and cream cheese together until smooth and set aside. Whip the cream and powdered sugar in a smaller bowl until stiff. Fold the mayonnaise mixture into the whipped cream, trying not to deflate the cream. Add the fruit and nuts carefully and gently fold. Carefully pour the salad into 2 refrigerator trays and freeze overnight. Remove the trays from the freezer at least 10 minutes before slicing.

CHRISTMAS CANDLE SALAD

Ingredients for 9 servings

1 lb	Cranberry sauce, can [jellied, not whole]
3 tbsp	Lemon juice
1 cup	Heavy cream, whipped
1/4 cup	Mayonnaise
1 cup	California walnuts, chopped [toasted, optional]
3 oz	Cream cheese, whipped
1/4 cup	Confectioners' sugar, sifted
	Birthday candles
	Small paper cups

Crush cranberry sauce with a fork and add lemon juice. Pour into small paper cups. Combine remaining ingredients and spread over the cranberry mixture. Freeze. Place a birthday candle on each when firm enough to hold it. May be made several days ahead. When ready to serve, tear the paper cups away. Place on lettuce and light candles just before calling guests into Christmas dinner. May not be the most practical salad, but it is very pretty at night.

Keep iceberg lettuce fresh in the fridge by wrapping it in clean, dry paper towel then storing the lettuce and paper towel in a sealed baggie.

HAM SALAD [THANKS, PATSY]

Cooking time: 1 hour to chill

Ingredients for 6 servings

3 cups	Baked holiday ham, cubed
1/2 cup	Mayonnaise
2 tbsp	Orange marmalade
2 cups	Sweet seedless red grapes, halved
1 cup	Sweet seedless green grapes, halved
1 cup	Celery, sliced
1 cup	Chopped walnuts, toasted

Combine mayonnaise and marmalade. Add grapes, celery, and ham. Mix, cover, and chill. Add walnuts just before serving.

Helpful hint: If the grapes are too tart [as grapes are during some seasons], try a sprinkle of sugar in the salad or add extra marmalade.

INSTANT COLESLAW

Ingredients for 6 servings

16 oz	Coleslaw mix [packaged]
	Poppy seed dressing

Just before serving, toss the dressing [a little or a lot, according to taste] with the coleslaw.

Helpful hint: Add other ingredients of choice.

ROSALIND'S SWEET AND TART COLESLAW

Ingredients for 8 servings

1 med	Green cabbage
3	Carrots, grated
2 stalks	Celery, sliced
1 cup	Mayonnaise
1/2 cup	Sour cream
2 1/2 tbsp	White vinegar
3 tbsp	Sugar
1/2 tsp	Celery seeds
1/2 tsp	Salt [or to taste]
1/2 tsp	Black pepper
	[or several grinds of fresh black peppercorn]

Whisk the mayonnaise, sour cream, vinegar, sugar, salt, pepper, and celery seeds together until well blended. Toss the dressing with the cabbage [which has been washed, quartered, and sliced thin], the grated carrots, and the sliced celery. Cover and refrigerate or serve at room temperature. If served the next day, keep in the refrigerator.

DOT'S CORN BREAD SALAD

Ingredients for 6 servings

8 1/2 oz	Box of Jiffy Corn Bread Mix
1	Egg
1/3 cup	Milk
4	Medium tomatoes [peeled and chopped]
1	Green bell pepper [chopped]
1	Medium onion [chopped]
1/2 cup	Sweet pickles [chopped]
9	Bacon slices [cooked and crumbled]

1 1/4 cup	Mayonnaise
1/3 cup	Pickle juice

Combine the first 3 ingredients and bake in an oiled 8-inch pan. Cool and crumble. Combine the next 5 ingredients. Set aside. Mix the mayonnaise and pickle juice. Set aside. Layer half of the corn bread crumbs. Layer half of the tomato mixture. Layer half of the dressing. Repeat. Let the salad rest for 2 hours. Keep refrigerated.

CRANBERRY MOUSSE

Ingredients for 9 servings

20 oz	Crushed pineapple [can], drain and save juice
1 pkg	Unflavored gelatin
6 oz	Strawberry Jell-O, [2 packages, 3 oz each]
1 cup	Water
1 can	Cranberry sauce
3 tsp	Lemon juice
1/4 tsp	Nutmeg
1/2 cup	Chopped pecans, toasted
1 tsp	Lemon zest
2 cups	Sour cream

Drain the pineapple, saving the juice. Mix the Jell-O, gelatin, pineapple juice, and water in a 2-quart saucepan. Stir and heat to boiling. Remove from heat and blend in the cranberry sauce, lemon juice, lemon peel, and nutmeg. Chill until mixture thickens. Blend in the sour cream. Fold in the pineapple and pecans. Pour into mold and chill until firm. Serve on lettuce with a dollop of mayo on top.

CRANBERRY SALAD

Ingredients for 8 servings

6 oz	Raspberry Jell-O [2 packages, 3 oz each]
2 cups	Boiling water
15 oz	Whole cranberry sauce
1 cup	Green apple, unpeeled and chopped or
	Celery, chopped fine
20 oz	Crushed pineapple [can], undrained
1 cup	Chopped pecans or walnuts, optional
	DRESSING
2 tbsp	Mayonnaise
2 tbsp	Sour cream
1/2 tsp	Sugar

Dissolve the Jell-O in the boiling water. Add the cranberry sauce and blend. Add the other desired ingredients and chill.

DRESSING: Blend the mayonnaise, sour cream, and sugar well. Spoon dressing on the individual servings. Garnish with parsley or mint leaves.

GRAPE SALAD DELIGHT OR DESSERT

Ingredients for 8 servings

2 cups	Red seedless grapes, halved or whole
2 cups	Green seedless grapes, halved or whole
1/2 cup	Sugar, granulated
8 oz	Cream cheese, softened
8 oz	Sour cream
1 tsp	Vanilla

1/4 cup	Light brown sugar
1/2 cup	Walnuts or pecans, chopped [reserved] and lightly toasted

Dry the grapes well after washing. Blend the cream cheese and granulated sugar. Add the sour cream and vanilla, mixing well. Fold in the grapes. Refrigerate until serving time. Sprinkle the brown sugar and nuts over the top before serving. This salad may be served from a bowl or on individual lettuce leaves. If layered, place half of the grapes in a glass container and then spread half of the cream cheese mixture, smoothing with the back of a spoon. Sprinkle half of the brown sugar and half of the pecans over the cream cheese. Repeat the layer. Cover and refrigerate.

Helpful hint: Granulated sugar or powdered sugar may be used instead of brown sugar. Also, more grapes may be added, if desired. Other fruits [blueberries, strawberries, peaches, kiwi, pitted bing cherries, plums, or raspberries] may be substituted for the grapes. Canned or frozen fruits are not recommended for this recipe.

GREEK SALAD

Ingredient for 6 servings

1/4 cup	Black olives
1	Red onion, sliced thin and divided
15	Cherry tomatoes, halved [more or less, as preferred]
8	Pepperoncini [or hot pickled green peppers]
4 oz	Feta cheese [block cheese], divided
5 sprigs	Oregano
1/2 cup	Lemon juice, fresh

1 1/2 cup	Olive oil
	Salt
	Pepper
	Lettuce, iceberg [1/2 head]

Cut the lettuce into quarters. Roughly slice the desired amount of lettuce and place into a large bowl. Add half of the thinly sliced onion, the black olives, the peppers, and broken chunks of feta cheese [all but 1/4 cup of the cheese]. Toss.

For the vinaigrette: Strip the oregano leaves off of the sprigs and add them in a food processor with the olive oil, 1/2 cup lemon juice, 1/4 cup feta cheese, 1/2 red onion, salt, and freshly ground pepper. Mix in the processor until all of the ingredients are well blended. Pour the desired amount of the vinaigrette over the salad. Refrigerate any unused vinaigrette.

Helpful hint: Romaine lettuce can be used. The other ingredients can vary according to taste.

MANDARIN ORANGE SALAD

Ingredients for 8 servings

3 oz	Package of orange Jell-O
8 oz	Cool Whip
8 oz	Sour cream
1 can	Mandarin orange sections, drained
8 oz	Pineapple tidbits [or crushed], drained
1 cup	Miniature marshmallows

Mix all of the ingredients together, cover, and chill in the refrigerator for 2 or 3 hours. [Can be served the next day.]

ROSALIND'S PASTA SALAD

Ingredients for 9 servings

8 oz	Shell pasta [cooked until barely tender]
4	Medium tomatoes [peeled, seeded, and chopped]
3	Stalks of celery [chopped small]
1/2	Cucumber [peeled, seeded, and chopped]
1/2	Bell pepper [chopped small]
8 oz	Bag of Four Cheeses

	DRESSING
1/2 cup	Mayonnaise
1/4 cup	Sugar
1 pkg	Package of Good Seasons Italian dressing [.7 oz]
1/2 cup	Oil
1/4 cup	White vinegar

Mix vegetables and cheese with cooled pasta in a bowl. Mix dressing ingredients well and pour over pasta mixture. Gently toss, cover, and refrigerate.

PEACH SALAD

Ingredients for 9 servings

1	Envelope plain gelatin
2	Packages peach gelatin, 3 oz each
1 1/2 cups	Boiling water
1 cup	Orange juice
3 tbsp	Lemon juice
	Zest of one lemon
1 1/2 cups	Mashed fresh peaches
1/4 cup	Sugar

Dissolve all gelatins in boiling water. Add other ingredients. Pour into an 11x7x2-inch Pyrex dish or a 6-cup mold. Refrigerate. Top with whip cream, Cool Whip, or mayonnaise. Garnish with fruit or a sprig of mint.

PEAR-COTTAGE CHEESE SALAD

Ingredients for 4 servings

8 oz	Cottage cheese
15 oz	Pear halves [can]
6 oz	Maraschino cherries [jar]
4	Lettuce leaves, washed and blotted

Place drained pear halves on lettuce leaves. Place a spoonful of cottage cheese in each pear. Top cottage cheese with a cherry. This can be made with peach halves also.

PINEAPPLE-PEAR SALAD

Ingredients for 10 servings

8 oz	Crushed pineapple [can]
16 oz	Pear halves [can]
6 oz	Lime Jell-O
6 oz	Cream cheese, softened
2 tbsp	Mayonnaise
2 cups	Boiling water
1 pkg	Unflavored gelatin [1/4 oz]

Drain the pineapple and pears, reserving the juice. Add enough water to the combined juices to make one cup of liquid. Dissolve the Jell-O and unflavored gelatin in the 2 cups of boiling water.

Remove from the heat and add the reserved liquid. Combine the cream cheese and mayonnaise, mixing well. Dice the pears. Stir the pears and pineapple into the cream cheese mixture and then into the gelatin. Pour the mixture into a lightly oiled 8-cup mold. Chill until firm.

PISTACHIO SALAD

Ingredients for 12 servings

3 1/3 oz	Instant pistachio pudding mix, package
8 oz	Frozen topping [Cool Whip], thawed
16 oz	Crushed pineapple [2 cans, 8 oz each]
1 cup	Miniature marshmallows
1/2 cup	Chopped pecans, toasted

Place thawed topping into a mixing bowl. Mix pudding mix into topping. Add pineapple, juice and all. Add marshmallows and pecans, mixing well. Pour into 8-inch Pyrex dish, cover, and refrigerate. Cut into squares when chilled. This salad may also be spooned into parfait glasses and topped with Cool Whip and a cherry for a dessert.

After boiling pasta or potatoes, cool the water and use it to water your house plants. The water contains nutrients that your plants will love.

RICH'S FROZEN FRUIT SALAD

Ingredients for 12 servings

8 oz	Cream cheese, softened
1/2 cup	Confectioners' sugar
1/3 cup	Mayonnaise
2 tsp	Vanilla extract
8 3/4 oz	Sliced can peaches, well drained
1/2 cup	Maraschino cherry halves, well drained
30 oz	Can fruit cocktail, well drained
6 1/2 oz	Can crushed pineapple, well drained
2 cups	Miniature marshmallows
1/2 cup	Whipping cream, whipped
	A few drops of red food coloring, optional

Put softened cream cheese in mixer, add confectioners' sugar, and blend in mayonnaise. Add vanilla. Fold in the fruit and marshmallows. Whip the cream and gently fold it into the mixture. Add the food coloring, if desired. Ladle into large paper soufflé cups or muffin liners. Freeze immediately. Defrost 15 minutes before serving, but do not allow them to get soft. Remove liners before serving.

This recipe and Rich's Chicken Salad were signature lunch salads at Rich's Magnolia Room in the downtown store for many years.

ROMAINE AND BLEU CHEESE SALAD

Ingredients for 6 servings

4 1/2 cups	Romaine hearts, torn into pieces
1 lg	Apple, unpeeled and chopped
1	Avocado [Hass], cubed
1/2 cup	Red onion, chopped
1/4 cup	Pecan pieces, toasted

BLEU CHEESE DRESSING

1/3 cup	Bleu cheese
2 tbsp	White vinegar
1 tsp	Dijon mustard
1/3 cup	Orange juice
8 oz	Plain yogurt

Toss all of the salad ingredients in a large bowl. In a small bowl, mash the blue cheese with a fork. Add the yogurt, vinegar, mustard, and juice, mixing well. Pour over the salad and toss.

ROSALIND'S SEVEN-LAYER SALAD

Ingredients for 10 servings

1	Large head of lettuce
16 oz	Frozen tiny green peas
1/8 tsp	Pepper
1/2 tsp	Salt
14 oz	Bacon
1	Bell pepper
1	Sweet onion
6	Celery stalks
6	Medium-size carrots
1 cup	Mayonnaise
2 tbsp	Sugar
2 tbsp	Parmesan cheese [in the shaker]

Cook peas in boiling water, salt, and pepper. Bring to a rolling boil for two minutes. Drain, cool, and blot excess water with paper towels. Fry bacon until crisp and microwave until bacon can be crushed into bacon bits. Wash and blot all of the veggies to avoid a wet salad. Tear lettuce into bite-size pieces and place half of it in a 10x3-inch glass bowl. The layers look pretty in a glass bowl. Chop the bell pepper and layer over lettuce. Chop the onion and layer over bell pepper. Chop the celery and layer over the onion. Grate the carrots and layer over the celery. Layer the cooled and blotted peas over the carrots. Add the remaining lettuce on top of the peas. Spread the mayonnaise over the lettuce, sealing the edges. This helps to blend the flavors. Sprinkle the sugar over the mayonnaise. Sprinkle the Parmesan cheese over the sugar. Sprinkle the bacon bits over the sugar. Seal with plastic wrap and refrigerate. [This salad is even better the second day.]

SHRIMP-MACARONI SALAD

Ingredients for 6 servings

7 oz	Macaroni, cooked as directed
1 lb	Shrimp, cooked
4 lg	Eggs, boiled and chopped
1 cup	Celery, chopped
1 cup	Mayonnaise
1/2 cup	French dressing
1/4 cup	Sweet pickles, chopped [or sweet pickle relish]
1/2 tsp	Dill
	Salt

Combine all of the ingredients in a large bowl, mixing well. Cover and chill.

SHRIMP AND PASTA SALAD

Ingredients for 4 servings

8 oz	Angel hair pasta
1 lb	Fresh shrimp
1/2 cup	Green onions
8 oz	Three Cheese Ranch dressing
	Tony Chachere's seasoning

Cook angel hair pasta according to directions on the box. Cook until just tender. Drain. Pour the dressing over the pasta while pasta is warm and toss. Cook the shrimp in boiling water seasoned with Tony Chachere's. Drain and cool. Chop green onions and toss, along with the shrimp, into the pasta. [The shrimp can be whole or chopped.] Serve immediately or cover and chill in the refrigerator. More dressing can be added, if desired. Boiled or baked chicken can be substituted for the shrimp.

SHRIMP AND RICE SALAD

Ingredients for 6 servings

2 lbs	Shrimp, cleaned and deveined
	Old Bay seasoning
1 cup	Rice
1/2 cup	Onion, chopped
1/2 cup	Green olives, chopped
1 cup	Mayonnaise
	Black pepper, if needed

Add the Old Bay seasoning to a pot of boiling water, enough to cover the shrimp. Add the shrimp and continue to boil until the shrimp curl up and begin to turn pink. Remove the shrimp and drain them in a colander, saving the water. Cut the shrimp into large pieces and let them dry on thick paper towels. [I like Bounty. They don't tear when wet.] Boil the rice [according to directions on the package] in the shrimp water. When the rice is tender, drain off any excess water and add the onion, olives, and seasoning [if desired]. Stir in the mayonnaise and the shrimp.

Helpful hint: The shrimp seasoning will settle on the bottom of the shrimp boiler. The flavor will be concentrated. You may want to check this before you add the rice. If too strong, pour off some of the broth and add water until it is the flavor that you like.

SPRING MIX SALAD

Ingredients for 8 servings

2 pkgs	Spring Mix salad greens
2 lg	Granny Smith apples, peeled and cored
1/2 cup	Walnut pieces, lightly toasted
	Bleu cheese
	Raspberry dressing [creamy]

Slice the apples [thin] lengthwise. Divide the salad greens in salad bowls. Place slices of apples over the greens. Sprinkle walnuts and bleu cheese over all. Add the dressing just before serving. Place extra dressing on the table in a small creamer or pitcher for guests to add to salads, if desired.

Helpful hint: If preparing the apples ahead of time, place the slices in a bowl of pineapple juice. Also, raspberry vinaigrette can be used, but it is a little tart and the apples are already tart. I prefer the dressing.

Pasta can be cooked ahead of time. Don't overcook it. Rinse in cold water, put in sealable bags, and refrigerate. When the sauce is ready and the guests have arrived, put the pasta in a colander, dip it in boiling water for a few seconds, and serve.

STRAWBERRY-PRETZEL SALAD

Ingredients for 12 servings

2 cups	Pretzels, crushed
1 1/2 stick	Butter or oleo, melted
1/4 cup	Sugar
8 oz	Cream cheese, softened
1 cup	Confectioners' sugar
9 oz	Cool Whip
2 pkg	Frozen strawberries [10 oz each]
2 pkg	Strawberry Jell-O [3 oz each]
2 cups	Boiling water

Mix the first 3 ingredients and press in a 13x19-inch Pyrex dish. Bake in a 350-degree oven for 10 minutes. Cool. Mix the cream cheese and 1 cup of sugar. Stir in the Cool Whip. Gently spread over the first layer. Cook the Jell-O and add the frozen strawberries. Cool in the refrigerator until mushy. If this mixture is too thin it will seep under the pretzel crust. Pour over the other layers, cover, and keep in the refrigerator. [This salad can be served as a dessert by topping with whipped cream and garnishing with sliced strawberries.]

STRAWBERRY-SPINACH SALAD

Ingredients for 6 servings

10 oz	Spinach, baby spinach in a bag
1 pt	Strawberries, washed and sliced

DRESSING

2/3 cup	White vinegar
2/3 cup	Sugar
1 tsp	Dry mustard
1 pinch	Salt
1/4 cup	Pure Wesson canola oil or a good olive oil
3/4 cup	Red onion, chopped or thinly sliced
1/8 tsp	Poppy seed

SUGARED PECANS

1 cup	Pecans, toasted and coarsely chopped
3 tbsp	Sugar

Toss the spinach and the strawberries in a bowl and toss with the dressing. Divide on individual serving plates. Top with the pecans.

DRESSING: Combine the vinegar, sugar, mustard, and salt in a small mixing bowl. Stir until well blended and the sugar is dissolved. Add the oil and mix well. Stir in the onion and poppy seeds.

PECANS: Place the sugar in a heavy skillet [black iron skillet is good] and place over medium-high heat. When sugar melts, remove from heat and stir in the pecans. Coat completely and spread on buttered foil to cool. Break into small pieces.

TOMATO ASPIC

Ingredients for 8 servings

1 pkg	Knox gelatin
1 3/4 cups	V-8 cocktail juice
1 tbsp	Lemon juice
1/2 tsp	Sugar
1/4 tsp	Salt
1/2 cup	Stuffed green olives, sliced
1/2 cup	Green pepper, chopped
1/2 cup	Celery, chopped
1/4 cup	Onion, diced [optional]
	Pepper, to taste
1 dash	Worcestershire sauce

Sprinkle the gelatin over 1/4 cup of the juice. Heat the rest of the juice, bringing it to a boil. Add the gelatin mixture. Add all of the ingredients and mix. Pour the mixture into an oiled mold. Cool and refrigerate overnight.

Helpful hint: A can of tomato soup can be used instead of the V-8 juice. Add a little water in the soup can and add to the soup. Boil lightly. Blend 8 ounces of softened cream cheese and 1 cup of mayonnaise into the soup, mix, and add the rest of the ingredients. Refrigerate.

Sandwiches

CHEESE SOUFFLÉ SANDWICHES

Ingredients for 80 servings

20 oz	Kraft Old English or Pimiento Cheese Spread [4 jars]
1 lb	Butter or oleo
1 1/2 tsp	Dill
1 1/2 tsp	Worcestershire sauce
1 tsp	Tabasco sauce
1 tsp	Onion powder
3	Loaves thin-sliced bread, frozen

Cream the cheese and butter. Add the seasonings and cream. Cut off the crusts of 3 slices of the frozen bread. Spread cheese mixture lightly on two slices of the bread and top with the third slice. Stack and cut into 4 squares or triangles with an electric knife. Spread mixture over the top and sides of the sandwich quarters. Repeat this procedure for the rest of the bread. Place on cookie sheets and bake in a 300-degree oven for 15–20 minutes or until lightly browned and bubbly. These may be made ahead of time, frozen on cookie sheets, and then transferred to freezer bags until ready to bake.

Helpful hint: These are great served at a morning party with coffee punch.

To hasten the ripening of avocados, place them in a paper bag with a banana or an apple. The gases released from the banana or apple will lessen the time it takes for avocados to ripen.

DARN GOOD CHILI DOGS

Ingredients for 8 servings

1 lb	Ground chuck [or lean ground beef]	1 tsp	Worcestershire sauce
1 small	Onion, chopped	1/8 tsp	Celery seed
2 tbsp	Yellow mustard	1/4 tsp	Tabasco sauce
2 tbsp	Brown sugar	1/3 cup	Ketchup
2 tbsp	Vinegar, apple cider	1/2 tsp	Salt
1 tbsp	Water		Pepper, to taste

Brown the ground beef and onion in a heavy skillet, seasoning with the salt and pepper. Drain off the grease. Mix the remaining ingredients together and add to the ground beef. Simmer long enough to let the flavors blend [5 or 10 minutes]. Serve over a good brand of hot dogs [steamed or boiled] and buns.

HAM AND SWISS CHEESE SANDWICHES

Ingredients for 3 dozen

2 sticks	Butter, softened
2 tbsp	Mustard [regular or spicy]
2 tbsp	Poppy seeds
1 tsp	Worcestershire sauce [optional]
1 med	Onion [Vidalia, if possible], grated
1 lb	Thinly sliced ham
2 cups	Swiss cheese, grated
3 doz	Petite dinner rolls

Mix the butter, Worcestershire sauce, mustard, poppy seeds, and onion together until blended. Slice the dinner rolls horizontally and do not separate. Spread the mixture evenly over the bottom halves. Place the ham on the rolls and sprinkle with the cheese. Replace the tops of the rolls and wrap well with foil. Bake in a 350-degree oven for 20 minutes. Cut and serve.

Helpful hint: These may be frozen and baked later for a morning party.

HAM AND CHEESE WRAP

Ingredients for 4 servings

4	Flour tortillas [8-inch, or your choice]
4 tsp	Cream cheese, softened
2 tsp	Dijon mustard
8 oz	Black Forest ham [sliced very thin in the deli]
8 oz	Cheese, finely shredded
1 jar	Onion and [or] pepper relish, drained well
	Fresh chives, chopped

Spread one tortilla with a teaspoon of cream cheese. Spread 1/2 teaspoon of mustard over the cream cheese. Place several slices of ham over all. Spread some of the relish over the ham. Sprinkle some of the grated cheese over the relish. Sprinkle the chopped chives over all. Repeat the procedure with the other tortillas. Roll up tightly and secure with toothpicks or wrap tightly in plastic wrap. Chill in the refrigerator overnight or heat in the microwave for a minute for a hot sandwich.

Helpful hint: I have used Monterey Jack and other cheeses, depending on the flavor desired. Also after chilling, slice the tortillas and serve as an appetizer. The chopped chives may be sprinkles over the appetizers as a garnish.

HAM AND RED PEPPER SANDWICHES

Ingredients for 2 servings

8 slices	Ham [thin, deli style ham]
1 slice	Roasted red pepper [packed in oil], blotted and sliced
2 slices	Mozzarella cheese [or cheese of your choice]
4 slices	Italian bread [or bread of your choice]
3 tbsp	Mayonnaise
1/2 tsp	Dijon mustard
2 tbsp	Butter, melted
2 tbsp	Parmesan cheese, freshly grated

Mix the mayonnaise and mustard together. Spread the bread with mayonnaise. Place the ham on two slices of bread. Place the sliced red pepper on the ham. Place the cheese slices on the peppers and cover with the remaining bread. Brush the top bread slice with butter and sprinkle with Parmesan cheese. Lightly oil a non-stick skillet with oil. [I do this with oil on a paper towel.] Carefully, turn the sandwiches onto the skillet. While the sandwiches are slowly cooking, brush the top sides with butter and sprinkle with Parmesan cheese. Turn the sandwiches with a spatula and press the sandwiches with a heavy [preferably a black] skillet. Turn the sandwiches again and press, making sure that the cheese is melted and the peppers are hot.

HOT HOAGIES

Ingredients for 6 servings

1 pkg	French rolls [6]	1/2 tsp	Cajun seasoning
1 stick	Butter, softened		[or seasoning of
2 tbsp	Onion, grated		choice]
1 tbsp	Mustard	12 slices	Swiss cheese
2 tbsp	Lemon juice	1 lb	Deli ham
1 tbsp	Poppy seeds		[or meat of choice]

Slice the bread horizontally. Blend the butter with the seasonings. Brush both halves of the bread with the butter mixture. Layer with the meat and cheese [break the cheese slices to make them fit] and put the rolls back together. Wrap well with foil. Bake in a 350-degree oven for 30 minutes. Serve warm.

MONTE CRISTO SANDWICH

Ingredients for 4 servings

8 slices	Bread [challah, brioche, Italian, or your choice], cut 1/2 inch thick	8 slices	Ham, thinly sliced [deli is good] Salt [dash] Pepper [dash]
1 tbsp	Dijon mustard	3 lg	Eggs, lightly
2 tbsp	Mayonnaise		beaten
8 slices	Provolone cheese [or Gouda, Swiss, or your choice]	1/3 cup	Milk
		4 tbsp	Butter
		2 tbsp	Vegetable oil
8 slices	Turkey, thinly sliced [deli is good]		Preserves, jam, or jelly Fresh fruit

Slice the bread at least 1/2 inch thick. Mix together the mayonnaise and mustard. Spread each slice of the bread with the mixture. Whisk together the eggs and milk, adding a dash of salt and pepper. Place 2 slices of the turkey, ham, and cheese on 4 slices of bread. Top with the remaining 4 slices of bread. Melt the butter in the oil. Cover the bottom of a heavy skillet with the butter mixture and place over medium-high heat. Dip both sides of the sandwiches in the egg mixture and place in the hot butter. Turn once and brown the other side. When brown, place the sandwiches onto a baking sheet. Bake in a 350-degree oven for 5–7 minutes, or until the cheese is melted. Serve warm.

Helpful hint: Ingredients may be changed according to taste. Only mayonnaise or only mustard may be preferred. Also, only ham or only turkey may be preferred. Serve with fresh strawberries or strawberry preserves, or again…your choice.

PIMIENTO CHEESE SANDWICHES

Ingredients for 8 servings

8 oz	Cheese [sharp or medium], shredded
4 oz	Pimiento, diced
1/2 cup	Mayonnaise, or to taste
	Black peppercorn, several grinds

Combine the cheese, pimiento [including the juice], and mayonnaise together and blend. Add several grinds of the peppercorns and blend. Spread a small amount of mayonnaise on slices of bread of your choice and add the pimiento cheese.

Helpful hint: This spread is good to serve on celery cuts as an appetizer.

EASY REUBEN SANDWICH

Ingredients for 5 servings

10 slices	Rye bread
14 oz	Can of corned beef, chilled
14 oz	Sauerkraut [can], well drained
4 tbsp	Butter
5 slices	Swiss cheese

Cover 5 slices of bread with well-drained sauerkraut. Cut the cold corned beef into 5 slices and place on top of the sauerkraut. Place a slice of cheese on top of the corned beef. Cover the cheese with the remaining bread and press slightly. Slowly brown both sides of the sandwiches in a buttered frying pan, adding more butter if needed.

SHRIMP SALAD SANDWICH

Ingredients for 4 servings

1 lb	Cooked shrimp, chopped small
3 stalks	Celery, chopped small
3 lg	Eggs, hard-boiled and chopped small
1/2 cup	Mayonnaise
3 grinds	Black pepper [or to taste]
1/2 tsp	Rosalind's Seasoned Salt
1 tsp	Celery seeds [or to taste]
8 slices	Whole wheat bread, lightly toasted
4	Lettuce leaves
	Tomato slices, optional
	Mayonnaise for bread slices, optional

Mix the shrimp, eggs, celery, and mayonnaise together in a bowl and mix well. Add the black pepper, salt, and celery seeds [according to taste], mixing well. Spread the toasted bread with mayonnaise. Place the shrimp salad on 4 bread slices, top with the remaining bread slices, and cut in half. The lettuce and tomatoes may be placed in the sandwich or served on the plate. [A hard-boiled egg wedge could be added to the plate also.]

Helpful hint: If the shrimp is boiled in spicy seasonings, check the mixture before adding salt and pepper.

SPICY TURKEY SANDWICH

Ingredients for 6 servings

12	Bread slices [white or your choice]
12 oz	Roasted turkey slices
8 oz	Pepper jack cheese, sliced thin
	Mayonnaise [optional]
	Butter, room temperature
	Strawberry jam, preserves, or fresh fruit

Spread mayonnaise thinly on one side of each slice of bread. Top 6 slices of bread with turkey slices and cheese. Place the remaining bread slices on top. Spread softened butter over the bread and brown in a heated skillet. Brown on both sides. Place the sandwiches in an ovenproof dish and keep warm in a 300-degree oven while completing all of the sandwiches. Serve warm with favorite jelly, preserves, or fresh fruit.

Sauces

ALFREDO SAUCE

Ingredients for 3 cups

1 cup	Heavy cream
1 cup	Half and half
1 stick	Butter
2 tbsp	Cream cheese
3/4 cup	Parmesan cheese
1 tsp	Garlic powder

Melt the butter in a small saucepan. Add cream cheese. When soft, add liquids and Parmesan cheese. Add garlic powder. Salt and pepper to taste. Serve with cooked noodles.

BARBECUE SAUCE

Ingredients for 5 pints

28 oz	Ketchup [2 bottles, 14 oz each]
1/3 cup	Mustard
1 1/2 cup	Brown sugar
1 1/2 cup	Red wine vinegar
1/2 cup	Steak sauce
1 tsp	Soy sauce
12 oz	Beer [can]
12 oz	Chili sauce
1 tbsp	Dry mustard
2 tbsp	Black pepper
1 cup	Lemon juice
1/4 cup	Worcestershire sauce
2 tbsp	Salad oil
	Tabasco [1 or 2 dashes]
	Garlic, optional

Mix all of the ingredients together in a large boiler. Heat and stir until all of the ingredients are blended. Store in the refrigerator in jars or empty ketchup bottles. Keeps several weeks.

BANANA-POPPY SEED DRESSING

Ingredients for 1 1/2 cups

1	Ripe banana
8 oz	Sour cream
1/4 cup	Sugar
1 tbsp	Poppy seed
1 tbsp	Lemon juice
1 tsp	Dry mustard
3/4 tsp	Salt
1 tbsp	Honey

Mash banana in a small bowl. Add the rest of the ingredients and mix well. Chill for 30 minutes or more. Serve over fruit such as slices of avocado and grapefruit on a bed of lettuce or young spinach.

BARBECUE CHICKEN SAUCE

Ingredients for 2 cups

2 sticks	Butter
1 cup	Lemon juice
1 tbsp	Worcestershire sauce
1/2 tbsp	Garlic salt
1/2 tbsp	Salt

Melt butter and add the Worcestershire sauce. Add the garlic salt. Add the lemon juice and salt. Do not boil. Brush over the chicken while cooking. Sauce for 5 chickens.

BASIC CREAM OR WHITE SAUCE

Ingredients for 1 cup

	THIN	1/2 tsp	Salt
2 tbsp	Butter	1/8 tsp	Pepper
1 tbsp	Flour	1 cup	Milk
1/2 tsp	Salt		
1/8 tsp	Pepper		THICK
1 cup	Milk	2 tbsp	Butter
		3 tbsp	Flour
	MEDIUM	1/2 tsp	Salt
2 tbsp	Butter	1/8 tsp	Pepper
2 tbsp	Flour	1 cup	Milk

In a small saucepan, melt the butter. Remove from the heat and add the flour, salt, and pepper, stirring until smooth. Return to the heat and slowly add the milk. Cook until thick and smooth, stirring constantly.

BÉCHAMEL: Substitute 1/2 cup of beef stock for 1/2 cup of milk in the thin or medium sauce. Add 1 teaspoon of lemon juice, if desired.

CHEESE: Add 1/2 cup of grated cheddar cheese [add 1 teaspoon Worcestershire and a dash of Tabasco, if desired] to a medium sauce.

CHICKEN A LA KING: Double the recipe for a medium sauce, substituting 1 cup of chicken stock for 1 cup of the milk. Add

2 beaten egg yolks [remember to temper the yolks], pimiento, sautéed green pepper, and chopped mushrooms. Add 1 tablespoon of cooking sherry or wine, if desired.

CURRY: In a medium sauce add 1 teaspoon of curry powder to the flour.

EGG: Add 1 finely chopped hard-boiled egg to a medium sauce.

HERB: Add 1/2 cup dry white wine reduced to 2 tablespoons to a medium sauce. Also, add 2 tablespoons of minced tarragon and parsley and 1 tablespoon of minced green or sweet onion. Add 1 tablespoon of softened butter just before serving.

SOUBISE: Press 4 boiled onions and 2 sprigs of parsley through a large sieve and add to a medium sauce.

TOMATO: Cook 1 cup of fresh or canned tomatoes, 1 rib of celery, 1 large slice of onion, 1/2 teaspoon of salt, a pinch of cayenne together for 20 minutes or until the tomatoes are tender. Press through a large sieve and gradually add to a medium sauce, stirring constantly.

VELOUTÉ: Substitute 1 cup of chicken stock for milk in a thin or medium sauce.

BLEU CHEESE SAUCE

Ingredients for 1 cup

3/4 cup	Mayonnaise [or sour cream]
2 oz	Bleu cheese
	Zest of 1 lemon
3	Grinds of fresh pepper

Mix the ingredients together and keep in an airtight container in the refrigerator. Serve on a roast beef sandwich or a steak sandwich.

BURGER SPREAD

Ingredients for 1 cup

1/3 cup	Mayonnaise
1/3 cup	Ketchup
1/3 cup	Yellow mustard

Mix the ingredients together, cover, and store in the refrigerator. When hamburgers are ready, spread on the hamburger buns.

CARAMEL-PECAN SAUCE

Ingredients for 2 cups

1 stick	Butter
3/4 cup	Light brown sugar, packed
1 cup	Heavy cream
1/2 cup	Pecans, chopped, lightly toasted

Heat the butter and sugar in a heavy saucepan for 2 or 3 minutes or until the sugar dissolves. Whisk in the heavy cream and slowly bring to a boil, stirring constantly. Cook and stir until the sauce thickens slightly [the sauce should hang slightly when lifting the whisk]. Add the nuts. Serve warm over ice cream or other desserts.

DILL SEAFOOD SAUCE

Ingredients for 1 cup

1 cup	Half and half
1 tbsp	Dill weed
1 tbsp	Lime pepper seasoning
2 tbsp	Lemon juice, freshly squeezed preferred
2 tbsp	Dijon mustard

Cook on very low heat for 10 minutes, stirring constantly. Serve with fish or other seafood. Refrigerate leftovers.

DURKEE-ASPARAGUS SAUCE

Ingredients for 3 cups

10 oz	Bottle of Durkee sauce
4	Eggs, whole
1 cup	Sugar
1/2 cup	Vinegar
1 cup	Oil
	Juice from 2 lemons

Beat eggs slightly. Add rest of the ingredients except for the Durkee sauce. Cook in a double boiler until thick. Cool slightly and add Durkee sauce. May be kept in the refrigerator for one month. Serve over cooked asparagus.

GREEN GODDESS DRESSING

Ingredients for 2 1/2 cups

2 cups	Mayonnaise
1 tbsp	Chives, minced
1 clove	Garlic, pressed or minced
1	Green onion, minced
2 tbsp	Parsley, minced
3/4 tube	Anchovy paste
8 tbsp	Tarragon vinegar

Place all of the ingredients into a blender and mix well. Serve as a salad dressing or as a vegetable dip.

HOLLANDAISE SAUCE

Ingredients for 1 cup

4	Egg yolks
2 tbsp	Lemon juice
1/2 lb	Butter, melted
1/4 tsp	Salt

Beat egg yolks in top half of a double boiler. Stir in lemon juice. Cook very slowly over low heat, never allowing the water in the lower pan to boil. Add butter a little at a time, stirring constantly with a wooden spoon. Add salt [and pepper, if desired]. Continue to cook slowly until thickened. Serve over asparagus or eggs Benedict.

NO-EGGS HOLLANDAISE SAUCE

Ingredients for 1 cup

1/2 cup	Yogurt, plain
1/2 cup	Mayonnaise
1 tsp	Lemon juice
1 tsp	Mustard, yellow

Mix all of the ingredients together and cook over low heat, while stirring, for 5 minutes. Serve over cooked broccoli or asparagus. Garnish with chopped pimiento or red bell pepper.

HONEY DRESSING

Ingredients for 2 servings

4 tbsp	Honey
1 tsp	Lemon juice
1 tsp	Lime juice
1/2 cup	Sour cream
1/2 tsp	Poppy seeds, optional

Whisk all of the ingredients together in a bowl. Cover and refrigerate. Serve chilled over fresh fruit such as cantaloupe or honeydew melon.

Helpful hint: To sweeten or to make more tart, adjust the amount of honey and/or juice.

EASY HONEY MUSTARD SAUCE

Ingredients for 1 1/2 cups

1 cup	Honey
8 tbsp	Yellow mustard

Mix well. Cover and refrigerate. Use the sauce within a month.

Helpful hint: This recipe is easy to halve or quarter.

JACK DANIEL'S MARINADE

Ingredients for 1 1/4 cups

1/4 cup	Jack Daniel's whiskey
1/4 cup	Soy sauce
1/4 cup	Dijon mustard
1/4 cup	Light brown sugar, firmly packed
1/4 cup	Green onions [including tops], minced
1 tsp	Salt, or to taste
	Pepper, to taste
	Worcestershire sauce, 1 or 2 dashes

Combine all of the ingredients and blend well. Use the marinade to brush on seafood or meat when grilling or use to marinate seafood, beef, chicken, or pork. Marinate the meats for several hours or overnight [in the refrigerator]. Marinate the seafood for at least 1 hour.

LEMON-BUTTER GRILLING SAUCE FOR CHICKEN

Ingredients for 1 cup

2 sticks	Butter
4	Lemons
1 tsp	Balsamic vinegar
3 tbsp	Worcestershire sauce
	[more or less, according to taste]
	Salt
	Pepper

Melt the butter in a small saucepan. Wash and cut the lemons in half. Squeeze the juice of the lemons into the butter. Add the salt, pepper, Worcestershire sauce, and vinegar. Drop 3 or 4 lemon halves into the butter. Let the sauce sit over very low heat while preparing the chicken. [This will let the oils of the lemon peel flavor the sauce even more.] Brush the sauce over the chicken while grilling. This is enough sauce for 4 chicken halves.

MARINARA SAUCE

Ingredients for 6 cups

1/4 cup	Olive oil
1/4 cup	Onion, diced
2 cloves	Garlic, diced
84 oz	Whole tomatoes [3 cans, 28 oz each], chopped
3 sprigs	Thyme
4 leaves	Basil, chopped small
1 1/2 tsp	Salt
	Black pepper, several grinds

Heat the olive oil in a large saucepan. Add the garlic and onion and stir until lightly browned. Add the tomatoes, reserving about half of the juice, and herbs. Bring to a boil, reduce the heat, and simmer until thickened. Remove the thyme. Salt and pepper to taste. Store leftovers in a covered container in the refrigerator for several days or freeze for several weeks.

MILK GRAVY

Ingredients for 2 cups

1/4 cup	Bacon grease
1/4 cup	Flour
1 1/2 cups	Milk, warmed
	Black pepper [several grinds of fresh, black pepper]
	Salt to taste

Heat the bacon grease in a heavy skillet. Add the flour and whisk or stir until smooth. Slowly add the milk [while stirring] and bring to a low boil. Simmer over very low heat until thickened. Add milk [as needed] to control the thickness. Season with pepper and salt. Serve hot.

Helpful hint: A cast-iron skillet is good to use for this recipe.

CHEESY MUSHROOM SAUCE

Ingredients for 3 1/2 cups

1 can	Cream of mushroom soup, undiluted
1 cup	Milk
1 1/2 cups	Cheddar cheese

Heat the milk and soup together slowly while stirring. When reaching a boiling point, add the cheese [cut into small cubes or grated]. When cheese has melted, serve over meats, rice, or potatoes. Garnish with chopped chives or chopped spring onion tops, if desired.

ORANGE SAUCE

Ingredients for 4 servings

6 med	Oranges [or 1/4 cup of juice]
1/4 cup	Vinegar
1/2 cup	Sugar
	Salt
	Pepper [a tiny pinch of white pepper]
	Zest of 3 oranges
	Flour and water

In a saucepan, melt the sugar in the vinegar. Add the orange juice and boil for about 5 minutes. Add the orange zest and thicken with a roux made with flour and water [1 or 2 tablespoons of all-purpose flour and enough water to dissolve the flour]. Add the roux to the sauce until desired thickness. Salt and pepper to taste. Serve with Cornish game hens or duck. Garnish with candied orange peel of 1 orange [recipe found in candy section].

RED PEPPER JELLY SAUCE

Ingredients for 18 ounces

16 oz	Red pepper jelly
1 sm	Clove of garlic, diced
1 tbsp	Olive oil
2 tbsp	Water

In a small saucepan cook the diced garlic in the olive oil. Add the pepper jelly and water. Heat thoroughly.

Helpful hint: This is my version of a sauce we had in a wonderful restaurant in Fairfax, Virginia. It was served over fried calamari and whole green beans [cooked crisp-tender] as an appetizer.

If you have leftover wine at the end of the evening, freeze it in ice cube trays. It makes for an easy addition to soups and sauces in the future.

BASIL PESTO

Ingredients for 1 cup

2 cups	Basil leaves, fresh
1/4 cup	Pine nuts, toasted
2 cloves	Garlic
1/2 tsp	Salt
1/4 tsp	Black pepper, freshly ground
1/3 cup	Olive oil, extra virgin
1/2 cup	Parmesan cheese, grated

Place the basil, pine nuts, garlic cloves, salt, and pepper into a blender and mix until finely chopped. Gradually add the olive oil [while the blender is running] until mixture is smooth and thickened. Pour mixture into a bowl and add the Parmesan cheese. Mix, cover, and refrigerate.

POPPY SEED DRESSING

Ingredients for 2 cups

3/4 cup	Sugar
1/3 cup	White vinegar
1 tsp	Salt
1 tsp	Dry mustard
4 1/2 tsp	Onion juice
4 1/2 tsp	Poppy seeds
1 cup	Vegetable oil

Beat the first 5 ingredients together with a whisk or electric hand mixer. Beat or whisk the oil in slowly. Stir in the poppy seeds.

Helpful hint: This dressing is good served with a green salad or with fruit such as avocado, grapefruit, and apple slices.

RASPBERRY SAUCE

Ingredients for 2 cups

1/2 pint	Raspberries, fresh
1/2 cup	Sugar
1/4 cup	Water
12 oz	Raspberry [seedless] jam
1 tbsp	Framboise liqueur

Place the water, sugar, and raspberries in a small saucepan and bring to a boil. Lower the heat and simmer for 4 minutes. Pour the jam, framboise, and cooked raspberries into a food processor bowl and process until smooth. Keep chilled until ready to serve.

RASPBERRY-POPPY SEED DRESSING

Ingredients for 2 cups

1 cup	Raspberries, fresh or frozen
1 cup	Canola oil
1 tsp	Poppy seed
6 tbsp	Red wine vinegar
10 tbsp	Sugar
1 tsp	Salt
1 tsp	Ground mustard [dry]

Combine the vinegar, sugar, salt, and mustard in a blender. Add the oil gradually while processing. Add the raspberries, cover, and blend well. Whisk in the poppy seeds and serve. Refrigerate leftovers.

RED SALAD DRESSING

Ingredients for 2 cups

1/2 cup	Whipping cream, whipped
1/2 cup	Mayonnaise
1/2 cup	Cranberry sauce [jellied]

Whisk the cranberry sauce and mayonnaise together and fold into the whipped cream. Refrigerate until ready to use. Serve over fruit or congealed salads.

RICE WINE VINEGAR DRESSING

Ingredients for 1 cup

1/2 cup	Sugar
1 cup	Rice wine vinegar
1/2 tsp	Salt
1/2 tsp	Freshly ground black pepper

Mix all of the ingredients together and whisk until the sugar is dissolved. Serve over a salad.

Helpful hint: Open and drain a can of asparagus spears. Place the spears on a lettuce leaf, add sliced or diced pimientos, and drizzle with this dressing.

SEAFOOD SAUCE

Ingredients for 1 1/4 cups

1 cup	Ketchup
1/4 cup	Lemon juice
1 tsp	Worcestershire sauce
	Horseradish

Mix ketchup and desired amount of horseradish. Add 1/4 cup lemon juice. Add Worcestershire sauce. Keep chilled until served. Good with boiled or fried shrimp.

Helpful hint: Add 1/2 cup of chili sauce and 2 or 3 dashes of hot sauce, if desired.

TARTAR SAUCE

Ingredients for 1 1/4 cups

1 cup	Mayonnaise
2 tbsp	Finely chopped dill pickles
1 tbsp	Finely chopped onion
1 tsp	Lemon juice
1/2 tsp	Capers, chopped
3	Drops of hot sauce
2 tsp	French dressing

Combine all ingredients and mix well. Keep refrigerated.

ROSALIND'S TARTAR SAUCE

Ingredients for 2 cups

1 cup	Mayonnaise
1/2 cup	Green onion, chopped small
1/2 cup	Dill pickle, chopped small
1/2 tsp	Rosalind's Seasoned Salt

Combine all of the ingredients in a bowl, mixing well. Store in an airtight container in the refrigerator.

Helpful hint: The sauce will keep in the refrigerator for several weeks.

REMOULADE SAUCE

Ingredients for 4 servings

1/4 cup	Whole-grain mustard
1/4 cup	Horseradish [prepared]
2 tbsp	Onion, minced
2 tbsp	Scallion, minced
2 tbsp	Celery, minced
1 tbsp	Sugar
1 3/4 tsp	Paprika
3/4 tsp	Worcestershire sauce
1/2 tsp	Garlic powder
2 tbsp	Red wine vinegar
2 tbsp	Oil [vegetable]

Beat all of the ingredients together on low mixer speed. Slowly add the oil in a steady stream. Cover and refrigerate for 6 hours. Pour the sauce over 24 cooked shrimp. Place the shrimp on shredded romaine lettuce. Extra sauce may be served with the salad. The sauce may be kept in the refrigerator for 3 or 4 days.

Seafood

CRAWFISH ÈTOUFÈE

Ingredients for 6 servings

1 lb	Crawfish tails		Pepper
1 stick	Butter		Cayenne pepper,
1 med	Onion, chopped		to taste
1	Green pepper,		Paprika, to taste
	chopped	1/4 cup	Fresh parsley,
1/2 cup	Celery, chopped		chopped
1 clove	Garlic, minced	1/4 cup	Green onion
	Salt		tops, chopped

Melt the butter in a skillet. Season the crawfish with the seasonings and add to the butter. Cook for 3 minutes and remove the crawfish from the butter. Put the celery, garlic, onion, and green pepper into the skillet. Cook until just tender. Return the crawfish to the skillet and add 2 cups of water. Cook for about 35 minutes over simmering heat, stirring occasionally. Add more water, if needed. Add the parsley and onion tops and cook another 10 minutes. Serve over fluffy, white rice.

ROSALIND'S CRAWFISH DEE-LISH

Ingredients for 6 servings

1 lb	Crawfish tail meat
1 stick	Butter
1 sm	Bunch of green onions, chopped
2 med	Celery stalks, chopped
2 tbsp	Flour
4 oz	Sliced mushrooms [can, drained]
2 cups	Half and half
3/4 tsp	Tony Chachere's creole seasoning
2 tbsp	Sherry or white wine

Melt the butter in a skillet or a heavy saucepan. Sauté the onions and celery in the butter. Stir in the mushrooms and seasoning [salt and pepper may be used instead of creole seasoning]. Add the flour and then the crawfish while stirring. Add the half and half, stirring constantly. If too thick, add 1/2 cup or less of water. Add the sherry and cook over low heat until blended and heated through [a small simmer]. Serve over white rice, pasta, crusty bread, or in patty shells. Garnish with chopped parsley or sliced onion tops.

Helpful hint: Milk scorches easily. Be careful to not overheat and keep stirring. Also, leftovers may be frozen.

GROUPER FILETS

Ingredients for 4 servings

1 lb	Grouper
1/2 stick	Butter
	Lemon pepper

Cut the grouper into 4 filets. Melt the butter in a shallow dish and butter both sides of the grouper. Sprinkle both sides with lemon pepper. Bake in a 350–400-degree oven until tender [or flaky].

GREAT GROUPER OR TILAPIA

Ingredients for 4 servings

4 lbs	Grouper filets [or fish of your choice]
6 oz	Texas Pete hot sauce [or hot sauce of your choice]
3/4 cup	Flour, self-rising
3/4 cup	Parmesan cheese, grated [in the shaker container]
	Oil for frying

Cut the fish filets into 4 servings. Place the fish and hot sauce into a ziplock bag. Marinate the fish for several hours or overnight. Whisk the Parmesan cheese and flour together. Shake the hot sauce off of the fish and dredge them in the flour mixture. Fry the fish filets in hot oil [350 degrees] until golden. Drain on paper towels which have been placed on top of a brown paper [grocery] bag.

Helpful hint: If more flour mixture is needed, it is simple to mix any amount half and half.

SALMON CROQUETTES

Ingredients for 4 servings

1 can	Pink salmon, 14.75 oz
2 1/2 tbsp	Flour
1	Egg
	Oil, for frying

Mix the can of salmon, egg, and flour in a mixing bowl. Mix well. When the oil is hot enough to sizzle, drop in large tablespoons of mixture. Fry until golden brown and turn once to brown the other side. Drain hot croquettes on paper towels.

SCALLOPS

Ingredients for 4 servings

16 med	Scallops, cleaned
1/8 cup	Olive oil, good extra virgin
2 tsp	Garlic, minced
1/2 tsp	Thyme, dried [or 1 tsp fresh, finely chopped]
1 tsp	Salt [preferably sea salt]
1/2 tsp	Black pepper, freshly ground
2 cups	Baby greens, spinach, or greens of choice

Mix the olive oil, garlic, thyme, salt, and pepper together in a bowl and add the scallops. Let marinate for 20 minutes. Heat just enough olive oil in a sauté pan to quickly cook the scallops until golden brown [1–2 minutes on each side]. Divide the greens between four plates. Place 4 scallops around each mound of greens.

SEAFOOD CASSEROLE

Ingredients for 8 servings

4 cups	Shrimp, cooked
2 cans	Crabmeat, drained and flaked
2 1/2 cups	Celery, sliced thin
2/3 cup	Onion, chopped small
1 cup	Mayonnaise
2 tsp	Worcestershire sauce
1 tsp	Salt
1/2 tsp	Pepper
1/3 cup	Butter
1 1/2 cups	Bread crumbs, fine
	Lemon slices, optional
	Parsley, optional

Cut the shrimp in half, lengthwise. Add the crabmeat, celery, onion, mayonnaise, Worcestershire sauce, salt, and pepper. Mix well. Spoon into a 1-1/2-quart casserole dish. Combine the butter and the bread crumbs. Sprinkle evenly over the casserole. Bake in a 350-degree oven for 25 minutes or until lightly browned. Garnish with lemon slices and parsley, if desired.

Helpful hint: Cans of lobster or other seafood can be used instead of, or in combination with, the canned crabmeat.

ROSALIND'S COCONUT SHRIMP

Ingredients for 4 dozen

2 lbs	Medium–large shrimp	1 tsp	Cayenne pepper
	[peeled and	1	Large egg
	deveined]	6 cups	Vegetable oil
20 oz	Flaked coconut		
1 cup	Flour, all-purpose		**DIPPING SAUCE**
3/4 cup	Beer [not dark]	1/2 cup	Pineapple preserves
3/4 tsp	Baking soda	1/4 cup	Orange marmalade
1/2 tsp	Salt	1/2 tbsp	Hot cocktail sauce

ANOTHER BATTER: Equal amounts of beer and self-rising flour or 7-Up and self-rising flour, rolling the shrimp in flour before dipping in the batter.

Whisk together the flour, beer, baking soda, salt, cayenne, and egg in a small bowl until the batter is smooth. Put the coconut into another small bowl. Heat the oil over medium-hot heat until it reaches 350 degrees. Dip shrimp into batter, letting the excess drip off. Dredge the shrimp into the coconut, covering completely and place on a tray. Fry the shrimp in batches of eight, turning once. The shrimp should fry to a golden brown. Lift with a slotted utensil and place on another tray. [Place a flat brown grocery bag on the tray and cover it with two layers of paper towels. This helps the shrimp to drain without becoming soggy.]

Helpful hint: To prevent scorching, loose coconut should be removed from the oil, by dipping or by straining. Also, cooked shrimp can be placed on a cookie sheet, covered with plastic wrap, and frozen. When ready to serve, remove from the freezer and place in a 400-degree oven (uncovered) for 10 minutes. The sauce will keep in an airtight container for a couple of weeks.

SHRIMP CREOLE

Ingredients for 4 servings

2 lbs	Shrimp, cleaned
4 oz	Tomato paste
1 med	Onion, diced
1 med	Green pepper, diced
6 tbsp	Butter
2 tbsp	Flour
1 clove	Garlic, crushed
1 tsp	Salt
1 dash	Pepper
1 dash	Cayenne pepper
1/2 tsp	Thyme
	White wine [optional]
1/2 cup	Hot water

Place the crushed garlic and salt in a heavy skillet. Add the butter and melt. Add the flour, stirring constantly to make a paste. Cook slowly for about 5 minutes, while stirring. Add the shrimp, stir, and coat well with the paste. Add the tomato paste and mix well. Add the remaining ingredients [except for the wine], cover, and cook on low heat for 10 minutes, or until the shrimp are pink. Add the white wine to thin, if desired, or add more water if needed.

SAUTÉED SHRIMP

Ingredients for 6 servings

2 lbs	Peeled and deveined shrimp
1/2 stick	Butter
0.7 oz	Package of dry Good Seasons Italian Dressing Mix

Melt butter in a saucepan. Blend in the dressing mix. Add the shrimp and sauté over medium heat until the shrimp are done [curled and pink]. Serve over cooked rice or pasta, using the liquid as a sauce.

Helpful hint: This can be served with crackers as an appetizer.

SHRIMP AND BOWTIE PASTA

Ingredients for 4 servings

1 lb	Shrimp [fresh, cleaned]
3 cups	Chicken [or fish] stock
4 cups	Cream, whipping or half and half
1 stick	Butter
1 med	Onion, chopped
1 med	Bell pepper, chopped
3 cloves	Garlic, minced
1 tbsp	Basil, chopped
3 tbsp	Butter, melted
3 tbsp	Flour
1/2 tsp	Black pepper, freshly ground
1/2 tsp	Cayenne pepper
6	Green onions, sliced thin
1 lb	Bowtie pasta, cooked until just tender
1/2 cup	Freshly shredded Parmesan cheese

Reduce the stock in a large saucepan by half. Add the cream and reduce again by half. Melt the butter in a sauté pan. Add the onion and bell pepper and sauté until almost tender. Add the garlic and basil and cook for 2 minutes. Add the shrimp and sauté for another 4 or 5 minutes. Blend the 3 tablespoons of melted butter with the flour. Slowly bring the reduced cream and stock mixture up to a boil. Whisk the flour mixture slowly into the cream mixture a little at a time. Add the black and cayenne peppers. Fold the shrimp mixture into the thickened sauce. Serve over the cooked pasta. Sprinkle the grated Parmesan cheese over the top and garnish with the sliced green onions. Some of the onions may be stirred into the mixture.

SHRIMP AND CRAB AU GRATIN

Ingredients for 4 servings

1 cup	Shrimp, boiled and chopped into small pieces
1 1/2 cups	Crabmeat, check and remove any shell
4 tbsp	Sherry or white wine
1 cup	Cream
4 tbsp	Flour
1 stick	Butter, divided in half
1/2 cup	Bread crumbs

Melt 1/2 stick of butter in a saucepan. Add the flour and stir. Add the cream slowly, stirring constantly until smooth. Add the wine or sherry and remove from the heat. Stir in the shrimp and crabmeat. Pour into buttered ramekins or a casserole dish. Sprinkle with the bread crumbs and dot with the remaining butter. Bake in a 400-degree oven until golden brown.

Helpful hint: Place the ramekins on a baking tray to catch any overflow. If desired, less butter may be used for topping.

SHRIMP FLORENTINE

Ingredients for 8 servings

8 oz	Spinach noodles [package]
2 lbs	Shrimp, peeled and deveined

1 can	Mushroom soup, undiluted
1 cup	Sour cream
1 cup	Mayonnaise
1/4 tsp	Dijon mustard
1/4 cup	Dry sherry [Woodbridge, Taylor, or any good sherry]
8 1/2 oz	Artichokes [can], drained and cut
3/4 cup	Cheddar cheese [sharp], shredded
1/2 cup	Butter

Cook the noodles according to the directions on the package for 5 minutes and drain. Line a 9x13-inch casserole dish with the noodles. Sauté the shrimp in the butter until pink and tender [about 5 minutes] and mix with the artichokes. Cover the noodles with the shrimp and pour any liquid over all. In a bowl combine the soup, mayonnaise, mustard, sour cream, and sherry. Pour the sauce over the shrimp and cover with the grated cheese. [May be refrigerated at this point. Remember to remove from the fridge and return to almost room temperature before baking.] Bake in a 350-degree oven for 30 minutes or until bubbly.

Helpful hint: Instead of shrimp, 1 1/2 pounds of cooked and cubed chicken can be used in this recipe. Both are very good! A good way to cook the chicken is to add a chicken bouillon cube, an onion, several stalks of celery, and a couple of carrots to the pot to enhance the flavor. Strain the chicken broth when done. Use a little of the broth in the casserole. [Angel hair pasta may be used instead of the spinach noodles.]

LADON'S SHRIMP GUMBO

Ingredients for 10 servings

1 rope	Sausage, diced	1 1/2 tbsp	Garlic, minced
1/2 cup	Olive oil	1/2 tbsp	Salt
2 cups	Nibblet corn	1/2 tbsp	Pepper
3 cups	Okra, cut	3 lbs	Shrimp
3 cups	Tomato, diced	1 cup	Chicken, cooked and diced
2 cups	Onion, chopped		
1 cup	Bell pepper, diced	1 cup	Ham, diced
1 cup	Celery, chopped	2 cans	Chicken broth

Sauté the vegetables in a skillet with olive oil or butter. Combine all of the ingredients except for the shrimp in a large pot. Bring the ingredients to a boil for 20 minutes. Add the shrimp. When the shrimp turns pink, lower the heat and let simmer. Stir occasionally. Serve the gumbo over cooked rice.

To thaw fish, place it in cold water until all the frost is removed. Then cook it as if it were fresh.

Side Dishes

BAKED APPLES AND CHEESE

Ingredients for 8 servings

3 lg	Apples, peeled and sliced
1 stick	Butter
1 cup	Sugar
3/4 cup	Self-rising flour
8 oz	Velveeta cheese

Place apple slices into an oiled 2-quart baking dish. Combine the other four ingredients with a pastry blender. [The butter can be melted in a saucepan on VERY low heat. Add the cheese. When the cheese has melted, add the sugar and flour]. Spoon the mixture over the apples. Bake in a 350-degree oven for 30 minutes or until bubbly.

Helpful hint: If the apples are small, another apple may be added. Gala apples are good for this dish. For a more tart dish use Granny Smith apples. This side dish is nice with ham.

CINNAMON SKILLET APPLES

Ingredients for 6 servings

4	Apples, peeled, cored, and cut into desired sizes
3/4 cup	Light brown sugar
1/3 cup	Butter
4 tsp	Cornstarch
1/2 tsp	Cinnamon
1 1/2 cups	Water

Melt the butter in a large skillet over medium heat. Dissolve the cornstarch in a little of the water. Stir the sugar and cinnamon into the melted butter. Add the water and apples. Cover with a lid and cook about 15 minutes or until the apples are desired tenderness. Stir occasionally and spoon the sauce over the apples.

Helpful hint: This dish is good with pork or spooned over vanilla ice cream.

ROSALIND'S BAKED BEANS

Ingredients for 8 servings

53 oz	Pork and beans
3/4 cup	Ketchup
3/4 cup	Brown sugar [dark]
1 tbsp	Worcestershire sauce
1 med	Onion [sweet], chopped
8 slices	Bacon

Drain some of the excess liquid off of the beans. Mix all of the ingredients, except the bacon, together in a bowl. Pour the mixture into a Pyrex dish. Place the bacon over the beans, covering the beans with single slices. Bake uncovered in a 350-degree oven for 45 minutes or until the bacon is cooked.

Helpful hint: Everyone has a favorite baked beans recipe. Try adding mustard or maybe cooked ground beef or sausage. Make it your own.

EASY NON-BAKED BEANS

Ingredients for 2 servings

15 oz	Pork and beans [can]
2 tsp	Dried onion flakes [in the spice section]
2 tbsp	Dark brown sugar
3 tbsp	Ketchup

Put all of the ingredients into a small saucepan. Slowly bring the beans to a simmer. Let the beans simmer long enough to absorb the flavors, stirring occasionally. Serve warm.

BAKED CRANBERRIES

Ingredients for 6 servings

2 cups	Cranberries, fresh
1 cup	Water
1 1/2 cups	Sugar
1/2 tsp	Cinnamon
1/2 cup	Walnuts, chopped and slightly toasted

Wash the berries and pick over to remove any unwanted ones. Combine the berries, water, and sugar in a one-quart casserole dish. Cover and bake in a 400-degree oven for 45 minutes. After 45 minutes, remove from the oven and sprinkle the cinnamon over the top of the berries. DO NOT STIR! Return to the oven uncovered for an additional 15 minutes. Sprinkle with the walnuts and serve hot or cold.

Helpful hint: Place the dish on a tray in case the cranberries boil over.

Optional: Cook 1 pound of cranberries, 2 cups of sugar, 1/3 cup of water, 2 cinnamon sticks, 1/8 teaspoon of nutmeg, and 1/2 teaspoon of allspice in a boiler until the mixture thickens slightly.

OR...

Cook cranberries, brown sugar, cinnamon sticks, the zest and juice of one orange together.

FRIED CHIPS

Ingredients for 4 servings

4 lg   Idaho potatoes
              Salt
              Oil

Peel and cut the potatoes lengthwise in 1/4-inch slices. Cut the slices into 1/4-inch strips. Heat oil in a deep pan [5 inches of oil] until it reaches 285 degrees. Cook potato strips for 10 minutes in small batches and spread on a parchment-lined baking sheet. [Can store in the refrigerator at this point.] When ready to serve, reheat the oil until it reaches 350 degrees and recook the potatoes until golden brown. Place paper towels over a brown grocery paper bag and drain the cooked potatoes. Season with salt.

The next time you have a cookout, place whole bananas in their skins right onto the grill. Cook for about eight minutes, turning several times. They're wonderful.

ROSALIND'S CORN BREAD DRESSING

Ingredients for 12 servings

CORN BREAD

3/4 cup	Flour [all-purpose], sifted
1 tsp	Salt, sifted with flour
2 tsp	Baking powder, sifted with flour
2 tbsp	Sugar
1 1/2 cups	Cornmeal [plain]
1 1/2 cups	Milk
2 lg	Eggs, lightly beaten with a fork
1/4 cup	Bacon drippings [or cooking oil]

DRESSING

1 cake	Corn bread
3 lg	Biscuits, baked [I like buttermilk biscuits]
6 slices	White bread, cubed
2	Hot dog [or hamburger] buns, several days old
4 cups	Chicken or turkey broth
2 cups	Celery, chopped
1 1/2 cups	Onion, chopped
4 lg	Eggs, beaten with a fork
1 stick	Butter
1 tsp	Salt
1 tsp	Black pepper
2 cans	Cream of chicken soup
1 can	Cream of celery soup

GRAVY

1 qt	Chicken broth
1 can	Cream of chicken soup
1/4 cup	Chopped celery
1/4 cup	Chopped onion
1 cup	Raw dressing

| 3 lg | Hardboiled eggs, chopped |
| 1/4 cup | Chopped chicken or giblets |

CORN BREAD: Sift the flour, salt, and baking powder together. Add the cornmeal and sugar. Combine the milk, eggs, and oil. Add the dry ingredients and mix well. Pour into an oiled pan or large iron skillet. Bake in a 375-degree oven for about 30 minutes or until top is golden brown.

Helpful hint: If using an iron skillet, place oil in it and let it heat in the oven while bringing the oven up to 375. Bread will brown better on the bottom.

DRESSING: Crumble the breads or process in a food processor to make crumbs with no large chunks. Cook the onion and celery in some chicken broth until tender. Put all of the ingredients in a large bowl and mix thoroughly. Add additional broth if it is too stiff. Reserve 1 cup of the raw dressing for the gravy. Pour into a large baking dish and bake in a 350-degree oven for about an hour or until golden brown.

Helpful hint: If using broth from a hen, strain the broth and omit the butter. Also, the raw dressing should be slightly thin, but not runny. The dressing will thicken while cooking.

GRAVY: Place the broth, soup, and cup of dressing in a saucepan. Cook over medium heat. Stir. To thicken, dissolve 2 teaspoons of cornstarch or 2 tablespoons of flour in 1/4 cup of cold water. If using flour, add more water. Add the other ingredients to gravy.

Helpful hint: You may want to use cream of celery soup instead of, or in addition to, the cream of chicken soup.

DEVILED EGGS

Ingredients for 16 servings

8 lg	Eggs
3 tbsp	Mayonnaise
3 tbsp	Pickles [I like sweet], chopped small
1 tbsp	Pickle juice
	Dash of salt
	Dash of pepper
	Dash of celery salt

Cover the eggs in a heavy saucepan with water and bring to a rolling boil. Turn off the heat, cover with a lid, and let them rest for 20 minutes. Drain off the hot water and cover with cold water. Remove the shells, rinse, blot, and slice in half lengthwise. Mash the yolks and add the remaining ingredients. Spoon the mixture back into the egg whites. Garnish with pimiento, parsley, or a dash of paprika.

Helpful hint: The egg whites may need to be blotted with a paper towel before filling. Also, adding mustard or dill pickles will give the eggs more spice.

BAKED FRUIT WITH ORANGE MARMALADE

Ingredients for 6 servings

15 oz	Pears or peaches [can], drained
	Orange marmalade
	Butter

Place fruit of choice with cut side up in a casserole dish. Spoon about a teaspoon of marmalade into each piece of fruit. Dot with butter. Bake in a 350-degree oven for 15–20 minutes. If marmalade isn't bubbly enough, turn broiler on for one minute. Serve warm.

Helpful hint: Mincemeat or other jams can be used at Thanksgiving or Christmas.

MACARONI AND CHEESE SUPREME

Ingredients for 6 servings

8 oz	Elbow macaroni
3 tbsp	Butter, divided
1 can	Cream of mushroom soup
1/4 cup	Onion, chopped fine
1/4 cup	Diced pimiento
1/4 cup	Green bell pepper, chopped small
1 cup	Mayonnaise
1/2 lb	Sharp cheddar cheese, grated

Cook the macaroni in seasoned water until just tender and drain. Sauté the onion and green pepper in 2 tablespoons of butter until just tender. Heat the undiluted mushroom soup. Add the onion, bell pepper, and pimiento to the soup. Cook [over very low heat] and stir for about 10 minutes. Cool slightly, add the mayonnaise, and mix. Place half of the macaroni into a buttered [using the remaining butter] 2-quart casserole dish. Spread half of the soup mixture over the macaroni. Sprinkle half of the grated cheese over the soup mixture. Repeat the procedure. Bake in a 350-degree oven for 30 minutes or until bubbly. This dish can be prepared ahead of time, covered, and refrigerated until ready to bake. Remove it from the refrigerator and return to room temperature before baking.

BAKED MACARONI AND CHEESE

Ingredients for 6 servings

8 oz	Cheese, grated
2 cups	Elbow macaroni
4 lg	Eggs, lightly beaten
3 cups	Milk
3 tbsp	Butter, melted
	Salt [optional]
	Pepper [optional]
	Additional cheese for topping

Cook the macaroni according to the directions on the box. Add the milk, beaten eggs, butter, salt, pepper, and cheese to the beaten eggs. Mix with the cooked and drained macaroni. Top with the additional cheese. Bake in a 350-degree oven for 30–45 minutes.

SAUTÉED MUSHROOMS

Ingredients for 4 servings

1 lb	Mushrooms, cleaned and sliced
1/2 stick	Butter, melted
3	Green onions with tops, chopped
1/4 cup	White wine
1/4 tsp	Pepper
1/8 tsp	Garlic powder
2 tsp	Worcestershire sauce

Sauté the green onions in the melted butter until tender. Stir in the remaining ingredients and cook [uncovered] until the mushrooms are tender, about 30 minutes.

BAKED VIDALIA ONIONS

Ingredients for 4 servings

4	Vidalia onions
4	Beef bouillon cubes
	Seasoned salt
	Butter

Peel onions and cut just enough out of the tops to place a bouillon cube into each one. Top the bouillon cube with a small pat of butter. Sprinkle with seasoned salt. Place in a baking dish and cover with foil. Bake in a 400-degree oven for 1 hour or until just tender. Excellent to serve at a cook-out.

VIDALIA ONION CASSEROLE

Ingredients for 6 servings

2 tbsp	Butter
2 tbsp	Flour
1 cup	Chicken broth
5 oz	Evaporated milk
3 cups	Vidalia onions, parboiled
1/2 cup	Slivered almonds
1/2 tsp	Salt
	Pepper to taste
1 cup	Crumbs
1/2 cup	Grated cheese

Peel 5 or 6 medium onions and cut into 6 sections. Cook in seasoned water until just tender, not mushy [about 10–15 minutes]. Drain. Melt butter in saucepan and stir in the flour. Add the broth and evaporated milk, stirring constantly until mixture begins to thicken and is smooth. Add the drained onions and the almonds. Pour into a buttered 1-1/2-quart casserole dish. Mix crumbs and cheese and sprinkle over onion mixture. Bake in a 375-degree oven for 30 minutes or until bubbly.

Helpful hint: One chicken bouillon cube dissolved in a cup of water can be substituted for the broth.

VIDALIA ONION PIE [THANKS, KAREN]

Ingredients for 8 servings

1 cup	Saltine cracker crumbs
5 tbsp	Butter, melted
2 1/2 cups	Vidalia onion slices [thin]
2 tbsp	Oil
2 lg	Eggs, slightly beaten
3/4 cup	Milk
	Salt [to taste]
	Pepper [to taste]
1/4 cup	Cheddar cheese, grated

Combine the crumbs and the melted butter. Press the mixture into an 8-inch pie pan or plate. Bake in a 350-degree oven for 8 minutes. Sauté the onion slices in the oil until tender and put them into the pie shell. Mix all of the remaining ingredients except for the cheese and pour over the onions. Top with the cheese. Bake in a 350-degree oven for 45 minutes.

SCALLOPED PINEAPPLE

Ingredients for 12 servings

3	Eggs
2 cups	Sugar
20 oz	Can crushed pineapple or tidbits, undrained
4 cups	Cubed fresh bread
	[6–8 slices cut into 1-inch squares]
1 cup	Butter or oleo [2 sticks]

Toast bread lightly and cut into cubes. [Kitchen scissors can be used.] Combine all of the ingredients in a mixing bowl. Pour into an oiled 12x7x2-inch baking dish or pan. Bake in a 350-degree oven for one hour or until golden brown.

PINEAPPLE AND CHEESE CASSEROLE

Ingredients for 8 servings

40 oz	Pineapple bits or chunks, drained
1 cup	Sugar
6 tbsp	Flour, all-purpose
6 tbsp	Pineapple juice [from drained pineapple]
2 cups	Sharp cheddar cheese, grated
1 stick	Butter, divided
1 stack	Ritz crackers, crushed

Save 6 tablespoons of the pineapple juice to add to the flour mixture when draining the cans of pineapple. Combine the sugar, flour, and reserved juice. Add the cheese. Melt half stick of butter and add to the mixture. Melt the other half of the butter in a small saucepan and add the crushed crackers, mixing well. Pour into a casserole dish. Sprinkle the buttered crumbs over the top of the pineapple mixture. Bake in a 350-degree oven for 30–40 minutes.

DELUXE POTATO CASSEROLE

Ingredients for 8 servings

2 lb	Hash brown potatoes, thawed
1 cup	Onion, chopped
1 can	Cream of chicken soup, undiluted
8 oz	Cheese, grated
8 oz	Sour cream
1 stick	Butter or margarine, melted

Mix all of the ingredients together except for the potatoes. When well mixed, add the potatoes. Pour the mixture into a 9x13-inch casserole dish. Bake in a 350-degree oven for 1 hour or until golden brown.

Helpful hint: To thaw potatoes in a hurry, punch 5 or 6 holes in the bag and microwave for two minutes.

CREAMED POTATOES

Ingredients for 8 servings

10 med	Potatoes, red skin or gold
1 stick	Butter
1/2 cup	Milk
1/8 cup	Mayonnaise
	Salt
	Pepper

Peel and cube the potatoes. Cook in seasoned water until tender. Drain the water from the potatoes, saving a little. In a small saucepan and over very low heat, melt the butter in the milk. Add the milk and butter to the potatoes while beating with a mixer. Add the mayonnaise last, beating well. If the potatoes are too dry, add some of the reserved water, discarding the rest. Keep warm over a large pan of hot water on the stove.

VARIATION: Keep leftover creamed potatoes in the fridge. Scoop out with a large ice cream scoop onto a baking sheet lined with foil or parchment paper. Sprinkle with paprika and freshly grated Parmesan cheese. Bake in a 375-degree oven for 20 minutes or until lightly browned on top. These are pretty and good. They can also be piped while warm with a large pastry tip.

ROASTED ONION-POTATOES

Ingredients for 6 servings

2 lbs	Potatoes of choice
1 pkg	Lipton onion soup mix [dry]
1/2 cup	Oil [vegetable or olive]

Peel and cut the potatoes into chunks. Mix all of the ingredients together and put into a baking dish or a roasting pan. Bake in a 350-degree oven for 45–55 minutes or until the potatoes are tender. Stir the potatoes with a fork several times. Optional: Sprinkle dried or fresh chopped parsley over the top. For a deeper flavor, chop some fresh rosemary and sprinkle over the top before baking.

ROSALIND'S LOADED POTATOES

Ingredients for 6 servings

6 med	Russet potatoes
1/2 stick	Butter
1/2 cup	Sour cream
3 tbsp	Mayonnaise
6 oz	Cheddar cheese, grated and divided
4 slices	Bacon, fried crisp and crumbled
	Salt [to taste]
	Pepper [to taste]
	Oil [vegetable or olive]
	Rosalind's Seasoned Salt

Line a baking sheet with foil. Scrub the potatoes with a vegetable brush and pat dry. Cover the skins of the potatoes with oil and then with seasoned salt. Bake in a 350-degree oven until fork tender. With a paring knife cut an oval on top of the potatoes just through the skin. Peel the top skin away and carefully scoop out the potatoes into a mixing bowl. Add the butter, sour cream, 4 ounces of the cheese, mayonnaise, salt, and pepper into the bowl and mix until well incorporated. Spoon the mixture into the potato skins. Sprinkle the remaining cheese on top. Return the potatoes to the hot oven and bake until reheated. Sprinkle the bacon bits over the tops the last couple of minutes of baking.

Helpful hint: More or less of the ingredients can be used, according to taste. Also, a little grated onion would be good in the mix.

SCALLOPED CHEESE POTATOES

Ingredients for 8 servings

6 lg	Potatoes
2 cups	Cheddar cheese, shredded
1/2 stick	Butter, melted
1 tsp	Salt
1/2 tsp	Pepper
1/3 cup	Onion, chopped small
1 1/2 cup	Sour cream

Boil the potatoes in seasoned water until just done, drain, and cool. Slice the cooled potatoes. Mix the remaining ingredients together. Gently fold in the potato slices. Pour the mixture into an oiled 2-quart casserole dish. Sprinkle with additional cheese, if desired. Bake in a 350-degree oven for 30 minutes or until bubbly.

SOUR CREAM POTATOES

Ingredients for 8 servings

12 med	Red skin potatoes, peeled and cut into large slices
1/3 cup	Onion, chopped
1/3 cup	Butter
1 cup	Cheese, shredded [optional]
16 oz	Sour cream
1 tsp	Salt
1/2 tsp	Pepper
1 1/2 cups	Corn flakes, slightly crushed

Boil the potatoes in seasoned water until just tender. Sauté the onions in the butter until translucent. Combine the potatoes, onions, sour cream, and cheese in a bowl and gently mix. Pour the mixture into a 12x8-inch casserole dish. Bake in a 350-degree oven until bubbly [30–35 minutes]. Top with the corn flakes and let bake the last 15 minutes.

Helpful hint: Crushed Ritz crackers may be used for the topping.

POTATO WEDGES

Ingredients for 4 servings

2 lg	Baking potatoes
1/2 cup	Mayonnaise
1/2 tsp	Hot sauce
1/8 tsp	Onion salt
1/8 tsp	Black pepper
2 cups	Bread crumbs
	[Parmesan or seasoned with herbs]
	Seasoned salt

Peel baking potatoes and slice lengthwise, cutting each potato into 8 wedges. Sprinkle with seasoned salt. Add the mayonnaise and the seasonings together [all of the remaining ingredients except for the bread crumbs]. Cover the potato wedges with the mayonnaise mixture and roll in the crumbs. Place the potatoes in an oiled baking dish. Loosely cover with foil and bake in a 350-degree oven until tender.

SENATOR RUSSELL'S SWEET POTATO CASSEROLE

Ingredients for 8 servings

3 cups	Sweet potato, cooked and mashed
1 cup	Sugar
2	Eggs
1/2 cup	Milk
1/2 cup	Butter, melted
1 tbsp	Vanilla

	TOPPING
1 cup	Brown sugar
1/3 cup	Flour
1/3 cup	Butter, melted
1 cup	Chopped pecans

Mix the first six ingredients together and pour into a casserole dish. Mix together the four topping ingredients and sprinkle over the top. Bake in a 350-degree oven for 40 minutes or until bubbly in the center. Dee-lish at Thanksgiving or Christmas.

PUMPKIN SOUFFLÉ

Ingredients for 8 servings

1 med	Pumpkin [cooked in 1/4 cup water and 1/4 cup sugar]
4 cups	Pumpkin, cooked [above]
1 stick	Butter
1 cup	White sugar
3	Eggs
1 tsp	Nutmeg
1 tsp	Ginger
1 tsp	Vanilla
1 1/2 cups	Milk [not too soupy]

Mash 4 cups of cooked and drained pumpkin. Add softened butter. Add slightly beaten eggs to cooled mixture. Mix seasonings and sugar. [Ginger, nutmeg, and vanilla can be increased to 2 teaspoons each, if desired.] Alternate sugar and milk to pumpkin mixture. Mix well and pour into a casserole dish. Bake in a 350-degree oven until firm. A topping of 1/2 stick of butter, 1 1/2 cups of brown sugar, and 1 1/4 cups chopped pecans can be sprinkled on cooked casserole and run under the broiler for a minute or two or until brown sugar melts.

BAKED RICE

Ingredients for 4 servings

2 cups	Rice [Uncle Ben's]
2 1/2 cups	Chicken broth [or stock]
1/2 cup	Onion, diced
1/4 cup	Celery, diced
1 1/2 tbsp	Butter

Combine the ingredients and pour into a casserole dish. Seal with foil. Bake in a 350-degree oven for 1 hour or until the rice is tender. Let the rice rest for about 10 minutes before serving. Serve a scoop in a bowl of gumbo.

BROWN RICE

Ingredients for 6 servings

1 stick	Butter or oleo
10 1/2 oz	Beef consommé [can]
10 1/2 oz	French onion soup [can]
7 oz	Mushrooms, slices or pieces [can or jar], drained
1 cup	Rice

Melt butter in a Pyrex dish. Mix all of the ingredients together. Bake in a 350-degree oven until rice is tender. Mushrooms will rise to the top and rice will be brown when done.

GREEN RICE

Ingredients for 8 servings

20 oz	Chopped broccoli [2 boxes, frozen]
8 oz	Cheez Whiz [jar]
1 cup	Chopped onion
1/4 cup	Chopped celery
3 tbsp	Butter
2 cans	Cream of mushroom soup, undiluted
2 cups	Cooked rice
	Buttered bread crumbs

Cook broccoli in seasoned water and according to directions. Drain well. Sauté onions and celery in butter until the onion is translucent. Add the soup and Cheez Whiz to the mixture and stir until well mixed. Add the cooked rice and drained broccoli, mixing well. Pour into a buttered 2-quart casserole dish. Top with buttered bread crumbs, crushed Ritz crackers, or crushed potato sticks. Bake in a 350-degree oven until bubbly and brown, approximately 35–40 minutes.

ORANGE RICE

Ingredients for 8 servings

2 cups	Rice, long grain
3 cups	Water
1 cup	Orange juice
1 tbsp	Orange zest
1/2 stick	Butter
1 1/2 tsp	Salt

Bring the water, salt, and orange juice to a boil in a large saucepan. Add the remaining ingredients and cook on a low boil. Cook covered for 20 minutes or until the rice is tender and fluffy. Serve with Cornish game hens or other festive meats.

RICE PILAF

Ingredients for 4 servings

1 cup	Rice
1 cup	Chopped onion
3 tbsp	Butter
2 1/2 cups	Chicken broth [or stock]

Salt
Pepper, freshly ground
Parsley, fresh, chopped, for garnish [optional]

Melt the butter in a heavy, deep skillet or saucepan. Add the onion and cook until tender. Add the rice and turn the heat to medium. Cook, while stirring, for 5 minutes or until the rice is glossy and beginning to turn color. Salt and pepper. Turn the heat to low and add the chicken broth [or stock] all at once. Stir several times and cover with the lid. Cook on low until the liquid is absorbed. [If the rice is not tender enough, add a little more chicken broth at this point.] Turn the heat off and let the rice rest, without lifting the lid. After about 30 minutes, fluff with a fork, adding a little more butter if desired.

ROSALIND'S SLICED BAKED TOMATOES

Ingredients for 4 servings

3	Slices of white bread
3	Small tomatoes, peeled and sliced
1/2 stick	Butter
2 tsp	Granulated sugar
	Dash of salt

Make bread crumbs by placing the bread slices in a 250-degree oven until crumbly. Bread crumbs already prepared work very well, but this is a good way to use day-old bread. Crumble dry toasted bread and add the salt, sugar, and melted butter. Mix well. Place a layer of tomato slices in a casserole dish and then a layer of the crumb mixture. Repeat the procedure ending with crumb mixture on the top. Bake in a 350-degree oven for 1 1/2 hours for tomatoes to be very well done [or less if desired].

SCALLOPED TOMATOES

Ingredients for 4 servings

2 lg	Eggs, slightly beaten
3/4 cup	Bread crumbs
3	Tomatoes, sliced thick
	Salt
	Pepper
2 tbsp	Butter
1 cup	Sharp cheddar cheese, shredded
	Paprika

Beat the eggs in a small bowl and place the bread crumbs in another. Dip each slice of tomato in the egg and then in the bread crumbs. Place the slices [side by side] on an oiled cookie sheet. Sprinkle them with salt and pepper and dot with butter. Bake in a 350-degree oven for 15 minutes. Remove the tray from the oven and sprinkle the tomatoes with paprika and the shredded cheese. Place back into the oven and bake for 5 minutes more. Serve warm.

STUFFED TOMATOES

Ingredients for 6 servings

6	Tomatoes, large
4 oz	Butter
1/2 cup	Green onions, chopped
2	Garlic cloves, minced
1/2 lb	Ham, finely chopped [can use shrimp or crabmeat]
1 cup	Bread, wet and squeezed
	Bread crumbs
	Salt
	Pepper
	Paprika
	Butter

Slice tops off of the tomatoes and scoop out. Chop the meat of the tomatoes. Sauté the onions in butter with garlic, chopped ham, and tomato. Add the wet bread and mix. Season with salt and pepper. Stuff the tomato shells and place in a baking dish. Cover with bread crumbs and paprika. Dot with butter and bake in a 350-degree oven for 10 minutes.

ROSALIND'S TOMATO PIE

Ingredients for 8 servings

4	Ripe tomatoes, peeled and sliced
9 inch	Deep-dish pie shell
1 cup	Mayonnaise
1 cup	Medium cheddar cheese, grated
1 cup	Mozzarella cheese, grated
	Salt
	Pepper
1/2 cup	Green onions, chopped
	Basil leaves, chopped

Bake the pie shell in a 400-degree oven for 5 minutes, making sure to prick with a fork to prevent air pockets. Slice the tomatoes, salt, pepper, and blot well on paper towels. Mix the mayonnaise and cheese in a bowl. Layer tomato slices in the bottom of the pie shell. Layer the chopped green onions and basil over the tomato slices. [Amount of basil and onions can vary, according to taste.] Cover with the cheese mixture. Bake in a 350-degree oven for 25 minutes or until the crust is a nice brown. Slice and serve warm.

Helpful hint: To make rosettes, take long strips of the tomato peel, turn them inside out and roll, making one edge smaller than the other. Place them in an airtight container, seam-side down, and keep in the refrigerator. When ready to serve the pie slices, place one rosette on top with a basil leaf.

Soups

ROSALIND'S GREAT NORTHERN BEAN SOUP

Ingredients for 8 servings

3 cups	Great Northern Beans [dry]
1	Ham hock or ham bone with meat remaining
1	Sweet or white onion, chopped
2 stalks	Celery, chopped
1	Clove garlic, minced
2 small	Russet potatoes, diced
	Salt, to taste
	Pepper, to taste
	Water

Soak the beans overnight in 2 quarts of water. Drain the water off of the beans and save. Place the beans and the ham bone in a heavy pot. Add enough water to the reserved water to make 2 1/2 quarts and pour it into the pot. Add the chopped onion, celery, salt, and pepper. Cook on medium heat. Place the potatoes and garlic in a small saucepan, cover with water [about a cup], and cook until tender. Cool a little and puree in a blender. Pour the potato mixture into the pot. Simmer for 1 1/2 hours or until desired tenderness of the beans. Check occasionally for tenderness and seasoning. When the beans are done, remove the ham bone and break up any large pieces of ham. Extra water may be needed.

ARTICHOKE AND SHRIMP BISQUE

Ingredients for 4 servings

4 tbsp	Butter
1	Onion, chopped
2	Potatoes, cut into cubes
14 oz	Chicken broth [can]
14 oz	Artichoke hearts [can], drained and cut
3 cups	Milk
1/2 tsp	Paprika
1/4 tsp	Black pepper, freshly ground
1/2 lb	Shrimp
	Chives, chopped for garnish

Cook the shrimp in seasoned water until just done and drain. Melt the butter in a large saucepan. Add the chopped onion and cook until tender. Cook the cubed potatoes in the chicken broth until tender. Pour off some of the liquid and add the potatoes to the onion. [Reserve some of the liquid to use to thin the soup, if needed.] Stir in the artichoke hearts, milk, paprika, and pepper. Put the soup into a blender or food processor and puree. Cut the shrimp into small pieces [reserving 4 shrimp] and add to the soup. Return to a boiler and heat to a boiling point. Slice the reserved shrimp lengthwise and arrange on top of each bowl of the bisque. Garnish with chives.

BROCCOLI SOUP

Ingredients for 6 servings

3 med	Broccoli heads
1 med	Onion, chopped
4 tbsp	Butter
4 tbsp	Flour
1 qt	Half and half
16 oz	Chicken stock
	Salt
	Pepper

Clean and cut the broccoli into small florets. Cook the broccoli in the chicken stock. Sauté the chopped onion in the butter. Add the flour to the butter and onion and stir in some of the chicken stock, making a paste. Add more stock and combine the two mixtures. Cook, while stirring, until it reaches the desired thickness. Adjust the seasoning by adding the desired amount of salt and pepper. Add the half and half while stirring.

Helpful hint: For a creamy soup omit the flour roux and add 1 can of cream of chicken soup [undiluted] and 12 ounces of Velveeta cheese the last few minutes of cooking.

BRUNSWICK STEW, Y'ALL

Ingredients for 10 quarts

12 cups	Chicken, cooked and chopped
6 cups	Pork, Boston butt seasoned with Rosalind's Seasoned Salt, cooked, and chopped
4 lg	Onions, chopped and cooked in chicken broth
6 med	Potatoes, cubed and cooked in chicken broth [optional]
3 cans	Diced tomatoes [28 oz each]
2 cans	Ro-Tel tomatoes and green chilies [10 oz each]
3 cans	Cream style corn [14 oz each]
3 cans	Whole corn [or white shoepeg]
16 oz	Petite green peas, frozen [cooked slightly in chicken broth]
12 oz	Chili sauce
2 cups	Ketchup
5 tbsp	Worcestershire sauce
4 tbsp	Lemon juice
4 tbsp	Apple cider vinegar
7 tbsp	Brown sugar
	Chicken broth [added to desired thickness]
7 drops	Hot sauce, optional

Cook the tomatoes. Add the rest of the ingredients, cover, and simmer. Cook very slowly for a couple of hours, stirring often. Place leftovers in quart or gallon bags and freeze. Makes enough to share with family and friends.

Helpful hint: If desired, use only chicken, pork, or leftover turkey for the meat in this recipe. Make it your own. This is easy to halve. Also good with Sour Cream Corn Bread.

TEX-MEX CHICKEN SOUP

Ingredients for 8 servings

4 lg	Chicken breasts
2 1/2 qts	Chicken stock
2 cups	Carrots, chopped [4 large]
1 cup	Celery, chopped [2 stalks]
2 cups	Onion, chopped [2 medium]
3	Jalapeno peppers, seeded and minced
3 cloves	Garlic, minced
28 oz	Crushed tomatoes
3 tbsp	Oil
1 tsp	Cumin, ground
1 tsp	Coriander, ground
8	White corn tortillas
	Salt
	Pepper

Cook the chicken breasts in enough seasoned [salt and pepper] water to cover the chicken until tender. Remove the skin and bones and cut into small chunks. Sauté the onions, carrots, and celery over medium heat for 15 minutes in the oil. Add the garlic and cook for another minute. Add the chicken stock, tomatoes, jalapeños, cumin, coriander, salt, and pepper. Simmer the soup for 30 minutes. Add the chicken and check the seasonings. Add the tortillas which have been cut into thin, short strips. Serve hot. Garnish with a dollop of sour cream, grated cheddar cheese, slices of avocados, or chopped cilantro leaves. Serve with crackers, toasted baguettes, or tortilla chips.

Helpful hint: Chicken is better if a couple of stalks of celery, a cut onion, and a couple of sliced carrots are added to the water while cooking.

CHICKEN AND RICE SOUP

Ingredients for 8 servings

1 cup	Rice, uncooked
3 qts	Chicken broth [saved from cooking chicken]
2 cups	Chicken, cooked and chopped
4 stalks	Celery, chopped
1 med	Onion, chopped
3	Carrots, chopped
2 tbsp	Butter
	Salt [to taste]
	Pepper [to taste]

Sauté the onion and celery in the butter until almost tender. Cook the carrots in a little chicken broth. In a boiler, cook the rice in two quarts of chicken broth. When the rice is almost done, add the carrots, onion, and celery. Add more chicken broth and adjust seasonings, if needed. Cook the soup on low heat for 30–40 minutes for the flavors to blend. Add chicken broth until the soup reaches the desired consistency. Serve hot.

CLAM CHOWDER

Ingredients for 8 servings

30 oz	Clams [3 cans]
1	Onion, chopped
3	Potatoes [large], cubed
1 can	Cream corn
1 can	Whole kernel corn [drained]
2 cups	Chicken broth [or 1 can]
1 pint	Half and half
3 tbsp	Butter
	Pepper

Sauté the onion in the butter until onion is translucent. Cook the potatoes in the chicken broth until they are mushy. [For a more hearty chowder, a couple more potatoes can be used.] Add the onion and the corn. Heat to steaming. Add the cans of clams [juice and all] and bring the heat up again. Check seasoning [pepper or your favorite spices]. Good served with Sour Cream Corn Bread or crackers.

GUMBO

Ingredients for 10 servings

1 cup	Flour, all-purpose
1 cup	Oil, vegetable
1 1/2 cups	Onions, chopped small
1 cup	Celery, diced
1 cup	Green pepper, chopped small
1 lb	Hot smoked sausage link, cut into 1/2-inch slices
1/2 lb	Smoked ham, cut into small cubes
1/2 lb	Shrimp
12 oz	Frozen okra, thawed
1 1/2 tsp	Salt
1/4 tsp	Cayenne pepper
1/4 tsp	White pepper
1/4 tsp	Cracked black pepper, ground
3	Bay leaves
3 qts	Chicken broth [may use reduced fat broth]
3 cups	Cooked chicken, chopped small
2 tbsp	Parsley [flat leaf], chopped
1/2 cup	Green onion tops, chopped
	Tabasco sauce, optional

Heat the oil in a large pot or Dutch oven and stir in the flour. Stir for 20 or 25 minutes over low heat until the mixture turns a dark brown, being very careful not to scorch the flour. [Stir constantly or the roux will scorch and will be bitter.] Add the onions, celery, and bell pepper and stir for another 5 minutes. Add the seasonings, sausage, and ham. Add the okra and stir. Cook for about 3 minutes. Stir in the chicken broth and mix well. Slowly bring the broth to a boil and reduce the heat. Simmer for 1 hour. Add the chicken and heat thoroughly. Add the shrimp and cook for about 5 minutes, or until the shrimp turns pink. Serve with hot sauce and a serving of Baked Rice.

TRUMAN'S OYSTER STEW

Ingredients for 4 servings

1 qt	Oysters [fresh]
1 1/3 stick	Butter
1 med	Onion, diced
1 tbsp	Flour [heaping], self-rising
1 1/2 qts	Milk, homogenized
	Salt [to taste]
	Pepper [to taste]

Place the oysters in a colander over a bowl for 30 minutes to catch liquids. Melt the butter in a large skillet, add the diced onions, and simmer for 20 minutes. Add the oysters to the butter and onions. Add the salt and pepper. Fry for 30 minutes or until most of the oyster moisture has evaporated. While the oysters fry, warm the milk in a heavy bottom 3-quart saucepan. Strain the saved oyster drippings and add them to the milk. Dissolve the flour in a small amount of water, stirring until smooth, and add to the milk. Add the oysters to the milk. While constantly stirring [milk scorches easily] gradually increase the heat until steaming but not boiling. ENJOY!

CREAM OF POTATO SOUP

Ingredients for 6 servings

4 tbsp	Butter
1	Medium onion, chopped
6	Medium potatoes, cubed
10 3/4 oz	Cream of chicken soup [can], undiluted
1/2 lb	Velveeta cheese
2 cans	Half and half [empty soup can]
14 oz	Chicken broth
	Pepper
	Garlic salt [optional]

Sauté onion in melted butter. Peel and cube the potatoes. Boil the potatoes in the chicken broth until potatoes are mushy. Stir in the onions and the undiluted cream of chicken soup. Cut the cheese in small pieces and stir into mixture until the cheese is melted. Add 1 1/2 or 2 cans of half and half while slowly heating and stirring. Add desired seasoning at this point. Make a day or two ahead and store in refrigerator until needed. Reheat very slowly and on low heat.

For BEER CHEESE SOUP: Use 1 can of half and half and 1 soup can of beer.

SWEET POTATO BISQUE

Ingredients for 6 servings

2 lg	Sweet potatoes, peeled and cubed
1 can	Corn [whole kernel], drained
1/2 cup	White onion, chopped
1 clove	Garlic, minced [optional]

2 tbsp	Canola oil [or 1 tbsp oil and 1 tbsp butter]
2 cups	Apple juice
2 cups	Chicken broth
2 tsp	Poultry seasoning
1/2 tsp	White pepper
1/2 tsp	Allspice
1/8 tsp	Cayenne pepper
1/2 cup	Heavy cream

Cover the cubed sweet potatoes in a boiler with just enough water to cover the potatoes and boil for 20 minutes or until tender. Sauté the onion and garlic in the oil until the onions are tender. Stir in the seasonings. Drain the potatoes and add the corn, onions, and chicken broth. Use an immersion tool to blend [or a blender]. Add the juice and blend. Add the cream and lightly blend.

If you happen to over salt a pot of soup, just drop in a peeled potato. The potato will absorb the excess salt.

SAUSAGE CHOWDER

Ingredients for 6 servings

1 lb	Sausage
1	Onion, chopped
3	Potatoes [large], cubed
1	Can of cream corn

1	Can of whole kernel corn [drained]
2 cups	Chicken broth [or 1 can]
2 cups	Milk [or 1 cup milk and 1 cup half and half]

Cook the sausage and onion in a skillet until the sausage is brown. Drain and blot as much grease from the sausage as possible. Cook the potatoes in the chicken broth. Add the sausage and the other ingredients and bring to a boil.

Helpful hint: This is very good served with Sour Cream Corn Bread.

SHRIMP AND CRAB CHOWDER

Ingredients for 10 servings

1 1/2 lbs	Shrimp, medium or small
1 lb	Crabmeat
1	Red bell pepper, chopped small
1 cup	Onion, diced
1 cup	Celery, diced
1 cup	Carrots, diced
3 cups	Potatoes, diced [I like red skins]
32 oz	Chicken broth [I like Swanson]
1 pint	Half and half
1 pint	Whipping cream
1/2 tsp	Thyme
3	Bay leaves
	Salt
	Pepper
	Olive oil
2 tbsp	Flour, heaping

Sauté the onion, red bell pepper, and celery in the olive oil until tender. Add the salt and the flour to make a roux. Add the chicken broth and stir until flour is well blended. Add the potatoes, carrots, thyme, and bay leaves. Heat to boiling and reduce the heat. Cook slowly until the vegetables are tender. Add the shrimp and crab meat and cook until done, being careful not to overcook the shrimp. Add the cream and half and half. Heat, while stirring. Check the seasoning. May add hot sauce, if desired. Remove the bay leaves before serving.

Helpful hint: Serve this when the president comes for dinner. The seafood is pricey.

TACO SOUP

Ingredients for 8 servings

2 lbs	Ground chuck
16 oz	Whole kernel corn
56 oz	Diced tomatoes
16 oz	Red kidney beans, undrained
16 oz	Pinto beans, undrained
2 cups	Onion, chopped
10 oz	Diced tomatoes with green chilies
1/2 tsp	Salt
3 tbsp	Brown sugar
1	Package of taco seasoning mix [Old El Paso]
2 oz	Package of Hidden Valley Ranch Mix
	Guacamole
	Sour cream
	Mozzarella cheese
	Doritos

Brown the meat and onions and drain well. Mix all of the ingredients except for the last four ingredients. Simmer for 30 minutes or more. Serve hot with tortilla chips. Top with cheese, guacamole, sour cream, or other preferred toppings.

ROSALIND'S VEGETABLE SOUP

Ingredients for 3 1/2 quarts

56 oz	Diced tomatoes [2 cans, 28 oz each]
3 tbsp	Brown sugar [optional]
14 oz	Butter beans, frozen
14 oz	Mixed vegetables, frozen
	[or cans of drained Veg-All]
16 oz	Okra, frozen
	Leftover ham bone with chopped bits of ham
	Salt
	Pepper
	Extra corn or any other vegetables desired

Cook tomatoes in a large pot with the ham bone and leftover ham pieces. Salt and pepper to taste. Add the brown sugar. [The brown sugar cuts the sharpness of the tomatoes.] Simmer. Cook the butter beans in seasoned water until tender. Add the vegetables to the pot and simmer until the flavors blend. Remove the bone and any fat or cartilage that may have been on the bone. Check the seasoning and add extra water if needed. Leftover soup can be frozen.

Helpful hint: This soup is good on a cold and rainy night served with Sour Cream Corn Bread.

Vegetables

ASPARAGUS QUICHE

Ingredients for 6 servings

8 oz	Cheddar cheese, shredded
1/4 lb	Asparagus spears [fresh]
1 1/2 cups	Half and half
4 lg	Eggs, slightly beaten
1/4 tsp	Salt
1/8 tsp	Pepper
6 slices	Bacon, cooked crisp and crumbled

	CRUST
1 cup	Flour, all-purpose
1/4 tsp	Salt
1/3 cup	Butter, cold
2 tbsp	Fresh chives, chopped
2 tbsp	Cold water

Combine the flour and salt together with a whisk. Cut the butter in with a pastry cutter, a fork, or two knives until the mixture resembles coarse crumbs. Stir in the water and chives until the flour is just moistened. Shape into a ball and flatten slightly with palm of hand. On a lightly-floured surface, roll the dough out into a 12-inch circle. Fold the dough in half twice and place it into a 10-inch [ungreased] quiche dish. Unfold and press firmly against the sides and bottom of the dish. Trim the crust, leaving 1/2-inch overhang. Roll the overhang up and crimp or flute the edge of the crust. Sprinkle the cheese over the bottom of the crust. Sprinkle the bacon bits over the cheese. Place the asparagus spears over the bacon in a spoke pattern. Combine the remaining ingredients in a small bowl. Pour evenly over the asparagus and cheese. Bake in a 350-degree oven for 40–45 minutes, or until golden and set in the center. Serve warm.

Helpful hint: Can be baked in a 9-inch glass pie plate if a quiche dish is not available.

BAKED ASPARAGUS
Ingredients for 6 servings

2 lbs	Asparagus, fresh
3 tbsp	Parsley, minced
2 tbsp	Butter, melted
2 tbsp	Olive oil, extra virgin
	Salt
	Pepper
	Slivered almonds, optional

Wash and drain the asparagus. Break off the tough ends of the asparagus. This can be done by holding the spears in both hands and slowly bending them. The spears will snap at the appropriate spot. Arrange the spears in one layer in a baking pan. Sprinkle with the parsley. Combine the butter and olive oil and drizzle over the asparagus. Sprinkle with the salt and pepper. Cover with foil and bake for 15–20 minutes in a 375-degree oven. If the asparagus is layered, increase the baking time for another 10–15 minutes. If desired, garnish with toasted almonds.

CREAMY-TOPPED ASPARAGUS
Ingredients for 6 servings

2	Cans of asparagus [10 1/2 oz]
1/2 cup	Sour cream
1/4 cup	Mayonnaise
1/4 cup	Parmesan cheese, grated

Drain asparagus well and arrange the spears on a buttered baking dish. Combine the remaining ingredients in a bowl and mix well. Spread the mixture over the asparagus. Broil in the oven until light brown and bubbly. Do not overcook. Serve immediately.

ARTICHOKE AND SPINACH CASSEROLE

Ingredients for 8 servings

20 oz	Spinach [2 packs, 10 oz each]
1/4 cup	Chopped onions [may use 1/2 cup]
3 tbsp	Butter
1 can	Artichokes [not pickled], cut in quarters
1 can	Water chestnuts [drained, rinsed, and sliced]
1 pint	Sour cream
	Salt to taste
1 cup	Parmesan cheese [reserve 1/4 cup to sprinkle on top]

Cook spinach according to directions and drain. Sauté onion in the butter. Mix all ingredients together. Pour into a casserole dish and sprinkle the reserved cheese over the top. Bake in a 350-degree oven for 30 minutes or until bubbly.

GREEN BEAN BUNDLES

Ingredients for 8 servings

1 can	Blue Lake whole green beans
4	Slices of bacon
6 oz	French dressing

Drain the beans. Cut the bacon in half and cook in the microwave oven until half done. Place 6 or 7 beans on each bacon half and roll. Place the rolls into a casserole dish with the cut-side down. Pour French dressing over tops of the bundles. Cover with aluminum foil and bake at 400-degrees for 10 minutes. Uncover and bake another 20 minutes or until bacon is brown.

SWEET AND SOUR BEETS

Ingredients for 4 servings

16 oz	Beets [can], drained, cubed, and save the juice
8 1/2 oz	Crushed pineapple [can], drained and save the juice
2 tbsp	Butter
1/2 cup	Brown sugar
1/4 tsp	Salt
1/3 cup	White vinegar
3 tbsp	Cornstarch [or flour]
1/2 cup	Raisins, seedless

Melt the butter in a saucepan. Add the flour, salt, and cornstarch, making a roux. Stir in the saved juices, mixing well. Add the vinegar and cook until thickened. Add the raisins and pineapple, heating through. Pour over the beets and let stand several hours to let the flavors blend. Reheat and serve warm.

BLACK-EYED PEAS

Ingredients for 8 servings

2 cups	Black-eyed peas [dry]
1	Ham hock or ham bone with meat left on it
	Salt
	Pepper
	Water

Soak the peas overnight in 1 1/2 quarts of water. Pour off the water and save. Place the peas in a heavy pot with the ham bone. Add the water and season. Cook slowly until the peas are done [tender]. Add more water, if needed. Remove the ham bone and break up any large pieces of ham. It is a tradition in the Deep South to cook and eat black-eyed peas and collard or turnip greens on New Year's Day. This ensures everyone who eats them wealth and good health for the rest of the year.

BROCCOLI QUICHE

Ingredients for 8 servings

2 bags	Frozen broccoli [10 oz each], thawed and chopped
1 med	Onion, finely chopped
1 cup	Bisquick
4	Eggs, slightly beaten
1/2 cup	Vegetable oil
1 cup	Sharp cheddar cheese, shredded
1 tbsp	Chopped parsley
1/2 cup	Light cream

Mix all of the ingredients together and blend well. Pour into an oiled 9-inch pie plate. Bake in a 350-degree oven for 40 minutes or until brown on top.

GLAZED CARROTS

Ingredients for 8 servings

1 lb	Baby carrots
2 oz	Orange marmalade
2 oz	Pineapple preserves
	Salt
1 dash	Pepper

Cook in salted water until just tender. Drain carrots and cover with orange marmalade and pineapple preserves. Steam and serve.

Helpful hint: Regular carrots can be used. Clean, slice, and prepare by the same procedure.

COPPER PENNIES [MARINATED CARROTS]

Ingredients for 8 servings

2 lbs	Carrots, peeled and cut into rounds
1	Can of tomato soup, undiluted
1 cup	Sugar
1	Bell pepper, chopped
1/2 cup	Oil [Wesson or other]
1	Can of sweet pickled onions, drained [or medium onion chopped]
3/4 cup	Vinegar

Cook carrots in water with a little salt. Drain and cool. Mix the other ingredients and cook for 15 minutes. Pour the liquid over the carrots and cook just a little longer. Do not overcook the carrots. May serve hot or cold. May be stored in the refrigerator for a couple of weeks.

CREAMED CELERY

Ingredients for 6 servings

4 cups	Celery, cut into 1-inch pieces
5 oz	Can of sliced water chestnuts
1 can	Cream of chicken soup, undiluted
1/4 cup	Pimiento, drained and chopped

1/2 cup	Soft bread crumbs
1/4 cup	Sliced almonds, toasted
2 tbsp	Melted butter

Cook celery in a small amount of water until crispy tender, about 8 minutes, and drain. Mix celery, water chestnuts, soup, and pimiento and place into a 1-quart casserole dish. Toss bread crumbs, almonds, and melted butter. Sprinkle over top. [Can sprinkle paprika over top.] Bake at 350 degrees for 35 minutes or until bubbly. Garnish with parsley.

Helpful hint: Pepperidge Farm stuffing [1/2 cup] can be used instead of bread crumbs to add a little zest.

ROSALIND'S EGGPLANT CASSEROLE

Ingredients for 8 servings

2 med	Eggplants
5 strips	Bacon
1 lg	Onion, diced
40	Saltine crackers, crushed small
1 lg	Egg
1/2 cup	Evaporated milk
4 oz	Cheddar cheese, shredded
	Salt
	Pepper

Peel and cut eggplants into 2-inch cubes. Place the eggplant into salted water and bring to a boil. Reduce the heat and simmer until tender [about 20 minutes]. Drain well and set aside. Chop the bacon into small pieces and cook until almost done and add the onions. Cook until the onions and bacon are lightly browned. Remove from the heat. Add the bacon and onions to the cooked and drained eggplant, scraping all of the drippings to the mixture. Add the crushed saltine crackers to the mixture. Stir thoroughly, adding the egg and milk. Season to taste. If the mixture is too stiff, add more milk. Spoon the mixture into a buttered 2-quart casserole dish. Sprinkle the cheese over the top. Bake in a 350-degree oven until bubbly, 25 minutes or more. Let the casserole rest a couple of minutes before serving.

MARINATED GREEN BEANS

Ingredients for 8 servings

3 cans	Whole green beans, drained
1	Purple onion, sliced thin
1 cup	Sugar
3/4 cup	White vinegar
1/2 cup	Water
3/4 cup	Oil
	Salt
	Pepper
1 clove	Garlic, mashed

Heat everything, except for the beans and the onion, together until the sugar dissolves. Pour the liquid over the sliced onion and drained green beans. Cover and refrigerate overnight.

Helpful hint: This dish is good served with Shrimp and Green Noodles.

HARVARD BEETS

Ingredients for 4 servings

16 oz	Can of sliced [or whole] beets
1/4 cup	Sugar
1 tbsp	Cornstarch
1/4 tsp	Salt
1 tbsp	Butter
2 tbsp	White vinegar

Drain beets, reserving the liquid. In a medium saucepan, combine sugar, cornstarch, and salt. Add vinegar and beet juice. Cook over medium heat, stirring constantly until thickened. Add beets and butter. Serve warm.

Helpful hint: If made ahead of time beet juice will thicken even more. I have served beets with 2 or 3 pineapple bits on top to add color to a luncheon plate.

BROCCOLI CASSEROLE

Ingredients for 8 servings

20 oz	Frozen, chopped broccoli [2 packages, 10 oz each]
1 can	Cream of mushroom [or cream of chicken] soup, undiluted
3 tbsp	Grated onion
2	Eggs, slightly beaten
1 cup	Mayonnaise
1 cup	Cheese, shredded
1	Stack of Ritz crackers
1/2	Stick of butter, melted
	Salt
	Pepper

Cook broccoli according to the directions on the package, seasoning with salt and pepper. Drain well. Combine all ingredients except for the crumbs and butter. Pour into a buttered casserole dish. Crush crackers and butter them in the melted butter. Top the broccoli mixture with the crumbs [or crushed potato chips]. Bake at 350 degrees for 40 minutes.

Helpful hint: This can be made ahead of time and frozen. Thaw and bake.

BRUSSELS SPROUTS [AND CARROTS] IN MUSHROOM SAUCE

Ingredients for 8 servings

20 oz	Frozen Brussels sprouts [2 packages, 10 oz each]
4	Carrots, sliced [optional]
1 tsp	Salt
1/2 cup	Boiling water
1 can	Cream of mushroom soup, undiluted
1/2 cup	Cheese, shredded

Simmer Brussels sprouts [and carrots] in the salted, boiling water. Cook until just tender. Drain and add the can of mushroom soup. Heat thoroughly. Add 1/2 cup of cheese and stir slightly. Serve immediately.

CARROT SOUFFLÉ

Ingredients for 6 servings

2 cups	Carrots, cooked and mashed
3 tbsp	Flour

3 tbsp	Butter
1 cup	Milk
1/4 tsp	Salt
3 lg	Eggs
1 tsp	Vanilla
3 tbsp	Sugar
1/2 tsp	Nutmeg

Melt the butter in a small pan and stir in the flour to blend. Gradually add the cup of milk, making a smooth sauce. Add to the remaining ingredients. Pour into a buttered casserole dish. Bake in a 350-degree oven for 40 minutes.

CARROT-PECAN CASSEROLE

Ingredients for 6 servings

3 lb	Carrots, peeled and sliced
2/3 cup	Sugar
1/2 cup	Butter, softened
1/2 cup	Chopped pecans, toasted
1/4 cup	Milk
2 lg	Eggs, lightly beaten
3 tbsp	Flour, all-purpose
1 tbsp	Vanilla
1 tsp	Orange rind, grated
1/4 tsp	Nutmeg, ground [fresh, if possible]

Cook the carrots in a small amount of water in a medium saucepan 10–15 minutes or until tender. Drain the carrots and mash. Stir in the next 8 ingredients. Spoon into a lightly-oiled 2-quart casserole dish. Bake in a 350-degree oven for 40 minutes. Garnish with carrot curls and fresh parsley.

CAULIFLOWER CASSEROLE

Ingredients for 4 servings

1 lb	Cauliflower, frozen
1/2 cup	Mayonnaise
1/2 cup	Sharp cheddar cheese, shredded
1/2 tsp	Dry mustard
1/4 tsp	Salt
1/8 tsp	Cayenne [red pepper]

Cook cauliflower in a small amount of boiling water, salt, and pepper for two minutes. Drain. Place cauliflower in a 1-quart casserole dish. Combine remaining ingredients and spoon over the cauliflower. Bake in a 350-degree oven until bubbly and lightly browned, approximately 15 minutes. Fresh cauliflower can be used. Boil the florets in a small amount of seasoned water for 10 minutes or until crisp-tender and drain.

CORN CASSEROLE

Ingredients for 6 servings

15 oz	Whole kernel corn [can]
15 oz	Cream corn [can]
1 stick	Butter, melted
1 cup	Sour cream
2	Eggs
2 tbsp	Sugar
1 box	Jiffy Corn Bread mix

Mix all of the ingredients together. Pour into a casserole dish. Bake in a 350-degree oven for 45 minutes.

OKRA AND TOMATOES

Ingredients for 6 servings

1 tbsp	Bacon grease
1 med	Onion, chopped
4 cups	Tomatoes, peeled, cored, and diced
4 cups	Okra, sliced [fresh or frozen]
1 cup	Chicken broth [or as much as needed]
	Salt
	Pepper
	Sugar

Cook the chopped onion in the bacon grease until it is tender and translucent. Add the remaining ingredients and cook until tender.

Helpful hint: Truman's mom was a fabulous cook. She always added as much sugar as salt when she cooked green vegetables. She said that it "cut the green taste."

PARTY PEAS

Ingredients for 8 servings

20 oz	Frozen English peas [tiny]
6 cups	Iceberg lettuce, shredded
1/2 stick	Butter
2 tsp	Salt
1/2 tsp	Pepper
1 cup	Water

Put all of the ingredients except for the lettuce in a large saucepan and bring to a boil. Boil for 4 or 5 minutes [a rolling boil]. Remove from the heat and add the lettuce, stirring lightly. Cover with a lid and let stand for 2 minutes. Drain and serve immediately.

SPINACH-ARTICHOKE CASSEROLE

Ingredients for 6 servings

20 oz	Chopped spinach [2 frozen packages], thawed and well drained
6 oz	Marinated artichoke hearts [jar], drained and chopped
6 oz	Cream cheese [2 packages, 3 oz each], softened
2 tbsp	Butter, softened
1/4 cup	Milk
1/4 tsp	Freshly ground pepper
2 tbsp	Parmesan cheese, grated

Combine the spinach and artichokes. Combine the cream cheese, butter, milk, and pepper. Combine the two mixtures and spoon into a lightly-oiled 1-1/2-quart casserole dish. Sprinkle with Parmesan cheese. Bake covered in a 350-degree oven for 30 minutes. Uncover and bake another 10 minutes.

Helpful hint: Spinach can be put in a clean cloth and squeezed out by wringing it like wringing water out of clothes.

Keep iceberg lettuce fresh in the fridge by wrapping it in clean, dry paper towel then storing the lettuce and paper towel in a sealed baggie.

SQUASH [GRANDMA BALMA'S RECIPE]

Ingredients for 8 servings

8	Tender yellow squash
1	Medium onion, chopped
2	Eggs, slightly beaten
	Salt
	Pepper
	Sugar
	Cooking oil

Wash squash with a vegetable brush, cut ends off, and slice. Heat oil in a large skillet or pan. Cook squash and onion together until tender. Add desired salt and pepper while the squash and onion are cooking. Add about as much sugar as salt to the squash to cut the green taste. When the liquid from the squash has cooked down, add the slightly beaten eggs and stir well. Cook 4 or 5 more minutes.

SQUASH CASSEROLE

Ingredients for 8 servings

6 cups	Squash, cooked and mashed
1	Medium onion, chopped and cooked with the squash
1 can	Cream of chicken soup, undiluted
1	Medium carrot, grated
1	Can sliced water chestnuts, drained and rinsed
1 cup	Sour cream
1 tsp	Salt
1	Stack of Ritz crackers
1 stick	Butter

Cook the squash and onion together in salted water until tender. Strain and mix with the soup, grated carrot, water chestnuts, and sour cream. Pour into a 10-inch casserole dish and top with crushed Ritz crackers [or saltines]. Melt a stick of butter or oleo and pour over all. Bake in a 350-degree oven until bubbly and golden brown.

CREAMED SPINACH

Ingredients for 8 servings

1 tbsp	Unsalted butter
1/2 cup	Yellow onion, diced
2 tbsp	Flour, all-purpose
1 cup	Milk, whole or 2%
1/2 cup	Cream, heavy
6 oz	Garlic and herbs spreadable cheese, Alouette or Boursin [found in the deli]
16 oz	Spinach, chopped and frozen
3 tbsp	Parmesan cheese, grated
1 tsp	Lemon zest
	Salt
	White pepper
	Cayenne
	Nutmeg
3 slices	White bread
2 tbsp	Unsalted butter
1 tbsp	Olive oil

Thaw and drain the spinach. Blot thoroughly with paper towels or a clean white kitchen cloth. Toast the bread slices in a 250-degree oven until they are completely dry and crumbly. Crumble the bread slices into a bowl and combine crumbs with the butter and oil. Season the crumbs with salt, pepper, or other preferred seasonings. Sauté the onion in the butter in a large saucepan. Cook over medium heat until the onion is soft. Add the flour and stir until the onion is coated. Whisk milk and cream into onion mixture, stirring constantly to prevent lumps from forming. Simmer for about 1 minute. Stir in the Alouette, Boursin, or other seasoned cheese spread. Stir until smooth. Add the spinach, Parmesan, lemon zest, and seasonings. Spray a baking dish with Pam. Pour spinach mixture into the dish and put the crumbs over the top, pressing lightly. Bake in a 400-degree oven for 25 minutes or until the crumbs are golden brown and the sauce is bubbly.

Helpful hint: Before baking, the dish can be covered and kept in the refrigerator. Remove from the refrigerator and let the dish get almost to room temperature before baking. Cold dishes and hot ovens do not get along very well.

VEG-ALL CASSEROLE

Ingredients for 6 servings

2 cans	Veg-All [16 oz each], drained
1 can	Water chestnuts, drained and diced
1 1/2 cups	Cheese, shredded
1 1/2 cups	Mayonnaise
1 cup	Onion, chopped
1 cup	Celery, chopped
1/2 stick	Butter or oleo
22	Ritz crackers, crushed

Combine the first six ingredients. Place in a casserole dish, cover, and bake in a 350-degree oven for 20 minutes or until bubbly. Melt the butter and mix with cracker crumbs. Spread topping evenly over the casserole and bake, uncovered, 10 minutes longer to brown. May be made a day ahead. Cover and store in the refrigerator.

Helpful hint: Whenever I use water chestnuts I drain them and rinse them in a colander. They sometimes have grit on them.

VEGGIE CASSEROLE

Ingredients for 6 servings

8 oz	Cans of the following, drained:
	Whole kernel corn
	English peas [LeSueur]
	White acre peas
	Baby lima beans
	Water chestnuts, sliced or chopped
	Pimientos [large can if preferred]
1 cup	Mayonnaise
	Ritz crackers, crumbled

Mix drained vegetables together with the mayonnaise. Pour into a casserole dish and sprinkle crushed Ritz crackers over the top. Bake in a 350-degree oven for 45 minutes or until bubbly.

Helpful hint: Ingredients [except for the crackers] can be mixed ahead of time, covered, and refrigerated.

Breakfast

BREAKFAST PIE

Ingredients for 8 servings

10 inch	Pie shell
1 1/2 cups	Swiss cheese, shredded
2 1/2 oz	Sliced mushrooms [jar], drained
12 slices	Bacon, fried crisp and crumbled
3 lg	Eggs, beaten
1/2 cup	Milk
1 cup	Whipping cream
1 dash	Pepper

Prick the pie shell with the tines of a fork and bake for about 4 minutes. Layer the cheese, and then the mushrooms, and then the crumbled bacon in the pie shell. Combine the remaining ingredients and pour over the bacon. Bake in a 350-degree oven for 45–55 minutes or until lightly browned and the center is set.

If you aren't sure how fresh your eggs are, place them in about four inches of water. Eggs that stay on the bottom are fresh. If only one end tips up, the egg is less fresh and should be used soon. If it floats, it's past the fresh stage.

EGGS BENEDICT

Ingredients for 4 servings

4	English muffins, separated and toasted
4 slices	Canadian bacon, cooked
8 lg	Eggs
1 pinch	Salt [sea salt, if possible]
1 tsp	White vinegar

HOLLANDAISE SAUCE

2	Egg yolks
2 tbsp	Lemon juice
10 oz	Butter, melted and hot
1 pinch	Salt [sea salt, if possible]
	Freshly ground pepper, according to taste

Combine the egg yolks and lemon juice in a blender and blend on medium speed. In a steady stream, drizzle in the hot butter until the eggs have emulsified and the ingredients are fully incorporated. Season with the salt and pepper. Keep warm in a heatproof bowl placed over, but not touching, hot water. Fill a medium saucepan with 5 cups of water and bring to a boil. Add a pinch of salt and the vinegar. Reduce the boiling water to a simmer. Carefully crack each egg into a small cup or bowl [do not disturb the yolk]. Gently slide the egg into the water. [If the white scatters, fold up the edges with a spoon.] Add more eggs, but do not crowd the pan. Cook each egg 2–3 minutes. Remove the eggs with a slotted spoon. Place the eggs on paper towels placed over a kitchen towel. Top each half of a toasted muffin with a slice of cooked Canadian bacon and a poached egg. Spoon the Hollandaise sauce over each egg and serve immediately while warm.

Helpful hint: The poached eggs may be placed on slices of bread to blot. Also, smoked salmon, ham, etc. may be used instead of Canadian bacon.

MAKE-AHEAD EGGS BENEDICT

Ingredients for 6 servings

3	English muffins, split and toasted
12	Thin slices of Canadian bacon [8 oz]
6 lg	Eggs
3 tbsp	Light cream or milk
1 tbsp	Butter
1/8 tsp	Salt
1/8 tsp	Pepper

TOPPING

1/4 cup	Soft bread crumbs [about 1 slice of bread]
1 tbsp	Chives, minced
1 tbsp	Butter, melted

SWISS CHEESE SAUCE

3 tbsp	Butter
3 tbsp	Flour, all-purpose
1/8 tsp	Nutmeg
1/8 tsp	Pepper
1 3/4 cups	Milk
6 oz	Processed Swiss cheese
1/3 cup	Dry white wine

Arrange the muffin halves in a 12x7x2-inch baking dish. Place 2 bacon slices on each muffin half. Beat together the eggs, cream, salt, and pepper. In a large skillet melt one tablespoon of butter over medium heat. Pour in the egg mixture. Cook without stirring until the mixture begins to set on the bottom and around the edges. Using a spatula, lift and fold the partially cooked eggs so that uncooked eggs flow underneath. Continue cooking over medium heat for 4 or 5 minutes or until the eggs are cooked but are still moist. Remove from the heat and spoon the eggs atop the muffins, dividing equally. Combine the crumbs, chives, and tablespoon of melted butter. Sprinkle the crumbs over the muffin stacks. Cover and chill in the refrigerator overnight.

For the SWISS CHEESE SAUCE melt 3 tablespoons of butter in a medium saucepan. Stir in 3 tablespoons of flour, 1/8 teaspoon of nutmeg, and 1/8 teaspoon of pepper. Add the milk all at once. Cook and stir until the mixture is thickened and bubbly. Stir in 6 ounces of processed Swiss cheese [torn into pieces]. When the cheese has melted, stir in 1/3 cup of dry white wine. Bake the muffin stacks in a 375-degree oven for 20–30 minutes or until heated through. Serve on individual plates with the hot cheese sauce over the top.

HAM QUICHE

Ingredients for 8 servings

1/2 cup	Onion, diced
1/2 cup	Green pepper, diced [optional]
3/4 cup	Ham, diced
4 tbsp	Butter
3 lg	Eggs, lightly beaten
1 1/2 cups	Half and half
1 tbsp	Cornstarch
1/2 tsp	Salt
1 pinch	Pepper
4 oz	Colby cheese, shredded [or cheese of your choice]
4 oz	Cheddar cheese, shredded
1/3 cup	Parmesan cheese
9 inch	Pie crust, deep dish

Prick the pie crust with the tines of a fork and bake until it is light brown. Set aside. Sauté the onions and peppers in the butter until tender. Add the ham and sauté until the flavors blend. Remove the pan from the heat. Mix the beaten eggs, cornstarch, milk, salt, and pepper in a bowl. Add the cheese and mix all together. Add the ham/onion mixture and blend. Pour the mixture into the crust. Place the quiche onto a baking sheet to prevent it from overflowing in oven. Bake in a 350-degree oven until the quiche is set in the middle and it is a golden brown on the top. Check the doneness of the quiche by inserting a small knife into the center. If the knife is clean when removing, the quiche is set.

Helpful hint: Cover just the crust with strips of foil the last few minutes of baking to prevent it from scorching. Remove from the oven and let it cool for about 5 minutes before slicing.

PANCAKES

Ingredients for 4 servings

2 cups	Bisquick
1 lg	Egg
1/2 cup	Oil
1/3 cup	Club soda

Mix all of the ingredients together thoroughly. Pour the batter onto a hot griddle or a waffle iron. Spread butter on top of the hot pancakes and serve with honey, syrup, or preserves.

Helpful hint: Pancakes can be made by simply mixing flour and milk together. Mama used only those two ingredients when cooking pancakes and they were so good.

Cakes

PECAN PIE CAKE

Ingredients for 24 servings

1 box	Yellow cake mix [Pillsbury classic yellow]
1 stick	Butter, melted
4 lg	Eggs
1/2 cup	Dark brown sugar
1 1/2 cups	White Karo syrup
1 tsp	Vanilla
2 cups	Chopped nuts [less, if desired]

Reserve 2/3 cup of the yellow cake mix for the topping. Mix the rest of the cake mix with the melted butter and one egg [the mixture will be thick]. Pat the batter into a 9x13-inch cake pan. Bake in a 350-degree oven for 20 minutes or until the cake is light brown. Beat the remaining 3 eggs with egg beater. Mix in the brown sugar, the reserved cake mix, 1 1/2 cups of white corn syrup, 1 teaspoon vanilla, and the chopped nuts. Pour the mixture over the partially baked cake. Return the cake to the oven and bake another 15–20 minutes or until an inserted pick comes out clean.

ANGEL FOOD CAKES

Ingredients for 6 servings

1/2 cup	Cake flour, sifted
2 tbsp	Cake flour, sifted
1/4 tsp	Allspice, sifted with the flour
7 lg	Egg whites
3/4 cup	Sugar
3/4 tsp	Cream of tartar

Sift the dry ingredients. Beat the egg whites and cream of tartar until foamy [about 1 minute]. Add the sugar gradually to the egg whites and beat until stiff and glossy and has tripled in volume. Fold the flour mixture into the egg whites in 3 additions, being careful not to deflate the egg whites. Grease and flour the bottom of jumbo muffin tins or individual angel food pans. Bake in a 350-degree oven about 30 minutes or until the cakes spring back when touched. Serve on dessert plates with Pineapple Curd [recipe is listed in FROSTINGS].

Helpful hint: A fresh pineapple can be sliced thin and slices baked in a 200-degree oven. Place the slices on the dessert plates and then the cake and pineapple curd. Or, the batter can be baked in a 10-inch tube pan.

APPLE CAKE

Ingredients for 1 serving

2 cups	Sugar
3 lg	Eggs
3 cups	Flour, all-purpose
1 1/4 cups	Cooking oil
1 tsp	Baking soda
1 tsp	Salt
2 tsp	Vanilla
3 cups	Apples [fresh], peeled, cored, and chopped
2 cups	Nuts, chopped

	FROSTING
1 cup	Dark brown sugar
1 stick	Butter
1/4 cup	Evaporated milk
1 tsp	Vanilla

Whisk the dry ingredients together. Mix all of the ingredients [except for the apples and nuts] thoroughly. Fold the nuts and apples in last. Oil and flour or spray a tube pan. Bake in a tube pan in a 350-degree oven for 1 hour and 25 minutes or in a 9x13-inch pan for 45 minutes. Check with a toothpick to test the cake. When inserted into cake, the toothpick should be clean when removed. Frost the cake while in the tube pan or serve with a dollop of sweetened whipped cream.

FROSTING: Cook all of the frosting ingredients over low heat, stirring constantly, bringing it to a full boil. Cook for 2 or 3 minutes. Cool and beat until the frosting reaches a spreading consistency.

Always keep an aloe vera plant near your kitchen. It's invaluable when you scrape your arm or burn your finger. Just break off a leaf and rub the gel from the inside on the injury.

APPLE CAKE SQUARES

Ingredients for 24 servings

2	Granny Smith apples, peeled, cored, and diced
2 cups	Flour, all-purpose
1/2 cup	Oil
1 tsp	Salt
1 tsp	Cinnamon
2 tsp	Baking soda
1 tsp	Vanilla

| 2 lg | Eggs |
| 1/2 cup | Nuts, chopped [optional] |

FROSTING

4 oz	Instant vanilla pudding mix
1 cup	Milk, cold
8 oz	Cool Whip

CARAMEL TOPPING

1 cup	Sugar, granulated
1/2 cup	Butter
1/2 cup	Buttermilk
1/2 tsp	Baking soda

Mix the sugar, oil, nuts [if desired], apples, eggs, and vanilla in a large bowl, stirring by hand. In another bowl, whisk the flour, salt, cinnamon, and baking soda until well incorporated. Add the dry mixture to the apple mixture and stir well with a wooden spoon. Spray or oil a 9x13-inch baking dish and pour the mixture in. Bake in a 325-degree oven for 45–50 minutes. Cool and cut into squares. This is good plain or with one of the following toppings:

FROSTING: Beat the milk and pudding together. Fold in the Cool Whip. Frost the cooled cake. Cut into squares. Keep in the refrigerator.
Or...

CARAMEL TOPPING: Combine all of the ingredients in a medium saucepan and bring to a boil. Reduce to a medium heat and cook for 15 minutes, stirring constantly. Remove from the heat and beat until smooth. Pour over the warm apple cake. Cut into squares. Need not refrigerate.

APPLE SPICE CAKE

Ingredients for 1 serving

3 cups	Flour, all-purpose
1 tbsp	Cinnamon [or 1 tsp of apple pie spice], ground
1 tsp	Baking soda
1 tsp	Salt
2 cups	Sugar
3 lg	Eggs
1 1/3 cups	Oil, vegetables
3 cups	Granny Smith apples [3 or 4], cored and cut into 1/2-inch pieces
1 cup	Chopped [small] pecans or walnuts, optional
1 tsp	Vanilla

CARAMEL SAUCE

1 cup	Light brown sugar
1 stick	Butter, unsalted
1/4 cup	Evaporated milk
1 pinch	Salt
1 tsp	Vanilla

Sift the dry ingredients together. [This can be done over a large piece of parchment paper.] Mix the oil, sugar, and eggs in mixing bowl and beat on high speed [with the paddle attachment, if possible] until a lemony color. Slowly add the flour mixture into the mixing bowl [on a low speed]. Mix until just incorporated. Add the apples [and nuts, if desired] and incorporate, not over-mixing. Pour the batter into a prepared tube or Bundt pan. I use a spray which contains flour. Bake in a 350-degree oven until a tester comes out clean [75–90 minutes]. Cool.

CARAMEL SAUCE: Combine the sauce ingredients in a saucepan. Cook over medium heat, while stirring, until thickened. Pour over the cooled cake or serve with the cake and a scoop of ice cream, reserving the sauce for the ice cream.

OPTIONAL TOPPING: Bring to a boil and cook for 2 minutes...1/2 cup of butter, 1/2 cup of brown sugar, and 2 teaspoons of milk.

BANANA POUND CAKE

Ingredients for 1 cake

1	Box of yellow cake mix
4	Eggs
1/3 cup	Oil
1/2 cup	Water
1 1/3 cups	Mashed bananas [3 or 4]
3 1/2 oz	Package of instant vanilla pudding mix
1/2 tsp	Ground cinnamon
1/2 tsp	Ground nutmeg
	FROSTING
1/4 cup	Butter
1 cup	Brown sugar [dark or light], firmly packed
2/3 cup	Whipping cream
1 cup	Confectioners' sugar
1 tsp	Vanilla
3/4 cup	Chopped and toasted pecans, optional

Put the cake ingredients into a mixing bowl. Beat with electric mixer until well mixed. Pour into a 10-inch greased and floured tube pan. Bake in a 350-degree oven for 1 hour or until done.

Check with a toothpick to determine when the cake is done. Cool slightly and frost.

FROSTING: Bring butter, brown sugar, and whipping cream to a boil over medium heat, stirring frequently. Boil for 1 minute. Remove from heat and add the confectioners' sugar and vanilla. Beat until smooth. Pour over the warm Banana Cake and sprinkle with nuts or add pecans to the frosting and pour over the cake.

OR...

Sprinkle sifted confectioners' sugar over the Banana Cake. It's good either way.

BROWN SUGAR CAKE

Ingredients for 10 servings

2 sticks	Butter, softened
2 cups	Brown sugar, firmly packed
1 cup	Granulated sugar
6	Eggs
3 cups	Flour [all-purpose], sifted
1/2 tsp	Salt
1/2 tsp	Baking powder
1 cup	Milk
1 tsp	Vanilla extract
1 tsp	Maple extract

BUTTERMILK GLAZE

1 cup	Sugar
1 1/2 tsp	Baking powder
1/2 cup	Buttermilk
1/2 cup	Butter

1 tbsp	Light corn syrup
1 tsp	Vanilla

Beat butter and sugar at medium mixer speed until light and fluffy. Add eggs one at a time, beating well after each addition. Combine dry ingredients and add to butter mixture alternately with milk. [Begin and end with flour mixture.] Mix in flavorings. Pour the batter into an oiled and floured 10-inch tube pan. Bake in a 350-degree oven for 1 1/2 hours, or until a wooden pick inserted in the center comes out clean.

BUTTERMILK GLAZE: Bring all ingredients EXCEPT for the vanilla flavoring to a boil in a large saucepan. Boil for 4 minutes over medium heat, stirring constantly until the glaze is a golden brown. Remove from heat and stir in the vanilla. Cool slightly. Pour over the cake while both are still warm.

THREE LAYER [BUTTERMILK] CAKE

Ingredients for 1 cake

2 cups	Sugar
1 cup	Crisco, solid
2 cups	Flour, all-purpose
1/2 tsp	Soda
1/2 tsp	Salt
4 lg	Eggs
1 cup	Buttermilk
2 tsp	Vanilla

Whisk or sift the flour, salt, and soda together. Cream the Crisco and sugar well. Beat in the eggs, one at a time. Add the vanilla to the buttermilk. Add the dry ingredients and the buttermilk to the sugar mixture alternately, beginning and ending with the dry ingredients. Pour the batter into 3 prepared cake pans [8- or 9-inch layer pans]. Bake in a 350-degree oven for 25–30 minutes. Frost with your choice of frosting.

Cottage cheese can be used in place of sour cream when making dips. Just place it in the blender until it is creamed.

BUTTERNUT CAKE

Ingredients for 1 cake

2 sticks	Butter
2 cups	Sugar
3 cups	Flour [all-purpose or cake flour]
1 cup	Buttermilk
2 tsp	Butternut flavoring
1 tsp	Soda
1/4 tsp	Salt
3 lg	Eggs, separated

	FROSTING
1 box	Powdered sugar [10 X]
1 stick	Butter, room temperature
8 oz	Cream cheese, room temperature
2 tbsp	Butternut flavoring
1 cup	Nuts, chopped

Beat the sugar and butter together. Beat the egg whites until they are stiff. Beat the salt, vanilla, and soda into the buttermilk until slightly foamy. Alternately add the flour and buttermilk to the butter mixture. Add the egg yolks one at a time, beating after each addition. Gently fold in the egg whites, trying not to deflate them. Pour the batter into 3 greased and floured cake pans. Bake in a 350-degree oven for 30 minutes or until done.

FROSTING: Cream the butter and cream cheese together and add the flavoring. Mix in the powdered sugar and add the nuts. Frost the layers and sides of the cake.

CARAMEL FROSTED CAKE

Ingredients for 1 cake

2 2/3 cups	Flour, all-purpose	1 tbsp	Vanilla
1 tsp	Salt		
1/4 tsp	Baking soda		**FROSTING**
2 sticks	Butter, room	2 sticks	Butter
	temperature	2 cups	Light brown sugar,
3 cups	Sugar		packed
6 lg	Eggs, room	1/2 cup	Evaporated milk
	temperature	1/2 tsp	Vanilla
8 oz	Sour cream	4 cups	Powdered sugar

Sift the flour, baking soda, and salt together. Set aside. Cream together the butter and sugar until fluffy. Add the eggs one at a time while beating. Alternate adding the flour mixture and sour cream to the butter mixture, starting and ending with the flour. Add the vanilla. Pour the batter into 3 oiled or sprayed 9-inch pans. Bake in a 350-degree oven for 30 minutes or until an inserted tester [toothpick] comes out clean. Cool before frosting.

FROSTING: Put the powdered sugar in a heatproof bowl and set aside. Melt the butter in a heavy saucepan. Add the sugar and evaporated milk. Boil over medium heat for 2 minutes, stirring constantly. Remove from the heat and add the vanilla. Pour the butter mixture over the powdered sugar and beat with a hand mixer [or whisk] until smooth. Cool slightly and frost the cake.

CHOCO-CHERRY CAKE

Ingredients for 1 cake

8 oz	Cream cheese, softened
12 oz	Cool Whip
2 cups	Confectioners' sugar [divided]
5 oz	Instant chocolate pudding
1 cup	Milk [no more]
6 oz	Maraschino cherries, drained and halved
1 box	Devil's food cake mix

Bake devil's food cake into 3 layers according to directions and cool. Mix cream cheese and 1 cup confectioners' sugar together and fold into Cool Whip. Spread mixture over 2 layers of cake. [Filling will be thick.] Mix chocolate pudding, milk, and 1 cup of confectioners' sugar together and frost top of third layer and sides of cake. Decorate top of cake with cherries and refrigerate. [Expect compliments on this creation.]

CHOCOLATE BLACKOUT CAKE

Ingredients for 1 cake

1 1/2 cups	Flour, all-purpose
2 tsp	Baking powder
1/2 tsp	Baking soda
1/2 tsp	Salt

1 stick	Unsalted butter
3/4 cup	Dutch-processed cocoa powder [or a good quality cocoa]
1 cup	Coffee, room temperature
1 cup	Buttermilk
1 cup	Light brown sugar, packed
1 cup	Sugar, granulated
2 lg	Eggs, room temperature
1 tsp	Vanilla

PUDDING

1 1/4 cups	Sugar, granulated
1/4 cup	Cornstarch
1/2 tsp	Salt
2 cups	Half and half
1 cup	Milk
6 oz	Unsweetened chocolate, chopped
2 tsp	Vanilla

FOR THE PUDDING: Whisk the granulated sugar, cornstarch, salt, half and half, and the milk in a saucepan. Add the chopped chocolate and cook over medium heat, whisking constantly, for 2 or 3 minutes until the mixture begins to bubble. Stir in the vanilla. Pour into a bowl and cover with plastic wrap, placing the wrap directly on top of the pudding. Let cool and then chill in the refrigerator [4 or 5 hours or overnight].

FOR THE CAKE: Whisk the flour, baking powder, baking soda, and salt together until blended. Melt the butter in a saucepan over medium heat. Stir in the cocoa powder and cook about 1 minute, or until it is slightly fragrant. Remove from the heat and whisk in the coffee, buttermilk, and sugars until dissolved. Cool slightly and whisk in the eggs and vanilla. Slowly whisk in the flour mixture. Bake in two 8-inch cake pans in a 325-degree oven for 35–45 minutes, or until inserted toothpick comes out clean. Remove the layers from the oven and let cool for 15–20 minutes. Invert onto a cooling rack and let cool completely. With a serrated knife, slice each cake layer in half, making 4 layers instead of two. Place one layer onto a cake plate and spread a cup of pudding over the top. Add two more layers, repeating the procedure. Spread pudding around the sides of the layers. If any pudding is left, add it to the top [or better yet, eat it…Yummy]. Crumble the last layer. Sprinkle the crumbs over the top and sides of the cake, pressing lightly.

CHOCOLATE FUDGE CAKE

Ingredients for 24 squares

1 stick	Butter, softened
1 cup	Sugar
4 lg	Eggs, room temperature
16 oz	Chocolate syrup
1 cup	Self-rising flour, sifted
1 tsp	Vanilla
	TOPPING
1 stick	Butter
2 oz	Unsweetened chocolate squares
1 cup	Evaporated milk
1 tsp	Vanilla
16 oz	Confectioners' sugar

Cream the butter and sugar together. Add the remaining ingredients and mix well. Pour the batter into an oiled 9x13-inch pan. Bake in a 350-degree oven for 40 minutes or until inserted pick comes out clean. While the cake is baking, melt the unsweetened chocolate squares and the remaining stick of butter in a heavy bottom saucepan. Add the evaporated milk, vanilla, and confectioners' sugar. Whisk the ingredients together over low heat until smooth. Remove the cake from the oven and pour the hot topping over the top. Return the cake to the oven and bake an additional 20 minutes or until it bubbles all over. Allow the cake to set for 6–8 hours or overnight. Serve with a scoop of vanilla ice cream.

Helpful hint: Place the baking dish on a large cookie sheet to catch any bubbly topping.

FIVE-MINUTE CHOCOLATE CAKE
[THE MOST DANGEROUS RECIPE IN THE WORLD]

Ingredients for 1 serving

4 tbsp	Flour, self-rising
4 tbsp	Sugar
2 tbsp	Cocoa
1 lg	Egg [beaten with a fork]
3 tbsp	Milk
3 tbsp	Oil
3 tbsp	Chocolate chips
1 small	Splash of vanilla
1 large	Coffee mug [microwave-safe]

Add the dry ingredients to the mug and mix well. Add the egg and mix thoroughly. Pour in the milk, oil, and vanilla and mix well. Add the chocolate chips and mix. Place the mug in the microwave and cook for 3 minutes at 1000 watts. The cake will rise above the top, but don't be alarmed. Let the cake cool slightly and turn onto a plate [or 2 plates], if desired. Why is this the most dangerous recipe in the world? Because we are only 5 minutes away from chocolate cake any time of the day or night!

ROSALIND'S EIGHT-LAYER CHOCOLATE CAKE

Ingredients for 1 cake

			FROSTING	
2 1/4 cups	Self-rising flour	2 1/2 sticks	Butter	
2 cups	Sugar	3 cups	Sugar	
5 lg	Eggs	1/2 cup	Cocoa	
1 cup	Oil	12 oz	Evaporated milk	
3/4 cup	Milk	1 tsp	Vanilla	
1 tsp	Vanilla	1 pinch	Salt	

Mix the cake ingredients well, adding the flour and milk alternately. Divide into 8 prepared cake pans. Bake in a 400-degree oven for about 4 minutes, or until done.

FROSTING: Melt the butter in a saucepan over medium heat. Whisk the cocoa and sugar together and add to the melted butter. Add the remaining ingredients and bring to a rolling boil, cooking for 4 minutes [or to a soft ball stage]. Cool slightly and frost.

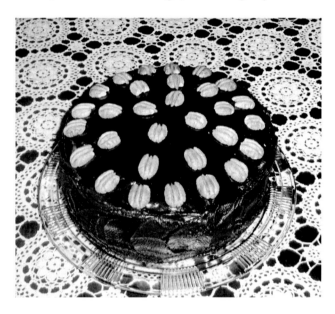

CHOCOLATE POUND CAKE AND FROSTING

Ingredients for 1 cake

3 cups	Flour, all-purpose	1 1/4 cups	Milk, whole
1/2 cup	Cocoa	3 cups	Sugar
1/2 cup	Shortening, solid	1/2 tsp	Baking powder
	[I like Crisco,	6 lg	Eggs, room
	regular or butter-		temperature
	flavored]	2 tsp	Vanilla
2 sticks	Butter, softened	1 pinch	Salt

	FROSTING [1]		FROSTING [2]
1/2 cup	Shortening, solid	2 1/4 cups	Sugar
2 cups	Sugar	3 oz	Semi-sweet
1/4 cup	Cocoa		chocolate
2/3 cup	Milk, whole		squares
1/4 tsp	Salt	3/4 cup	Milk, whole
2 tsp	Vanilla	2 1/4 tbsp	Karo [light corn] syrup
		3/4 stick	Butter
		2 tsp	Vanilla
		1 cup	Pecans, chopped and lightly toasted [optional]

Whisk the flour, cocoa, baking powder, and salt together and set aside. Cream the butter, shortening, and sugar together until blended. Add the eggs one at a time, beating after each addition. Add the dry ingredients alternately with the milk, beginning and ending with the dry ingredients. Add the vanilla. [I usually add the vanilla to the milk. It get dispersed more evenly.] Bake in a greased and floured tube pan at 325 degrees until an inserted pick comes out clean [about 1 hour and 50 minutes]. Cool before frosting.

FROSTING [1]: Cook all of the ingredients in a heavy saucepan. Let the mixture boil for 2 minutes. Remove from the heat and beat occasionally while cooling. When spreading consistency, frost the cooled cake.

FROSTING [2]: Cook the sugar, milk, chocolate, and Karo syrup in a heavy bottom saucepan until boiling. Cook until a candy thermometer reaches 230 degrees. Add the butter and vanilla.

Beat the mixture until it is a spreading consistency. [Add the pecans, if desired.] Frost the cooled cake.

Helpful hint: If a candy thermometer is not available, drop a little mixture into a cup of cold water. If the chocolate forms a soft ball, remove from the heat. Also, place 4 strips of wax or parchment paper [about 2 inches wide] under the 4 sides of the cake. After frosting the cake, slip the paper out and discard. This recipe makes a big and pretty cake.

CREAMY CHOCOLATE PUDDING CAKE

Ingredients for 1 cake

1 box	Chocolate fudge cake mix	8 oz	Cool Whip
1/4 cup	Sugar	1/2 cup	Powdered sugar
4 lg	Eggs		**FROSTING**
8 oz	Sour cream	1/4 cup	Powdered sugar
1/3 cup	Oil	4 oz	Chocolate pudding mix, instant
1/4 cup	Water	1 cup	Milk
	FILLING	8 oz	Cool Whip
8 oz	Cream cheese, softened		

Mix cake ingredients together. Pour into 4 prepared cake pans. Bake in a 350-degree oven until done. Cool completely. Mix the filling ingredients and spread between the layers. In a clean bowl, mix the milk, sugar, and pudding together and fold in the Cool Whip. Spread over the top and sides of the cake. Refrigerate.

SWISS CHOCOLATE CAKE

Ingredients for 1 cake

1 box	Swiss chocolate cake mix

FROSTING

12 oz	Cool Whip, thawed
8 oz	Cream cheese, softened
1 1/2 cup	Confectioners' sugar
8	Hershey bars with almonds

Bake the cake into 4 layers according to directions on the box and cool.

FROSTING: Mix the cream cheese and confectioners' sugar together. Chop the candy bars in a food processor or chopper. Fold the candy bars and Cool Whip into the cream cheese mixture. Frost cake and keep refrigerated.

CREAM-FILLED CHOCOLATE CAKE

Ingredients for 1 cake

2 cups	Flour, all-purpose		**FILLING**
1/2 cup	Unsweetened cocoa	8 oz	Cream cheese, softened
1/2 cup	Butter, softened	1/4 cup	Sugar
1 1/2 cups	Sugar	1	Egg
1 cup	Water	1 tsp	Vanilla
3	Eggs		
1 1/4 tsp	Baking powder		**GLAZE**
1 tsp	Baking soda	1 cup	Confectioners' sugar, sifted
1 tsp	Vanilla		
		3 tbsp	Milk
		1/2 tsp	Vanilla

In a small bowl combine all filling ingredients. Beat with a mixer at a low speed for 2 or 3 minutes or until smooth, scraping down sides of bowl often. Set aside. In a large mixing bowl combine cake ingredients, beating at a low speed and scraping sides of bowl often until all ingredients are moistened. Increase speed and beat batter 2 or 3 minutes at a high speed until smooth. Pour 3 cups of the cake mixture into a greased and floured 12-cup Bundt pan. Spoon filling over batter without letting it touch the sides of the pan. Cover with the remaining batter and bake for 50–60 minutes in a 350-degree oven or until toothpick comes out clean. Let cake rest in the pan for 20 minutes. Remove from pan. Mix 1 cup of sifted confectioners' sugar, 3 tablespoons of milk, and 1/2 teaspoon of vanilla and pour over warm cake or...sprinkle sifted confectioners' over top of cake. Pretty served with a fresh strawberry or two and a sprig of mint.

Helpful hint: If the filling is slightly chilled, it is less likely to run to the sides of the pan, which ruins the looks of this creation but not the taste.

DEVIL'S FOOD AND WHITE ICING CAKE

Ingredients for 1 cake

2 cups	Flour, all-purpose	1 1/2 cups	Buttermilk
1/2 cup	Cocoa	1 tsp	Vanilla
1 tsp	Baking soda		
1 tsp	Baking powder		**FROSTING**
1/4 tsp	Salt	3	Egg whites,
2 cups	Sugar		whipped
2 sticks	Butter, softened	1 cup	Sugar
3 lg	Eggs, room	1 cup	Light corn syrup
	temperature	1 tsp	Vanilla

Sift the first 5 ingredients together and set aside. Cream the butter and sugar together, adding the eggs one at a time. Add the vanilla to the cup of buttermilk. Add the flour and buttermilk mixtures to the butter and egg mixture, starting and ending with the flour. Divide the batter between 3 oiled or sprayed cake pans. Bake in a 350-degree oven for 25 minutes or until inserted tester [toothpick] comes out clean.

FROSTING: Combine the sugar and syrup in a saucepan over medium heat. Bring to a boil. Beat the egg whites in a heatproof bowl until stiff. Pour the hot syrup mixture slowly into the egg whites. Add the vanilla and beat until stiff. Frost the layers.

FRUITCAKE

Ingredients for 2 cakes

24 oz	Dates, pitted
1 lb	Candied red and green cherries [extra for decoration]
1 lb	Candied yellow pineapple
2 lb	Pecan halves [extra for decoration]
2 cups	Flour, all-purpose
2 tsp	Baking powder
1/2 tsp	Salt
1 cup	Sugar
4 lg	Eggs
	Light corn syrup

Grease the bottoms and sides of two 9-inch tube pans with detachable bottoms with butter-flavored Crisco and line with parchment paper. Cut the dates in half, crosswise. [If using kitchen shears, dip the shears in water occasionally.] Cut the pineapple into pieces. Cut the cherries in half. Place all of the fruit into a very large bowl. Sift the flour, salt, and baking powder [all together] over the fruit. Mix, with a large spoon or hands, until all of the fruit is coated. In a smaller bowl, beat the eggs until they are frothy. Add the sugar to the eggs gradually and beat well. Add the egg mixture to the larger mixture and incorporate, using a large spoon or hands. Add the pecan halves and mix until well coated with the mixture. Pack the mixture into the pans and press down with hands. Decorate the tops of the cakes with the extra cherries and pecans. Bake in a 275-degree oven for 1 1/2 hours or until the top is no longer wet. Let the cakes rest for 5 minutes before removing from the pans [run a knife or spatula between the parchment paper and the cake pan.] Remove the paper. Brush the tops completely with light corn syrup while the cakes are very warm.

Helpful hint: If baking individual fruit cakes, spray the pans with a very good baking spray and place the extra cherries and pecans into the pans before packing the batter into the pans. Bake in a 275-degree oven for less time [start checking in 1 hour]. Let rest after baking until the sides begin to release the cake. Carefully use a small knife and insert between the cakes and pans and turn out onto a cooling rack. Brush the tops with light syrup while warm. Wrap with a clear wrap when cool enough to prevent drying.

HUMMINGBIRD CAKE

Ingredients for 1 cake

3 cups	Flour, all-purpose
2 cups	Sugar
1 tsp	Baking soda
1 tsp	Salt
1 tsp	Cinnamon
3 lg	Eggs, beaten
1 cup	Bananas, chopped
1 cup	Oil
1 1/2 tsp	Vanilla
8 oz	Crushed pineapple [can]
1 cup	Pecans, chopped
1 cup	Shredded coconut, optional

	FROSTING
8 oz	Cream cheese, softened
1 stick	Butter, softened
1 box	Powdered sugar
1 tsp	Vanilla

Combine the flour, sugar, soda, salt, and cinnamon. Add the eggs and oil, stirring [not beating] until the flour mixture is moistened. Stir in the vanilla, pineapple, pecans, and bananas with a large or wooden spoon. Bake in 3 greased and floured [9-inch] cake pans in a 350-degree oven. Remove from the oven when an inserted toothpick comes out clean and cool in the pans.

FROSTING: Combine the cream cheese and butter, beating until smooth. Add the powdered sugar and vanilla. Beat until light and fluffy. Spread between the layers, on the top, and sides of the cake.

Optional: Sprinkle chopped pecans on the top of the cake.

ICEBOX FRUITCAKE

Ingredients for 3 rolls

16 oz	Honey graham crackers [1 box], crushed into crumbs
6 cups	Miniature marshmallows
2 sticks	Butter or margarine
6 oz	Red maraschino cherries [2 jars], with juice [or 1 green and 1 red]
4 cups	Chopped pecans, slightly toasted
15 oz	White raisins [1 box]

Chop cherries and nuts. Crush crackers into crumbs. Melt butter and marshmallows in a saucepan. Combine marshmallow mixture with crumbs and cherry liquid. Add cherries, raisins, and pecans. Mixture will be sticky. Form long rolls of mixture on wax paper. Roll into logs. Wrap logs in aluminum foil and refrigerate. Slice and serve.

Helpful hint: Emptied paper towel rolls can be cut down one side and mixture [wrapped in wax paper] can be placed inside to chill. This makes a more perfect roll. Yield: 3 long rolls. This mixture can also be rolled into bite-size balls and rolled in powdered sugar for a festive holiday sweet. Keep chilled.

GRANNIE SUE'S ICEBOX FRUITCAKE

Ingredients for 24 portions

16 oz	Honey graham crackers [box]
10 oz	Marshmallows [package]
12 oz	Evaporated milk [can]
2 jars	Cherries [1 red and 1 green], halved
15 oz	Golden raisins [box]
6 oz	Coconut
4 cups	Nuts [assorted, chopped]

Warm evaporated milk in a medium to large saucepan. Melt marshmallows in cream and stir. Crush crackers and add remaining ingredients to the crumbs. Mix dry ingredients. Pour marshmallow/cream over all and mix until blended. If weak, add more cracker crumbs. Press into a 9x13-inch glass dish, cover well, and keep in the refrigerator. This will keep for several weeks.

LEMON-CHEESE CAKE

Ingredients for 1 cake

1 cup	Butter, softened	3	Lemons, juice
2 cups	Sugar		and grated rind
3 cups	Cake flour, sifted	4	Eggs
3	Eggs	2 tbsp	Butter, melted
1 cup	Buttermilk		
1/2 tsp	Baking soda		**WHITE ICING**
1 tsp	Vanilla flavoring	1 1/2 cups	Sugar
1 tsp	Lemon flavoring	1/4 tsp	Cream of tartar
		1/4 tsp	Salt
	LEMON-CHEESE	1/3 cup	Cold water
	FILLING	2 tsp	Light corn syrup
1 1/2 cup	Sugar	2	Egg whites
		1 tsp	Vanilla

CAKE: Cream butter and sugar. Add the eggs one at a time, beating well after each addition. Alternately, add flour and baking soda with buttermilk. Bake in 4 greased and floured 9-inch cake pans about 20 minutes or until done. While warm, frost tops with the lemon filling.

LEMON FILLING: Beat the eggs slightly and add the other ingredients. Place in top of a double boiler over boiling water and stir the mixture until it is thickened and is a bright yellow. Spread between layers. [Can microwave by cooking on high 2–3 minutes, stir, and cook 2–3 minutes longer.]

WHITE FROSTING: Put all of the ingredients except for the vanilla flavoring in a double boiler. Cook over boiling water for 7 minutes, beating with an electric beater. Remove from heat and add vanilla, beating for one minute. Frost top and sides of lemon-cheese cake. [Makes enough to ice a two-layer cake with plenty of frosting in the middle.]

MISSISSIPPI MUD CAKE

Ingredients for 24 servings

2 sticks	Butter, room temperature
2 cups	Sugar
4 lg	Eggs
1 1/2 cups	Flour, all-purpose
1/2 cup	Cocoa
1/2 tsp	Salt
1 cup	Nuts, chopped
10 oz	Miniature marshmallows
	GLAZE
1 stick	Butter
1/2 cup	Cocoa
1/2 cup	Milk
1 tsp	Vanilla

Cream together the butter, sugar, and eggs. Sift the flour, cocoa, and salt together and mix into the butter mixture. Stir in the nuts. Pour the batter into a lightly-oiled 9x11-inch pan. Bake in a 350-degree oven for 30 minutes or until done [insert toothpick to test]. Remove the pan from the oven and spread the marshmallows over the top. Broil the marshmallows for about a minute or until slightly melted.

GLAZE: Melt the butter in a saucepan and whisk in the cocoa, milk, and vanilla, whisking until smooth. Drizzle the glaze evenly over the marshmallows. Cool and cut. Serve with a scoop of vanilla ice cream.

NEIMAN MARCUS CAKE

Ingredients for 24 servings

1 lg	Egg
1 stick	Butter, melted
1 cup	Pecans, chopped
1 box	Duncan Hines cake mix, butter flavor
1 box	Powdered sugar [16 oz]
8 oz	Cream cheese, softened
2 lg	Eggs
1 tsp	Almond extract

Mix the first four ingredients. Pat into a lightly-oiled 9x13-inch dish. Mix the remaining ingredients together. Pour the cream cheese mixture over the cake mixture and smooth. Bake in a 350-degree oven for 10 minutes. Turn the oven down to 325 degrees and bake an additional 30 minutes. May serve with various toppings including whipped cream, chocolate sauce, or fruit pie filling. I like it plain.

ORANGE CAKE

Ingredients for 1 cake

1 box	Yellow cake mix
2/3 cup	Cooking oil
2/3 cup	Orange juice [or apricot nectar]
4	Eggs
3 oz	Orange Jell-O [1 box]

GLAZE

1/3 cup	Orange juice [or apricot nectar]
2 cups	Confectioners' sugar

Combine cake mix and Jell-O with a wire whisk. Add orange juice and oil. Add eggs and mix thoroughly. Bake in a greased tube pan in a 325-degree oven for 1 hour or until inserted toothpick comes out clean. [This can be baked in a greased 9x13-inch pan and cut into squares.]

For glaze: Mix confectioners' sugar and juice and pour over hot cake. [For variation, substitute milk for juice and lemon or strawberry Jell-O for orange Jell-O.

ORANGE-PINEAPPLE CAKE

Ingredients for 1 cake

1 box	Duncan Hines All-butter cake mix
1 stick	Butter or oleo, or 1/2 cup oil
4	Eggs
8 oz	Mandarin orange slices [can]
1/2 cup	Mandarin oranges' liquid

FROSTING

3 1/3 oz	Instant vanilla pudding mix
11 oz	Crushed pineapple [can]
12 oz	Cool Whip

Beat the cake mix, butter [or oil], and liquid in a mixer bowl at medium speed until smooth. Add eggs, one at a time, mixing 1 minute after each addition. Add oranges, mixing just enough to slightly chop them. Divide batter and bake in three 8-inch cake pans at 350 degrees for about 25 minutes or until done. Cool...

FROSTING: Mix the pudding and the pineapple juice together. Add the pineapple. Fold into the Cool Whip and frost the cooled cake. Keep in the refrigerator. This cake tastes better the second day. It mellows.

PINEAPPLE CAKE

Ingredients for 1 cake

2 cups	Flour, self-rising
1/2 cup	Crisco [butter-flavored Crisco, optional]
1 1/2 cups	Sugar
2 lg	Eggs
1 cup	Milk
1 tsp	Vanilla

FROSTING

20 oz	Crushed pineapple [can], drained
1 stick	Butter
3 tbsp	Flour
1 1/2 cups	Sugar
1/2 cup	Milk

Beat the sugar and Crisco until smooth. Add the vanilla to the milk. Add 1/2 cup of milk to the sugar mixture and blend. Add the eggs and mix well. Alternate the flour and the rest of the milk to the batter. Bake 3 layers in a 350-degree oven until done.

FROSTING: Drain the pineapple. In a small mixing bowl, whisk 1 1/2 cups of sugar with 3 tablespoons of flour. Melt the butter in a heavy saucepan. Mix the milk, sugar mixture, and the melted butter in the saucepan and cook over medium-low heat. Bring this to a rolling boil for about 2 minutes while stirring. Reduce the heat and stir in the drained pineapple. Cook [while stirring] over low heat 4 or 5 more minutes until it thickens. It will hang from the spoon when held up over the pan. Frost the cake. YUMMY!

PINEAPPLE CAKE SQUARES

Ingredients for 24 servings

2 cups	Cake flour
2 cups	Sugar
2 tsp	Baking soda
2 lg	Eggs, beaten
1 tsp	Vanilla
20 oz	Crushed pineapple [can]

	FROSTING
1/2 stick	Butter, softened
3 oz	Cream cheese, softened
1 cup	Confectioners' sugar
	Chopped nuts, optional

Mix the cake ingredients together, using the pineapple juice as the liquid. Add the pineapple last, mixing well. Pour into a buttered and floured 9x13-inch pan. Bake in a 350-degree oven for 30–40 minutes. Begin checking with a toothpick after 30 minutes.

FROSTING: Mix the frosting ingredients and spread over the cake. Sprinkle with nuts, which have been slightly toasted, if desired.

PINEAPPLE DESSERT TOPPING

Ingredients for 3 cups

2 lg	Eggs, beaten
1 cup	Pineapple juice
3 tbsp	Butter
3/4 cup	Sugar
1 tbsp	Flour, all-purpose
1 cup	Whipping cream
1 tbsp	Powdered sugar

Whisk the flour and sugar together in top of a double boiler. Add the beaten eggs, pineapple juice, and butter. Cook over boiling water, stirring constantly, until the mixture is thickened [it will coat a spoon]. Remove from the heat and cool. [May place the container in a bowl of ice to cool more quickly.] Whip the cream, adding the powdered sugar. Fold the whipped cream into the cooled pineapple mixture, cover, and chill. Serve over fresh fruit, pound cake, or angel food cake.

PISTACHIO CAKE

Ingredients for 1 cake

1 box	White cake mix
4	Eggs
1 cup	Water
1 cup	Cooking oil
1/2 cup	Chopped pecans [optional]
3 drops	Green food coloring [optional]
3	Small boxes of instant pistachio pudding
10 oz	Cool Whip

Preheat oven to 275 degrees. Combine cake mix, eggs, water, oil, and two packages of pudding mix, mixing well after each addition. Pour the batter into an oiled or sprayed tube cake pan or Bundt pan and bake at 275 degrees for 10 minutes. Bake at 300 degrees for another 10 minutes. Bake at 325 degrees for 35 minutes or until inserted wooden pick comes out clean. Cool cake. Gradually add the remaining package of pistachio pudding mix to 10 oz of Cool Whip and spread the frosting over the cake. Keep cake in the refrigerator.

SWEET-POTATO-BOURBON BUNDT CAKE

Ingredients for 1 cake

1 1/2 cups	Brown sugar, firmly packed
1/3 cup	Butter, room temperature
2 lg	Eggs
1 cup	Sweet potato, cooked and mashed
2 3/4 cups	Flour, all-purpose
3/4 cup	Milk
1 tsp	Vanilla

1/3 cup	Bourbon [or apple juice, if preferred]
1 tbsp	Baking powder
1 tsp	Pumpkin pie spice
3/4 tsp	Salt
3 tbsp	Pecans, chopped small
	Cooking spray with flour

BOURBON SYRUP

1 cup	Sugar
1 tsp	Butter
1/2 tsp	Vanilla
2 tbsp	Bourbon
1/2 cup	Water

With a paddle attachment mix the butter, brown sugar, and eggs together until light and fluffy. Add the sweet potato and combine. Mix the dry ingredients together with a whisk and add the vanilla to the milk. Add the flour and milk to the batter and mix until just incorporated. Lightly spray a 10- or 12-cup Bundt pan and sprinkle with the pecans. Pour in the cake batter. Bake in a 325-degree oven for 60 minutes or until inserted pick comes out clean. Remove from the pan and cool on a wire rack. Brush the top of the cake with the bourbon syrup. Serve remaining sauce with the cake slices.

BOURBON SYRUP: Bring the sugar and 1/2 cup of water to a boil in a small saucepan. Cook for 5 minutes. Add the butter, bourbon, and vanilla. Cook until the mixture is the consistency of syrup, about 5 minutes.

SWEET POTATO CAKES

Ingredients for 1 dozen

1 stick	Butter, softened	1 tsp	Vanilla
1 cup	Sugar	1/3 cup	Buttermilk
2 lg	Eggs, room temperature	1/2 cup	Pecans, chopped
1 1/4 cups	Flour, all-purpose		**CARAMEL SAUCE**
1 tsp	Baking soda	1 stick	Butter
1/4 tsp	Salt	1/4 cup	Light brown sugar, packed
1/2 tsp	Ginger, ground		
1/2 tsp	Cinnamon, ground	1 cup	Heavy cream
15 oz	Sweet potato [can], drained and mashed		

Beat the butter and sugar together on medium speed until smooth. Add the eggs, one at a time, incorporating them. Add the sweet potatoes. Combine the flour, salt, ginger, cinnamon, and baking soda in a bowl, either whisking or sifting them together. Add the flour mixture to the butter and beat on low speed until blended. Add the milk, vanilla, and nuts, mixing until smooth. Spray jumbo muffin tins with a good spray and divide the batter evenly into each cup. Bake in a 350-degree oven 15–20 minutes or until an inserted pick comes out clean.

CARAMEL SAUCE: Melt the butter and sugar in a non-stick pan for 2 or 3 minutes or until the sugar dissolves. Whisk in the heavy cream. Bring the mixture slowly to a boil, stirring constantly. Cook until the sauce thickens slightly. Serve warm over the potato cakes. [For a different flavor, add 1/2 teaspoon of instant coffee granules to the sugar mixture.] A scoop of vanilla ice cream is good with this dessert, but this dessert stands on its own, also.

CHOCOLATE CHIP POUND CAKE

Ingredients for 1 cake

1 box	Yellow cake mix with pudding
1/2 cup	Sugar
3 1/3 oz	Instant chocolate pudding mix [box]
2/3 cup	Vegetable oil
2/3 cup	Water
4	Eggs
8 oz	Sour cream
6 oz	Semi-sweet chocolate chips
1 tsp	Vanilla flavoring
	TOPPING
1/2 cup	Confectioners' sugar, sifted

Combine cake mix, sugar, and pudding mix in a large mixing bowl and whisk until blended and lumps are gone. Add oil, eggs, and water, mixing well. Blend in the sour cream and vanilla. Add chocolate chips and stir. Bake in a greased and floured 12-cup Bundt pan or a prepared 10-inch tube pan for 1 1/2 hours in a 350-degree oven or until inserted toothpick comes out clean. Let cool for 20 minutes and turn onto cake plate. Sprinkle with sifted confectioners' sugar or...glaze with one cup of confectioners' sugar mixed with 3 tablespoons milk and 1/2 teaspoon of vanilla.

CHOCOLATE POUND CAKE [COLD OVEN]

Ingredients for 1 cake

5	Eggs, separated
8 oz	Sour cream

1/4 tsp	Baking soda
1 cup	Butter, softened
3 cups	Sugar
2 1/2 cups	Flour, all-purpose
1/2 cup	Cocoa, unsweetened powder
1 tbsp	Vanilla

EASY FUDGE ICING

3 cups	Sugar
3 tsp	Cocoa, powder
3/4 cup	Evaporated milk
2 tbsp	White corn syrup
1/2 cup	Butter
1 tbsp	Vanilla
1 cup	Pecans, chopped or whole [optional]

Beat egg whites in a medium bowl until stiff. Set aside. Combine sour cream and baking soda in a small bowl. Set aside. Cream butter and sugar in a mixing bowl. Add the egg yolks and mix well. Combine the flour and cocoa. Add the flour mixture and the sour cream to the butter, alternating. Add the vanilla, mixing well. Fold in the egg whites. Pour the batter in an oiled tube pan. [I use a wax paper liner as well.] Place in a COLD oven. Bake at 325 degrees for 1 hour and 20 minutes or until inserted toothpick comes out clean. Cool before frosting.

FUDGE ICING: Combine the sugar, cocoa, milk, corn syrup, and butter in a large saucepan. Cook over medium heat, stirring constantly, until the mixture reaches a full boil. Boil, while stirring, for 2 minutes. Drop a little in a cup of cold water. When mixture reaches the soft ball stage, remove from heat and add the vanilla. Beat until spreading consistency. Spread over the cake and place the pecans on top.

COCONUT POUND CAKE

Ingredients for 1 cake

2 sticks	Butter, room temperature	6 lg	Eggs
1 stick	Oleo, room temperature	3 cups	Flour [all-purpose], sifted
8 oz	Cream cheese, room temperature	2 tbsp	Cold water
		2 tsp	Coconut flavoring
3 cups	Sugar	4 oz	Coconut [can, flaked]

Cream butter, oleo, and cream cheese [should be at room temperature]. Add sugar slowly and mix well. Add eggs, one at a time, mixing after each egg. Add flour gradually. Add water, coconut flavoring, and the coconut. Pour into a greased and floured tube pan. Place in a cold oven. Bake for 1 1/2 or 1 3/4 hours at 275 degrees or until inserted toothpick comes out clean.

KAREN'S QUICK AND EASY POUND CAKE

Ingredients for 2 loaves

2 1/2 cups	Gold Medal self-rising flour
2 cups	Sugar
1 cup	Crisco vegetable oil
1 cup	Milk
4	Eggs
1 tsp	Vanilla or to taste

Preheat the oven at 325 degrees. Mix all of the ingredients together. Pour the batter into 2 greased and floured loaf pans. Bake for 1 hour and 15 minutes.

Helpful hint: Karen suggests that only the ingredients listed in the recipe be used for best results.

LEMON CREME POUND CAKE

Ingredients for 1 cake

1 lb	Butter, softened	2 tsp	Vanilla flavoring
8 oz	Cream cheese, softened	2 tsp	Lemon flavoring
3 cups	Sugar		**GLAZE**
9 lg	Eggs	1 cup	Powdered sugar
3 cups	Flour, all-purpose, sifted	1/2 cup	Lemon juice

Cream the first two ingredients and gradually add the sugar. Beat until light and fluffy. Add the eggs one at a time, beating after each addition. Add the flour gradually. After the first addition of the flour, add the flavorings. Pour into a prepared 10-inch tube pan or a Bundt pan. Bake in a 325-degree oven for 1 1/2 hours or until inserted toothpick comes out clean. Cool and drizzle the confectioners' sugar/lemon juice glaze over the top, letting it run down the sides. Serve with a big scoop of vanilla ice cream.

Helpful hint: If the batter is too much for the size of the tube pan, use the excess batter for cupcakes or a small loaf cake.

ROSALIND'S COLD-OVEN POUND CAKE

Ingredients for 1 cake

3 cups	Flour [all-purpose], sifted
1/2 tsp	Baking powder, sifted with flour
2 sticks	Butter, room temperature
3 cups	Sugar
1/2 cup	Crisco, butter flavored
6 lg	Eggs
1 1/2 tsp	Vanilla
3/4 cup	Buttermilk

Sift together the flour and baking powder. Add the vanilla to the milk. Cream the butter, Crisco, and sugar together. Add the eggs one at a time. Alternate adding the flour and milk to the butter mixture. Lightly oil the bottom and sides of a tube pan. Line the bottom with wax paper. Pour the batter into the pan, place in a COLD oven, and bake in a 325-degree oven for 1 1/2 hours or until inserted pick comes out clean.

GOLDEN LEMON POUND CAKE

Ingredients for 1 cake

1 cup	Butter, softened	1 tbsp	Lemon peel,
2 cups	Sugar		grated
4 lg	Eggs	1 tbsp	Lemon juice
3 cups	Flour, all-purpose		
1/2 tsp	Baking powder		**GLAZE**
1/2 tsp	Baking soda	1 1/4 cups	Powdered
1/2 tsp	Salt		sugar
3/4 cup	Buttermilk	2 tsp	Lemon juice
		3 tbsp	Milk

Measure the dry ingredients together in a bowl and mix with a whisk. In another bowl, mix the sugar and butter together and beat until creamy. Add one egg at a time, beating after each addition. Reduce the mixer speed and add the flour mixture alternately with the buttermilk and lemon juice. Stir in the lemon zest. Pour into a prepared 12-cup Bundt pan or tube pan. Bake in a 325-degree oven for 55–65 minutes or until inserted toothpick comes out clean. Cool for 10 minutes before removing from the pan. Cool.

GLAZE: Stir together the powdered sugar, lemon juice, and milk. Drizzle the glaze over the cooled cake. If necessary, add more milk to the glaze mixture.

Helpful hint: This batter makes 3 dozen cupcakes if baked in regular muffin tins. Pink or green sugar crystals on top of the glaze look pretty for Easter or a party.

MAHOGANY POUND CAKE

Ingredients for 10 servings

2 1/2 cups	Flour	6 lg	Eggs, room
1/2 cup	Cocoa		temperature
1 cup	Butter, softened	1 tsp	Vanilla
2 cups	Sugar	1/4 tsp	Baking soda
1 cup	Brown sugar	1 cup	Sour cream

Sift the flour and cocoa together and set aside. Cream the butter, sugar, and brown sugar together and beat until light and fluffy. Add the eggs one at the time, beating after each addition. Add the vanilla. Mix together the sour cream and baking soda. Add the flour mixture and the sour cream mixture alternately. Pour the batter into a well-greased and floured 10-inch tube pan. Bake in a 325-degree oven until inserted tester comes out clean, about 1 1/2 hours. Cool and dust with confectioners' sugar OR drizzle with a glaze of 1 cup confectioners' sugar, 3 tablespoons milk, and 1/2 teaspoon of vanilla while cake is still warm.

SOUR CREAM POUND CAKE

Ingredients for 1 cake

1 cup	Crisco, butter flavored
3 cups	Sugar
5 lg	Eggs
3 cups	Flour, all-purpose
1/4 tsp	Baking soda
1 cup	Sour cream
1 tsp	Vanilla

Mix sugar and Crisco well. Add the eggs, one at a time, beating well after each addition. Add the flour and sour cream alternately, starting and ending with the flour. Add the soda and vanilla. Pour into a well-oiled [and wax-paper-lined, if preferred] tube pan. Bake in a 325-degree oven for 1 hour and 15 minutes or until inserted toothpick comes out clean.

RED VELVET CAKE OR CUPCAKES

Ingredients for 1 cake

2 1/2 cups	Flour, all-purpose
1 1/2 cups	Sugar
1 tsp	Salt
1 tsp	Baking soda
1 tsp	Cocoa powder
2 lg	Eggs, room temperature
1 cup	Buttermilk, room temperature
1 1/2 cups	Vegetable oil
1 tsp	White vinegar
2 tbsp	Red food coloring [1 oz]
1 tsp	Vanilla flavoring

CREAM CHEESE FROSTING

1 lb	Cream cheese, room temperature
2 sticks	Butter, room temperature
4 cups	Confectioners' sugar, sifted
1 tsp	Vanilla
	Crushed pecans

Sift together the flour, sugar, salt, baking soda, and cocoa powder. In another bowl, whisk the oil, vinegar, buttermilk, eggs, vanilla, and food coloring together. Mix the dry ingredients into the wet ingredients and mix until just combined and a smooth batter is formed. Divide the cake batter evenly among 3 oiled or sprayed 9-inch cake pans. Place the pans in a 350-degree oven. Bake for 30 minutes or until the cake pulls away from the sides of the pans. Place the cakes on a cooling rack, baked side up, and let them cool completely.

FOR FROSTING: Mix the cream cheese, butter, confectioners' sugar, and vanilla together on low speed with a handheld mixer or in a standing mixer with the paddle attachment until incorporated. Increase the mixer speed to high and beat another 5 minutes or until the frosting is light and fluffy, stopping occasionally to scrape down the sides with a spatula. Chill slightly in the refrigerator and frost the top and sides of the cake. Press the top and/or sides of the cake with the pecans.

Helpful hint: When frosting the cake, place one layer on a cake plate with the baked side down. Spread about 1/3 inch of the frosting on the first layer. Place another layer on top of the first layer and repeat the process. Place the third layer on top with a baked side up. Frost the top and sides of the cake.

FOR CUPCAKES: Line a cupcake pan with 24 paper liners, filling them 2/3 full. Bake in a 350-degree oven, 20–22 minutes, turning halfway through the baking. Cool completely. Frost with cream cheese frosting using a butter knife or pipe it on with a big star tip. Garnish with chopped pecans, a strawberry, raspberry, or cherry.

SEVEN-UP CAKE [THANKS, MARY ANN]

Ingredients for 1 cake

2 sticks	Butter
1/2 cup	Crisco
3 cups	Sugar
5	Eggs
3 cups	Flour, all-purpose
1/2 tsp	Salt
2 tsp	Vanilla
3 tsp	Lemon extract [or 4 tsp vanilla]
7 oz	7-Up [bottle]
	VANILLA GLAZE
2 cups	Confectioners' sugar, sifted
3 tbsp	Milk
2 tbsp	Butter
1/2 tsp	Vanilla
	FROSTING
8 oz	Cream cheese, softened
1 stick	Butter, softened
1 box	4X Sugar

Cream butter, Crisco, and sugar. Add eggs one at a time, beating continually. Add rest of the ingredients except the 7-Up and mix well. Fold in the 7-Up. Bake at 325 degrees in a greased and floured tube pan for 1 1/2 hours, or until tester comes out clean. Top with the glaze or the frosting.

VANILLA GLAZE: Sift the powdered sugar into a bowl. Heat 3 tablespoons of milk and 2 tablespoons of butter over low heat stirring constantly until butter just melts. Add to the sugar and whip until smooth. Stir in vanilla and spoon over the warm cake.

CREAM CHEESE FROSTING: Mix the softened cream cheese, softened butter, and 4X sugar together. Beat until smooth. Spread over the cooled cake.

Helpful hint: This cake is delicious with either topping.

CARROT SHEET CAKE

Ingredients for 1 cake

2 cups	Sugar
2 cups	Flour, all-purpose
1/2 tsp	Cinnamon
1 tsp	Salt
2 tsp	Baking soda
1 1/2 cups	Oil
4 lg	Eggs
1 sm	Bag of carrots [8 or 10], grated

	ICING
1 box	Powdered sugar
1/2 stick	Butter, room temperature
8 oz	Cream cheese, softened
2 tsp	Vanilla
1/2 cup	Chopped pecans, lightly toasted

Mix the sugar, flour, cinnamon, salt, and soda together with a whisk or by sifting. Mix the oil, eggs, and carrots together in a blender. Add to the flour mixture and blend well. Pour into an oiled 13x9-inch pan. Bake in a 350-degree oven until inserted toothpick comes out clean.

ICING: Beat the butter and cream cheese until smooth. Add the powdered sugar and vanilla and beat until well blended. Spread over the cake. Sprinkle the nuts over the top.

CHOCOLATE SHEET CAKE

Ingredients for 1 cake

1 stick	Butter, softened
1 cup	Sugar
4 lg	Eggs
1 tsp	Vanilla
1 cup	Flour, all-purpose
1/8 tsp	Salt
1 tsp	Baking powder
16 oz	Chocolate syrup [can]
	FROSTING
1 stick	Butter
1/2 cup	Chocolate chips
1 cup	Sugar
1/3 cup	Evaporated milk
1 pinch	Salt
1 tsp	Vanilla
1/2 cup	Nuts [optional]

Cream the butter and sugar together until light and fluffy. Add the eggs one at a time, beating after each addition. Sift the dry ingredients together. Add the dry mixture to the creamed butter, beating until incorporated. Add the vanilla and chocolate syrup to the batter. Pour into an oiled 13x9-inch baking pan. Bake in a 350-degree oven for 30 minutes or until inserted pick comes out clean.

FROSTING: Melt the butter in a saucepan. Add the milk, sugar, and chocolate chips. Bring to a boil for 2 or 3 minutes, while stirring. Remove from the heat and add the vanilla and nuts. Pour the frosting over the warm cake.

WHITE SHEET CAKE

Ingredients for 1 cake

2 cups	Flour, all-purpose
2 cups	Sugar
1 tsp	Salt
1 tsp	Baking powder
2 sticks	Butter, room temperature
1 cup	Water
1/2 cup	Sour cream
2 lg	Eggs, slightly beaten
1 tsp	Almond extract
1 cup	Pecans, chopped

	BUTTER FROSTING
1 stick	Butter
1/4 cup	Milk
1/2 tsp	Almond extract
3 cups	Confectioners' sugar

Whisk the flour, sugar, salt, and baking powder together and set aside. Combine the butter and water in a small saucepan and bring to a boil while stirring. Combine the two mixtures and stir.

Add the sour cream, eggs, and almond extract and mix. Pour into a prepared 15x10-inch jelly roll pan. Bake in a 350-degree oven for 20–25 minutes or until an inserted toothpick comes out clean. Spread the frosting over the warm cake and sprinkle with the chopped pecans. Cut into squares and serve.

BUTTER FROSTING: Combine the butter and milk in a saucepan and bring to a boil over medium heat while stirring. Remove from the heat and add the almond extract. Gradually whisk in the confectioners' sugar. Spread over the warm cake and sprinkle the pecans over the top.

SNOWBALL CAKE

Ingredients for 1 cake

2 pkgs	Plain gelatin
4 tbsp	Cold water
1 cup	Boiling water
2 cups	Crushed pineapple, juice and all
1 cup	Sugar
1/2 tsp	Salt
1	Angel food cake, baked from mix or bought from a bakery
16 oz	Carton of Cool Whip
	Coconut and maraschino cherries, if desired

Mix cold water with gelatin and allow to stand for a short time. Add the boiling water and mix. Add the pineapple, sugar, and salt. Place in the refrigerator to partially gel. Break the angel food cake into bite-size pieces in a large bowl and set aside. Add about 12 ounces of Cool Whip to the gelatin mixture. Stir in the cake pieces and mix well. Pour mixture into a large bowl lined with plastic wrap, leaving enough wrap to cover the top of the bowl. Place the bowl in the refrigerator overnight, or until the mixture has jellied into a solid. Turn the cake out onto a cake plate and frost with the remaining Cool Whip. Sprinkle with coconut and decorate with cherries. Keep refrigerated.

SOCK-IT-TO-ME CAKE

Ingredients for 1 cake

1 box	Butter Recipe Golden cake mix [Duncan Hines]
1 cup	Sour cream
1/2 cup	Oil [Crisco]
1/4 cup	Sugar
1/4 cup	Water
4 lg	Eggs

	FILLING
1 cup	Pecans, chopped
2 tbsp	Brown sugar
2 tsp	Cinnamon

	GLAZE
1 cup	Confectioners' sugar
2 tbsp	Milk

Blend together the cake mix, oil, sugar, water, and eggs. Add the sour cream and mix. Pour 2/3 of the batter into a sprayed or greased and floured 10-inch Bundt pan. Combine the filling ingredients and sprinkle over the batter. Pour the remaining batter over the filling. Bake in a 350-degree oven for 55 minutes or until an inserted pick comes out clean. Let the cake rest for about 10 minutes and turn it onto a cake plate. Blend the confectioners' sugar and milk with a small whisk. Drizzle the glaze over the warm cake.

TEA CAKES

Ingredients for 3 dozen

3/4 cup	Butter	1 tsp	Baking powder
1 1/2 cups	Sugar	1/2 tsp	Salt
2 lg	Eggs	1 tsp	Vanilla
2 3/4 cups	Flour, all-purpose		

Mix the flour, salt, and baking powder together in a small bowl. Cream the butter and sugar, adding the eggs one at a time. Add the vanilla. Mix in the dry ingredients. Drop onto a lightly-oiled baking sheet. Bake in a 350-degree oven for 8–10 minutes.

Helpful hint: If frosting, reduce the amount of sugar to 1 cup instead of 1 1/2 cups.

TEA CAKES, ROLLED

Ingredients for 4 dozen

3 1/2 cups	Flour, all-purpose
1 cup	Sugar
1 lg	Egg
1/2 cup	Butter or butter-flavored Crisco
1/4 cup	Buttermilk
1 tsp	Baking soda
1 tsp	Vanilla

Beat the sugar, butter, and egg together until creamy. Add the soda and vanilla to the buttermilk. Add the milk to the butter mixture. Add the flour slowly until thick enough to handle. Roll the dough on a floured surface to 1/2 inch thick or desired thickness. Cut with a cookie cutter. Bake in a 350-degree oven on a lightly oiled cookie tray for about 12 minutes.

Candies

CANDIED CITRUS PEEL

Ingredients for 2 pounds

5	Navel oranges [or 3 large grapefruit]
3 1/2 cups	Sugar [divided]
1 1/2 cups	Water

Score the peel of each fruit into quarters, cutting through the rind and white pith. Pull peel from the fruit, refrigerating the fruit for another use. [The peel should amount to 14 oz.] Cut orange peel lengthwise or grapefruit crosswise, about 1/4-inch wide. Boil peel and water [on high heat] in a 4-quart saucepan for 5 minutes. Drain. Repeat the boiling process 2 more times, using fresh water each time. Combine 2 1/2 cups sugar with 1 1/2 cups water in a 12-inch skillet. Cook over high heat, stirring constantly, until mixture boils and sugar dissolves. [Candy thermometer should register 230 degrees.] Add the drained peel to syrup in the skillet and stir to coat evenly. Reduce the heat, partially cover, and simmer for 1 hour. Gently stir occasionally. Peel should absorb most of the syrup. Remove the lid and continue to simmer, stirring gently, until all of the syrup has been absorbed. Place the remaining cup of sugar on a sheet of wax paper. Lightly roll the peel onto the wax paper with tongs. Let peel dry on wire racks for 12 hours or until peels are dry on the outside and moist on the inside. Store in an airtight container for one month at room temperature.

CHOCOLATE CHIP MERINGUES

Ingredients for 4 dozen

3 lg	Egg whites
1/8 tsp	Salt
3/4 cup	Sugar
4 oz	Chocolate chips
1 tsp	Vanilla
1 cup	Pecans, chopped small

Beat the egg whites until soft peaks form. Mix the sugar and salt together and add to egg whites 1 tablespoon at a time, beating after each addition. Add the vanilla along with the sugar. When the whites are very stiff, fold in the chocolate chips and pecans, being careful not to deflate. Drop the mixture on baking sheets which have been lined with non-stick foil. Bake in a 175-degree oven for 4–5 hours. Turn the oven off and leave in the oven for several hours [or overnight] with the oven light on. These add a gourmet touch to a parfait or a dish of ice cream with maybe a drizzle of chocolate sauce and a dollop of whipped cream.

CHOCOLATE-COVERED MARSHMALLOWS

Ingredients for 48 pieces

10 oz	Jet-puffed marshmallows
1 1/2 cups	Granulated sugar
2/3 cup	Evaporated milk
2 tbsp	Butter
1/4 tsp	Salt
2 1/4 cups	Miniature marshmallows
1 3/4 cups	Milk chocolate morsels [or 11.5 oz package]
1 tsp	Vanilla extract
1 cup	Chopped pecans or walnuts [toasted]

Line a cookie sheet with foil. In a medium, heavy-duty saucepan combine sugar, evaporated milk, butter, and salt. Bring ingredients to a full rolling boil over medium heat, stirring constantly for 4–5 minutes. Remove from heat. Stir in miniature marshmallows, morsels, and vanilla extract. Stir for 1 minute or until marshmallows are completely melted. Spear a large marshmallow with a wooden skewer and dip it into the chocolate mixture, covering completely. Roll the chocolate-covered marshmallow in pecans and place it on the foil-lined tray to cool. A small, shallow bowl works well for holding the pecans. The chocolate mixture may need to be rewarmed on a very low heat 2 or 3 times.

CHOCOLATE COVERED RITZ BITS

Ingredients for 110 pieces

9 1/2 oz	Ritz Bits Sandwich Crackers with peanut butter [1 box]
16 oz	Chocolate candy coating

Melt the chocolate in top of a double boiler with the water hot but not boiling. Drop individual Ritz Bits into chocolate, turning with a small fork or other utensil. Place the chocolate-covered Bit on a large tray lined with wax paper. Cool completely and store in an airtight container.

Helpful hint: I like the milk chocolate, but the white chocolate is good also.

CRUNCH BARS

Ingredients for 1 batch

35	Saltines, Original Premium
1/2 cup	Butter [1 stick]
1/2 cup	Light brown sugar, firmly packed
1 cup	Chopped nuts, lightly toasted [pecans or walnuts]
15	Hershey bars [1.55 oz each]

Line a cookie sheet with foil. Unwrap the candy bars, checking to make sure they will cover the saltines when placed on them. If needed, unwrap more. Place saltine crackers on foil as closely as possible. Boil butter and sugar in a saucepan for 3 minutes, adding the nuts before removing from the heat. Quickly spread over the crackers. Bake in a 400-degree oven for 7 minutes. Remove from oven, quickly place Hershey bars over the top, and smooth with a knife or the back of a spoon. Score with a paring knife. Cool completely and cut along the lines that were scored.

Helpful hint: These can be broken into desired pieces instead of being cut. Store cool candy in an airtight container or a ziplock bag.

DIVINITY

Ingredients for 1 batch

3 cups	Sugar
1 cup	Water
3/4 cup	White corn syrup
2	Egg whites
1 tbsp	Black walnut flavoring
2 cups	Nuts

Cook corn syrup, sugar, and water to a hard ball stage, about 20–25 minutes. Beat egg whites until stiff. Add syrup and beat 10 minutes, adding flavoring and nuts. When mixture has lost its gloss, drop by tablespoons onto wax paper.

Helpful hint: Start testing the syrup after 20 minutes. Do this by dropping a little syrup into a cup of cold water and then drop the ball on the stove top. If it "pings," the syrup is ready.

EASTER EGG NEST

Ingredients for 3 dozen

1 stick	Butter
1 cup	Brown sugar, light or dark
1 tbsp	Corn syrup
6 oz	Chow mein noodles [package]

Melt the sugar in a saucepan. Add the brown sugar and syrup. Boil for 3 minutes, stirring constantly. Add the noodles and stir until all are coated. While hot, drop a small amount in a miniature muffin pan and press in the center, forming a nest. Fill the nests with candy eggs or jelly beans. Larger nests can be made by using larger muffin pans.

ENGLISH TOFFEE [CAIRO STYLE]

Ingredients for 48 pieces

1 cup	Sugar
2 sticks	Butter
3 tbsp	Water
1 tsp	Vanilla

| 8 | Hershey bars [unwrapped ahead of time] |
| 1 cup | Chopped pecans [optional] |

Butter a 13x9-inch pan. Melt butter and sugar in a saucepan. Add water. Bring to a rolling boil on medium-high heat for about 10 minutes, stirring constantly, until mixture turns to a walnut-brown color. Add vanilla and nuts. Stir well. Immediately pour into pan. Smooth mixture and lay chocolate bars across top. Smooth chocolate with a knife, covering all areas. Score with a paring knife immediately.

Helpful hint: This is a work-fast recipe. It is best to have all ingredients and utensils handy. Yield: Approximately 48 squares. Delicious!

FUDGE

Ingredients for 16 pieces

1 stick	Butter
2 cups	Sugar
5 oz	Evaporated milk [can]
1/8 tsp	Salt
6 tbsp	Cocoa
1 1/2 tsp	Vanilla
1 cup	Pecans [or nuts of choice]

Sift the sugar, salt, and cocoa together. Melt the butter in a heavy saucepan. Add the milk and dry ingredients. Bring to a boil, while stirring, and cook for 7 minutes. Add the vanilla and nuts. Pour into a buttered 8x8-inch Pyrex dish or pan. Cool before cutting.

Helpful hint: This recipe can be used for frosting. Reduce the cooking time to 4 minutes.

FABULOUS FUDGE

Ingredients for 60 pieces

4 1/2 cups	Sugar
12 oz	Evaporated milk [can]
1 1/2 tsp	Vanilla
24 oz	Semisweet chocolate morsels
15 oz	Sweet chocolate bar [Hershey or Symphony]
7 oz	Marshmallow cream [jar]

Bring the sugar and milk slowly to a boil in a large saucepan, stirring constantly. Boil for 5 minutes, constantly stirring. Combine the vanilla and the remaining ingredients in the top of a double boiler, stirring until the chocolate is melted. Add to the hot milk mixture, stirring until smooth. Pour into a well-buttered 13x9-inch Pyrex dish. Cool and cut into squares.

WHITE CHOCOLATE FUDGE

Ingredients for 2 pounds

8 oz	Cream cheese, softened
4 cups	Powdered sugar, sifted
1 1/2 tsp	Vanilla extract
12 oz	Vanilla candy coating, melted
3/4 cup	Chopped pecans

Beat the cream cheese at medium speed with an electric mixer until smooth. Gradually add the sugar and vanilla, beating well.

Stir in the candy coating and the pecans. Spread in a buttered 8-inch square pan. Refrigerate until firm. Cut into small squares.

FUDGE WREATH

Ingredients for 3 pounds

16 oz	Semisweet chocolate morsels
12 oz	Butterscotch morsels
14 oz	Sweetened condensed milk [not evaporated]
1 cup	Walnuts, chopped
1/4 cup	Currants
	Red candied cherries [about 12]
	Green candied cherries [3]

Line a cake pan with plastic wrap [8 inch is good]. Place the empty milk can in the center [wash first]. Put the milk and candy morsels in a heavy saucepan. Melt over low heat. Add the chopped walnuts and currants and mix. Pour into the prepared pan. Cut the red cherries in half and cut again. Place the pieces on the chocolate in a poinsettia design [you will want to make 7 or 8]. Cut the green cherries into smaller pieces and place 3 slivers around each poinsettia. Let set well before serving on your Christmas buffet or giving as a gift.

Helpful hint: Before removing candy from the pan, gently turn the can until it can be removed.

GRAHAM CRACKER PRALINES

Ingredients for 1 batch

48 pieces	Graham crackers
1 cup	Brown sugar
2 sticks	Butter
1 cup	Chopped nuts

Place graham crackers on large baking tray [with sides], covering surface. Boil brown sugar and butter for 2 minutes. Add chopped nuts. Pour hot mixture evenly over crackers and bake for 10 minutes in 350-degree oven. Cut while hot. Yield: 48 pieces.

HAYSTACKS

Ingredients for 2 1/2 dozen

12 oz	Butterscotch morsels
5 oz	Chow mein noodles [can]
1 cup	Salted peanuts
3 tbsp	Peanut butter

Melt the butterscotch morsels in a saucepan over medium heat. Add the peanut butter and blend. Add the peanuts and the chow mein noodles. Stir until the peanuts and noodles are covered. Drop spoonfuls of the mixture onto wax paper and let cool.

MARSHMALLOWS

Ingredients for 64 pieces

2 1/2 tbsp	Gelatin, unflavored
1 cup	Water, divided

1 1/2 cups	Sugar
1 cup	Light corn syrup
1/4 tsp	Salt
2 tsp	Vanilla
1 tbsp	Water
	Powdered sugar
	Cooking spray

Lightly coat an 8x8-inch [2-inch deep] pan with a good cooking spray, dust heavily with powdered sugar, and set aside. Dissolve the gelatin in the mixer bowl with 1/2 cup of water. Let rest for 25 minutes. Combine the remaining 1/2 cup of water, sugar, corn syrup, and salt in a heavy 2-quart saucepan. Cook, while stirring, over medium-low heat until the sugar is dissolved. Increase the heat to medium-high and bring to a boil, while stirring. Cook over medium heat [or lower, if necessary to keep mixture from boiling over] for about 15 minutes until candy thermometer registers 244 degrees. With the mixer set on low to med-low speed, pour the hot sugar mixture into the gelatin mixture. Increase the speed to high and beat about 15 minutes. Add the vanilla to 1 tablespoon of water and add to the mixture and beat until combined. The mixture should be thick, white, and nearly tripled in volume. Spoon the mixture into the prepared pan. The mixture will be sticky. Let stand, uncovered, overnight. The next day, loosen by running a knife around the pan. Turn on to a cutting board which has been dusted with confectioners' sugar. Cut into 1-inch squares with a long, thin knife. Dust the squares with additional powdered sugar.

Helpful hint: Using a stand mixer is almost a must for this recipe unless someone can assist you. The syrup is dangerously hot while pouring. It is always good to have a bowl of cold water handy in the event you get some hot syrup on you. This is a good thing to do while making any cooked candy.

CHOCOLATE MERINGUES

Ingredients for 3 dozen

2 lg	Egg whites, room temperature
1/8 tsp	Salt
1/2 tsp	Vanilla
1/4 tsp	Cream of tartar
2 tbsp	Cocoa [powder]
1/2 cup	Sugar

Beat the egg whites until they are foamy. Add the salt and cream of tartar while beating. Whisk the sugar and cocoa powder together. Gradually add the sugar mixture to the egg whites and beat until stiff peaks form. Add the vanilla and beat until just blended. Spoon onto baking sheet that has been lined with foil or parchment paper. Bake in a 175-degree oven for 4–5 hours, or until the meringues are firm and are lightly browned. Cool in the oven and store in an airtight container.

If two pots become stuck together after stacking, it's not impossible to unstick them. Put ice in the inner pot and dunk the outer pot in hot water. The warm water will expand the outer pot and the ice will contract the inner pot, making the pots separate.

CHOCOLATE MICE

Ingredients for 2 dozen

2 oz	Milk chocolate candy coating
24	Maraschino cherries with stems
24	Mini chocolate chips
48	Sliced almonds

Blot the cherries well and let dry. Melt the chocolate in a heatproof bowl over steaming water. Dip the cherries into the chocolate by holding the stems. Let them almost dry on wax paper. Using tweezers, place a chocolate chip on the opposite side of the cherry stem [or the tail] for the nose. Place an almond slice on each side of the top of the cherry for the ears.

Helpful hint: The almond slices are fragile, so this is tedious. These mice add a special touch to a Christmas dessert. [Not a creature was stirring…not even a mouse.]

OREO BALLS [THANKS, NANCY]

Ingredients for 3 dozen

15 1/2 oz	Oreo cookies
8 oz	Cream cheese [room temperature]
	Chocolate of choice

Crush the cookies or process in a food processor. Mix in the softened cream cheese. Roll the mixture into balls and chill in the refrigerator. Dip the balls in melted milk chocolate. Let the chocolate become firm. Drizzle the chocolate balls with white or dark chocolate [or with both]. Store in an airtight container in the refrigerator.

SUGARED PEANUTS

Ingredients for 1 batch

4 cups	Raw peanuts, shelled
2 cups	Sugar
1 cup	Water

Mix sugar and water in an iron skillet. Add peanuts and bring to a boil for 20 minutes over medium heat, stirring, until liquid and sugar crystallize on peanuts. Spread on large cookie sheet and bake in a 325-degree oven for 15 minutes. Separate any large clusters while baking. Food flavorings may be added during the boiling process, if desired [vanilla, cinnamon, etc.]. Cool and store in an airtight container.

Helpful hint: Ziplock bags are great!

PEANUT CRISPIES

Ingredients for 35 pieces

1 cup	Sugar, granulated
1 cup	Light corn syrup
1 cup	Peanut butter, creamy
1 tsp	Vanilla
6 cups	Rice Chex cereal
9 1/2 oz	Salted peanuts [I use Planters]

Combine the sugar, corn syrup, and peanut butter in a large [5 qt] non-stick boiler. Cook over medium-low heat until boiling, stirring gently. Boil 2–3 minutes, while stirring, or until the sugar is completely dissolved. Add the vanilla and blend. Add the peanuts and cereal and fold until all is covered with the peanut butter mixture. Pour into a buttered 9x13-inch Pyrex dish. Let cool and cut.

CANDIED SPICED PECANS

Ingredients for 2 quarts

2 qts	Pecans [approximately 2 pounds; Elliotts, if possible]
3/4 cup	Sugar
3/4 tsp	Salt
2 tsp	Cinnamon
1/3 tsp	Cloves, ground
1/2 tsp	Allspice, ground
1/2 tsp	Nutmeg, ground
1 lg	Egg [white only]
2 1/2 tbsp	Water

Whisk all of the ingredients, except for the pecans, together in a mixing bowl. Add the pecans and mix until they are well coated. Line a large jelly roll tray with non-stick foil. Spread the pecans on the tray. Bake the pecans in a preheated 275-degree oven for 45–55 minutes or until the coating is dry. Stir the pecans every 10–15 minutes to separate. Store in airtight containers, or quart jars.

Helpful hint: I save plastic mayonnaise jars to store nuts, etc. in. Also, they are good to freeze leftover soup in.

PEPPERMINT MERINGUES

Ingredients for 4 dozen

2	Egg whites
1/4 tsp	Cream of tartar

3/4 cup	Sugar
1 dash	Salt
1 tsp	Peppermint extract
3 drops	Green food coloring
6 oz	White chocolate morsels

Beat the egg whites, salt, and cream of tartar until frothy. Gradually add the sugar and beat until stiff and glossy, approximately 15 minutes. Add the food coloring and peppermint extract. Fold in the chocolate morsels. Spray cookie sheets with Pam or line them with non-stick aluminum foil. Drop small spoonfuls onto the prepared cookie sheet. [A very small ice cream scoop works nicely.] Bake in a 250-degree oven that has been preheated for 25 minutes. Bake for 20 minutes. Remove from the oven and let rest until slightly cooled. Place in an airtight container.

Helpful hint: These are fragile and will not last over 2 or 3 days without crumbling. Red food coloring can be used and semisweet chocolate morsels. All good!

PRALINES

Ingredients for 1 batch

2 cups	Light brown sugar, packed
2 cups	Granulated sugar
4 tbsp	Corn syrup, light
4 tbsp	Butter
1 cup	Condensed milk [not evaporated]
2 tsp	Vanilla
3 cups	Pecan pieces
1 pinch	Salt

Combine the sugars, corn syrup, butter, salt, and milk in a heavy saucepan and place over medium heat. Stir with a wooden spoon until the sugar dissolves. Cook, while stirring, about 8 minutes. The mixture should become a caramel color and very bubbly. Add the vanilla and pecans, stirring until the mixture reaches soft ball stage, 240 degrees on a candy thermometer. Pour onto non-stick foil and quickly spread. Cool and cut into desired sizes or break into pieces.

Helpful hint: Make sure that the boiler is large enough to contain the mixture when it begins to boil and bubble.

ROLO PRETZELS

Ingredients for 1 batch

40 pcs	Rolo candy
40	Snyder's Butter Snaps pretzels
40	Pecan halves
	Butter
	Salt

Toast pecans halves in 250-degree oven for 45 minutes, stirring occasionally. Melt butter. Brush pecans with the melted butter and sprinkle with salt the last 10 minutes of baking. Place the pretzels on a baking tray and top each one with a Rolo candy. Bake in a 300-degree oven for 5 minutes and remove from oven. Top each Rolo with a toasted pecan and press gently. Cool and store in an airtight container.

Helpful hint: Elliott pecans look pretty on this goodie. Delicious!

PRETZEL WREATH

Ingredients for 8 servings

1 pkg	Small pretzels, shaped like a butterfly
1 pkg	Milk chocolate candy coating
1 pkg	Dark chocolate candy coating
1 pkg	White chocolate candy coating
	Candy mold for leaves

Draw a circle [desired size of the wreath] on the back of wax paper or parchment paper. Place the pretzels around the circle [on the top side of the paper] to form the wreath. Melt the milk chocolate coating [according to the direction of the coating being used] and dip the lower half of the pretzels in the coating, placing each pretzel back in place on the paper. Make sure some of the chocolate is touching the pretzel next to it. Melt the dark chocolate and pour it into several of the leaf molds, place in the freezer for a couple of minutes, turn over, and release the chocolate leaves. Melt the white chocolate coating and place some of it in 4 or 5 small molds, such as molds for chocolate covered cherries. Place the coating in the freezer long enough to be firm. Release the white coating and roll each one in the palms of your hands so that the heat from your hands will help to form white balls or berries. If the chocolate gets too soft, place it back in the freezer briefly. When the leaves and berries have hardened, dip the berries lightly in the white chocolate and place each berry at the top of the wreath or you can put a little chocolate on the berry with a toothpick. The chocolate leaves work better if you put a little dark or milk chocolate directly onto the wreath and position the leaf on the applied chocolate. Place each leaf with the inside point toward the berries. After all of the chocolate has hardened, check to make sure all of the pretzels are firmly connected. If not, apply more of the milk chocolate with a toothpick or a candy-making tool. Run a spatula or a thin knife under the wreath to release it from the paper.

Helpful hint: A round plate is good to use to draw the circle.

CARAMELIZED SNACK MIX

Ingredients for 1 batch

6 cups	Corn Chex cereal
6 cups	Rice Chex cereal
2 cups	Brown sugar, firmly packed
1 cup	Butter
1/2 cup	Light corn syrup
1/2 tsp	Baking soda
16 oz	Dry roasted peanuts

Spray a large roasting pan with a baking spray. Place the cereal and nuts into the pan. Combine brown sugar, butter, and syrup in a 3-quart saucepan. Cook over medium-high heat until mixture comes to a boil [8–10 minutes]. Continue cooking for 1 minute, stirring constantly. Remove from heat and add the baking soda, mixing well. Pour the syrup mixture over the cereal and toss gently until it is coated. Bake for 40–50 minutes in a 250-degree oven, stirring every 15 minutes, or until coating is set. Cool and store in an airtight container or ziplock bags.

Helpful hint: May add more cereal or cereal of your choice.

TRUFFLES [CAIRO STYLE]

Ingredients for 30 pieces

1/3 cup	Whipping cream
2 cups	Double chocolate chips [Ghirardelli's]
6 tbsp	Unsalted butter, cut into small pieces
1/3 cup	Confectioners' sugar
3/4 cup	Finely chopped pecans, slightly toasted

Bring the cream to a simmer in a small saucepan. Remove from the heat and stir in the butter. Microwave the chocolate chips for 1 minute. [If not melted, repeat the process at 30-second intervals.] Add the melted chocolate to the cream mixture, stirring until smooth. Pour the mixture into a shallow bowl. Cool, cover, and refrigerate until firm [approximately 2 hours]. Pour the coatings into pie plates. Scrape a spoon across the chocolate and form it into a 1-inch ball. Dip spoon into warm water if needed. Roll ball in hands and then in the coating, first the sugar and then the nuts. Shake the pans with the toppings to coat evenly. Transfer to an airtight container and refrigerate. Keep in the refrigerator for 2 weeks or freeze up to 3 months. The same procedure can be used with the Ghirardelli milk chocolate and topped with 1/3 cup of unsweetened cocoa or pecan meal.

GLAZED WALNUTS OR PECANS

Ingredients for 1 1/2 cups

1 1/2 cups	Walnuts or pecans
2 cups	Sugar
2 cups	Water

Boil the water, sugar, and nuts in a medium saucepan for 10–15 minutes. Drain any excess water. Spread the nuts on a baking sheet lined with non-stick foil or lightly-oiled parchment paper. Bake in a 250-degree oven for 12–15 minutes or until the nuts are lightly toasted.

WHITE CLOUDS

Ingredients for 3 dozen

2	Egg whites
1/4 tsp	Cream of tartar
1/2 cup	Sugar
1 tsp	Vanilla extract
1 cup	Pecans, finely chopped and toasted slightly
6 oz	Semisweet and white chocolate morsels, swirled

Beat egg whites, at room temperature, and cream of tartar at high speed for 1 minute with an electric mixer. Gradually add sugar, 1 tablespoon at a time. Beat until stiff peaks form, about 3–4 minutes. Carefully stir in the pecans and morsels with a large spoon or spatula. Drop by spoonfuls onto trays which have been lined with non-stick aluminum foil. Place in a preheated 350-degree oven and TURN HEAT OFF. Leave trays in the oven for 8 hours without opening the oven door. Store in an airtight container.

Cookies

RICH'S BROWN SUGAR BARS

Ingredients for 30 bars

1 stick	Butter
1 lb	Light brown sugar
4 lg	Eggs
2 tsp	Vanilla
1 tsp	Orange zest
2 cups	All-purpose flour, sifted
2 tsp	Baking powder
1/4 tsp	Salt
1 cup	Candied fruit [or dried fruit]
1 cup	Nuts, chopped

Beat the brown sugar and butter together on medium-low speed until light and fluffy. Add the eggs one at a time, beating after each addition. Beat in the vanilla and the orange zest. Sift together the flour, baking powder, and salt into small mixing bowl. Add the flour mixture to the butter mixture and mix on low speed until about half combined. Add the nuts and fruit and mix until just combined. Spread the batter into an oiled 11x16-inch pan. Bake in a 325-degree oven for 25 minutes. Cut into bars.

SYMPHONY BROWNIES

Ingredients for 24 servings

1 box	Brownie mix [13x9 family size]
	Oil, water, and eggs
18 oz	Almonds and Toffee Chips Symphony Bars
	[3 bars, 6 oz each]

Mix brownies according to the cake-like directions on the box. Pour 1/2 of the batter in a 13x9x2-inch Pyrex baking dish which has been sprayed with Pam. Place the 3 Symphony bars on top of the batter. Pour the rest of the batter over the candy and smooth it with a spatula. Bake the brownies in a 345-degree oven for 45 minutes or until a toothpick inserted around the edge comes out clean.

BUTTERSCOTCH BROWNIES

Ingredients for 24 bars

1/2 stick	Butter
1 cup	Light brown sugar
1 lg	Egg
1 cup	Flour, all-purpose
1/2 tsp	Baking powder
1/2 tsp	Vanilla
1/2 cup	Nuts, chopped

Melt the butter over low heat. Remove from the heat and add the sugar. Stir until well blended. Cool. Stir in the slightly beaten egg. Sift the flour and the baking powder together and add to the mixture. Stir in the vanilla. Add the nuts. Pour into a greased and floured baking pan. Bake in a 350-degree oven for 20–25 minutes. Cut while warm.

CREAM CHEESE BROWNIES

Ingredients for 24 servings

4 oz	Chocolate square [unsweetened]
1 cup	Butter
2 cups	Sugar
4 lg	Eggs
1 1/2 cups	Flour, all-purpose
1/2 tsp	Salt
2 tsp	Vanilla
1 cup	Nuts, chopped

FILLING

16 oz	Cream cheese, softened
1/2 cup	Sugar
1 lg	Egg
2 tsp	Vanilla

Mix all of the filling ingredients until smooth. Slowly melt the butter and chocolate in a small saucepan, stirring frequently. Cool. Beat the sugar, vanilla, eggs, and chocolate mixture together on medium speed. Mix the flour and salt together. Add the flour, beating on low speed for about a minute. Stir in the nuts. Spread 1/2 of the batter in an oiled 13x9-inch baking pan. Slowly spread the filling over the batter. Carefully spread the rest of the batter over the filling. Bake in a 350-degree oven for 45–50 minutes or until an inserted pick comes out clean.

BUTTER COOKIES

Ingredients for 2 1/2 dozen

2 sticks	Butter, room temperature
1 cup	Sugar
1 lg	Egg
2 1/2 cups	Flour, all-purpose
1 tsp	Baking powder
1 tbsp	Vanilla
2 tbsp	Orange juice

FROSTING

3 cups	Powdered sugar
1/3 cup	Butter, softened
1 tsp	Vanilla
1 1/2 tbsp	Milk [more or less]
	Food coloring, optional

Mix the first 3 ingredients together in a bowl and beat until creamy. Add the flour, baking powder, vanilla, and orange juice and mix on low speed. Beat until blended. Divide the mixture into thirds and wrap in plastic wrap. Refrigerate for 2 hours or overnight. Remove 1/3 of the chilled dough from the refrigerator and roll out on a floured surface until 1/4-inch thickness or thinner. Cut with 3-inch cookie cutters. Place at least 1 inch apart on an ungreased cookie sheet. Bake in a 375-degree oven for about 10 minutes or until the edges are lightly browned. Cool completely. Repeat the procedure. For the frosting, combine the powdered sugar, 1/3 cup of softened butter, vanilla in a small mixing bowl. Beat on low speed, adding just enough milk for desired spreading consistency. If desired, tint with food coloring. Frost the cooled cookies.

BLACK FOREST CHERRY SQUARES

Ingredients for 24 bars

	CRUST
8 oz	Chocolate wafers, crushed
1/2 cup	Sugar
10 tbsp	Butter, melted

	FILLING
1 box	Confectioners' sugar [10X]
3 oz	Cream cheese, softened
1 stick	Butter, softened
1/2 tsp	Almond extract
2 cans	Cherry pie filling

	TOPPING
2 cups	Cool Whip
1 tsp	Almond extract [optional]

Blend the crushed cookies with the sugar and butter. Pat into a 9x12-inch baking dish or pan. Bake in a 350-degree oven for 5–10 minutes. Cool. Mix the confectioners' sugar, cream cheese, butter, and almond extract. Spread over the crust. Spread the pie filling over the above. Gently fold the almond extract into the whipped topping and spread over the pie filling. Cover and refrigerate. Cut and garnish with chocolate curls or a maraschino cherry [patted dry] with a stem.

CHESS SQUARES

Ingredients for 2 dozen

1 box	Cake mix [yellow, butter flavored]		**TOPPING**
		8 oz	Cream cheese, softened
1 lg	Egg		
1 stick	Butter, melted	1 box	Confectioners' sugar
1 cup	Nuts, chopped		
		2 lg	Eggs
		1 tsp	Vanilla

Combine the first 4 ingredients together and press into a 9x13-inch baking dish. Beat the remaining ingredients together and pour over the bottom layer. Bake in a 325-degree oven for 1 hour. Cool and cut.

CHOCOLATE CHERRY BARS

Ingredients for 36 bars

1 pkg	Devil's food cake mix [2-layer size]
21 oz	Cherry pie filling [can]
2 lg	Eggs, beaten
1 tsp	Almond extract
1 cup	Sugar
5 tbsp	Butter
1/3 cup	Milk
1 cup	Semisweet chocolate chips

Combine the cake mix, pie filling, eggs, and almond extract in a bowl, mixing well. Spoon into a greased and floured 9x13-inch baking pan. Bake in a 350-degree oven for 25–30 minutes or until done [the edges will separate from the sides of the pan]. In a saucepan bring the sugar and milk to a boil, stirring constantly. Boil for 1 minute, stirring constantly. Add the chocolate chips and stir until smooth. Pour the mixture over the hot cake. Cool. Cut into bars.

ROSALIND'S CHOCOLATE CHIP COOKIES

Ingredients for 7 dozen

2 1/4 cups	All-purpose flour
1 tsp	Baking soda
1/2 tsp	Salt
2 sticks	Butter [salted], softened
3/4 cup	Sugar, granulated
3/4 cup	Dark brown sugar, lightly packed
2 lg	Eggs, room temperature
1 tsp	Vanilla
12 oz	Milk chocolate chips [not semisweet]
1 1/4 cups	Pecans, chopped [or a heaping cup]

In a small bowl, whisk together the flour, salt, and baking soda. Set aside. In a larger bowl, cream together the butter, sugars, eggs, and vanilla. Gradually add the flour mixture, mixing until well incorporated. Mix in the chocolate chips and then the nuts. Very lightly oil a cookie sheet with a paper towel [too much oil will cause the cookies to spread]. Drop the batter onto the cookie sheet with a small spoon or a very small ice cream scoop [about an inch in diameter]. Bake in a 350-degree oven for about 12 minutes or until the edges begin to turn a golden brown. Remove the cookies from the oven and let rest for about a minute and remove with a spatula. Wipe the cookie sheet clean with the oiled paper towel, cool, and repeat. Place the cookies into a container that has a lid. When the cookies are almost room temperature, place the lid on the container to prevent cookie from getting too dry.

Helpful hint: Place the butter on the kitchen counter the night before mixing. It will mix perfectly.

WHITE CHOCOLATE CHIP COOKIES

Ingredients for 5 dozen

2 1/4 cups	Flour, all-purpose
2/3 cups	Cocoa
1 tsp	Baking soda
1/4 tsp	Salt
2 sticks	Butter, room temperature
2 lg	Eggs
1 tsp	Vanilla
2/3 cup	Brown sugar [packed]
3/4 cup	Sugar, granulated
12 oz	White chocolate chips [or morsels]

Combine the flour, baking soda, cocoa, and salt in a bowl and whisk together until blended. Beat the sugars, butter, and vanilla together in another bowl until creamy. Add the eggs one at a time, beating after each addition. Gradually add the flour mixture and blend. Stir in the white chocolate chips. Drop small amounts on very lightly oiled baking sheets. Bake in a 350-degree oven for 10 minutes. Let cool on the baking sheet for a couple of minutes before lifting, cooling, and storing in an airtight container.

CHOCOLATE-FILLED COOKIES

Ingredients for 6 dozen

2 sticks	Butter, room temperature
1/2 cup	Sugar
2 cups	Flour, all-purpose, sifted
1 tsp	Vanilla
	Hershey's Chocolate Kisses [unwrapped]

Cream the butter, sugar, and vanilla together on medium speed until light and fluffy. Reduce the mixer speed and add the flour slowly, beating after each addition, until well blended. Cover the dough with plastic wrap and chill in the refrigerator for an hour. Using a very small ice cream scoop or a spoon, scoop a small amount of dough and wrap around each chocolate kiss, making sure to cover all of the candy. Place them on an ungreased cookie sheet. [If the dough is too soft, place the trays in the refrigerator for a few minutes to firm up. The cookies will retain their shapes better.] Bake in a 375-degree oven for 15 minutes.

CONGO SQUARES

Ingredients for 24 servings

2 1/4 cups	Light brown sugar
3/4 cup	Butter [1 1/2 sticks]
2 1/2 cups	Self-rising flour
3 lg	Eggs
1 cup	Semisweet chocolate chips
1 cup	Pecans, chopped [optional]

Melt the butter and mix with the brown sugar. Stir well. Let the mixture cool slightly. Add the eggs one at a time, mixing after each addition. Add the flour slowly, mixing well. Stir in the chocolate chips [and pecans] last. Pour in an oiled or sprayed 9x13-inch baking dish or pan. Bake in a 350-degree oven for 30–35 minutes. Cool and cut. Can serve with whipping cream, ice cream, or as is.

DATE NUT SQUARES

Ingredients for 24 bars

2 sticks	Butter
1 box	Brown sugar
2 lg	Eggs
2 1/2 cups	Flour, all-purpose
1/4 tsp	Salt
1/2 tsp	Soda
8 oz	Dates, chopped
1 cup	Pecans, chopped

Mix the flour, salt, and soda together. Cream the butter and sugar together. Add the eggs one at a time. Mix all together and add the chopped dates and pecans. Bake in a 13x9-inch oiled baking pan in a 350-degree oven for 25 minutes.

FIG NEWTON BARS

Ingredients for 90 bars

1 lb	Fig Newtons, bag
	Confectioners' sugar
	[enough to cover all of the bars]

Cut each Fig Newton bar crosswise into three equal pieces. Place on a cookie sheet. Bake in a 350-degree oven for 10 minutes. While baking, put the confectioners' sugar into a ziplock bag [I use a quart bag]. Remove the Fig Newtons from the oven and put them into the bag with the sugar. Seal the bag and gently roll the Fig Newtons in the sugar. When covered, remove the Fig Newtons and cool on a tray or rack. This is better done in 2 batches.

Helpful hint: Apple Newtons are good also. However, I did not like the non-fat Fig Newtons. That figures.

FRUIT BARS

Ingredients for 40 servings

1 cup	All-purpose flour, unsifted
1 1/2 cups	Light brown sugar
1 stick	Butter
2	Eggs
2 tsp	Vanilla flavoring
1 tsp	Cinnamon, ground
2 cups	Pecans, chopped
1/2 lb	Candied cherries, halved
1/2 lb	Candied pineapple, cut

Grease 9x13-inch baking pan and flour well. Cream the butter, sugar, and spices. Add the eggs and beat. Whisk the flour and the cinnamon together and add to the butter mixture. Stir in the fruit. Bake for 1 hour in a 300-degree oven, checking after 45 minutes to prevent over-cooking. Cut into 40 squares and store in an airtight container.

Helpful hint: Red and green cherries can be used instead of the pineapple or a combination of the three can be used.

FRUIT WAFERS

Ingredients for 6 dozen

12 oz	Vanilla Wafers [box], finely crushed
1 cup	Green candied pineapple, chopped fine
1 cup	Red candied cherries, chopped fine
2 cups	Pecans, chopped small
14 oz	Sweetened canned condensed milk [not evaporated]
	Sifted confectioners' sugar

Combine all of the ingredients except for the powdered sugar, mixing well. Divide into equal portions and roll into logs. Roll each log in the confectioners' sugar and wrap in plastic wrap. Refrigerate until firm [several hours or overnight]. Slice before serving.

FRUITCAKE COOKIES

Ingredients for 9 dozen

1 cup	Light brown sugar
2 sticks	Butter, softened
3 lg	Eggs
2 cups	Flour, all-purpose
1 tsp	Cinnamon
1 tsp	Baking soda
1/2 cup	Milk
1 lb	Candied cherries, cut
1 lb	Candied pineapple, cut
8 oz	Pitted dates, chopped
2 cups	Pecans, chopped

Sift the dry ingredients together. Cream the butter and sugar together and add the eggs. Add the flour mixture and milk alternately to the butter/sugar mixture. Add the fruits and pecans. Drop by spoonfuls onto a cookie sheet which has been lightly oiled. Bake in a 325-degree oven for 15–20 minutes. Cool and store in an airtight container.

Helpful hint: If these cookies get too soft, pop them back into a 300-degree oven for five minutes or more to firm up. Sometimes this Georgia humidity even gets to food stored in airtight containers.

FRUITCAKE SQUARES

Ingredients for 40 servings

1 1/2 cups	Light brown sugar, not packed
1 stick	Butter or margarine
1 cup	Unsifted all-purpose flour
2	Eggs
1 pound	Candied red cherries, cut
1/2 pound	Candied green pineapple, cut
2 cups	Chopped pecans
2 tsp	Vanilla flavoring
1 tsp	Ground cinnamon

Cream butter and brown sugar. Add eggs and beat well. Mix in the flour and add vanilla, cinnamon, and flour. Stir in cherries, pineapple, and nuts. Pour into a greased and floured 9x13-inch pan. Bake in a 300-degree oven for approximately 1 hour. Check after 45 minutes of baking. Cut into 40 squares and store in an airtight container.

Helpful hint: Spray knife with cooking spray if fruit sticks to knife.

LEMON SQUARES

Ingredients for 2 dozen

CRUST

1 cup	All-purpose flour, unsifted
2 tbsp	Sugar
1/8 tsp	Salt
1/3 cup	Butter, softened

MIXTURE

2	Eggs, beaten
1/2 cup	Pecans, chopped
1 cup	Light brown sugar, packed
1 cup	Flaked coconut
1/8 tsp	Baking powder
1 tbsp	Lemon juice
1 tsp	Lemon zest
1 tsp	Vanilla

GLAZE

2/3 cup	Powdered sugar
1 tbsp	Lemon juice
1 tsp	Lemon zest

Mix all of the crust ingredients together until it resembles coarse meal. Press into a 9x13-inch pan or baking dish. Bake at 350 degrees for 15 minutes. Combine all of the mixture ingredients and spread over the baked crust. Bake 30 minutes. Loosen edges and spread on the lemon glaze. Cool and cut into squares.

ROSALIND'S LEMON SQUARES

Ingredients for 3 dozen

1 stick	Butter, softened
1 cup	Flour [all-purpose], sifted
1/4 cup	Confectioners' sugar

TOP LAYER

1 cup	Sugar
2 tbsp	Flour [all-purpose]
1/2 tsp	Baking powder
2 lg	Eggs, slightly beaten
3 tbsp	Lemon juice [fresh]
	Confectioners' sugar [for dusting]

Combine the first 3 ingredients. Pat the mixture into a 9-inch square pan. Bake in a 350-degree oven for 15 minutes. Combine the top layer ingredients. Pour the mixture over the baked bottom layer. Bake in a 350-degree oven for 25 minutes. While warm, sprinkle with 3 tablespoons of confectioners' sugar over the top. Cut into 1-1/2-inch squares.

Oil your measuring cup or spoon before measuring molasses or honey. The ingredient will slip right out for an accurate measurement.

MACADAMIA CHIP COOKIES

Ingredients for 5 dozen

2 sticks	Butter, room temperature
1 1/2 cups	Sugar
1 cup	Light brown sugar, firmly packed
2 lg	Eggs, room temperature
1 1/2 tsp	Vanilla
3 cups	Flour, all-purpose
1/2 tsp	Salt
1/2 tsp	Baking soda
6 1/2 oz	Macadamia nuts, roughly chopped
11 oz	White chocolate chips [I like Ghirardelli]

Whisk the flour, baking soda, and the salt together until incorporated. Cream the butter and the two sugars until fluffy. Add the vanilla and the eggs one at a time. Mix well. Add the flour mixture in several additions. Stir in the white chocolate chips and the nuts. Drop teaspoonfuls of batter onto ungreased cookie sheets. [A very small ice-cream scoop works well.] Bake in a 350-degree oven for about 12 minutes. [The cookies will be lightly brown around the edges and on the bottom.]

ALMOND MACAROONS

Ingredients for 30 cookies

2/3 cup	Condensed milk [not evaporated]
3 cups	Coconut
1 tsp	Almond extract
2	Drops of red food coloring
15	Candied cherries, halved

Stir extract and food coloring into the condensed milk until it is evenly blended. Fold in the coconut until it mixed well. Drop by teaspoon onto a greased cookie sheet or one covered with non-stick foil. Top with a cherry half or a blanched almond. Bake for 10 minutes in a 350-degree oven.

MADELEINES

Ingredients for 3 dozen

1 1/2 cups	Cake flour
1/2 tsp	Baking powder
1/8 tsp	Salt
2 sticks	Unsalted butter, clarified
3 lg	Eggs
1 tsp	Vanilla
3/4 cup	Sugar
2 tsp	Lemon zest
	Confectioners' sugar
	Butter for pans

To clarify the butter: Melt the butter in a small saucepan. Let the solids settle to the bottom. Pour 3/4 cup of butter into a measuring cup. Discard the solids. Lightly butter [not the clarified butter] the madeleine pans. Dust with flour, tapping out the excess. Sift the flour, salt, and baking powder together. Sprinkle the lemon zest over the flour. In another bowl, beat the eggs until light. Add the vanilla. Gradually add the sugar, beating until the mixture is thick and the volume has increased four times its original size. Fold in the flour. Fold in the clarified butter. Spoon the mixture in the madeleine pans filling them 1/2 full. Bake in a 350-degree oven about 18 minutes or until the centers spring back when lightly pressed. Turn the madeleines out on a wire rack and lightly dust with confectioners' sugar, using a small sifter. Store in an airtight container, placing wax paper between the layers.

MARSHMALLOW-CRISPY TREATS

Ingredients for 2 dozen

1/2 stick	Butter
10 1/2 oz	Miniature marshmallows
6 cups	Crispy rice cereal

Melt the butter in a large, heavy bottom saucepan. Add the marshmallows and melt while stirring. When the butter and marshmallows are blended, remove from the heat and add the cereal. Mix until all of the cereal is evenly coated. Spread the mixture in a buttered 13x9x2-inch dish or pan. Cool and cut.

OATMEAL LACE COOKIES

Ingredients for 6 dozen

2 1/2 cups	Quick oatmeal
2 1/4 cups	Light brown sugar
3 tbsp	Flour, self-rising
1/4 tsp	Salt
2 sticks	Butter, melted
1 tsp	Vanilla
1 lg	Egg, slightly beaten

Pulse the oatmeal a few times in a food chopper. Mix in the flour, sugar, and salt. Stir in the butter, vanilla, and egg. Cover the cookie sheets with foil. Drop 1/2 teaspoons of batter onto the cookie sheets, leaving 2 or 3 inches between them. Bake in a 360-

degree oven for about 7 minutes or until lightly brown and lacy looking. Lift the foil onto a cooling rack and let the cookies cool and become crispy. Peel the cookies off of the foil and store them in an airtight container.

PECAN CRESCENTS

Ingredients for 5 dozen

2 sticks	Butter, room temperature
2 1/3 cups	Flour, all-purpose
2/3 cup	Confectioners' sugar
2 cups	Pecans, chopped small
1 tsp	Vanilla
1/2 tsp	Almond extract
	Confectioners' sugar for coating

Cream the butter and sugar, adding the flavorings, flour, and then the pecans. Scoop out small spoonfuls and shape into crescents. Place on an ungreased cookie sheet. Bake in a 350-degree oven for 20 minutes. Roll in confectioners' sugar while hot. Cool and store in an airtight container.

Helpful hint: The dough can be rolled into balls or rolled out and cut with a cookie cutter. I have heard these cookies called Wedding Cookies.

PECAN PIE BARS

Ingredients for 36 portions

2 cups	Flour, all-purpose
1/2 cup	Powdered sugar
1 cup	Butter, chilled

14 oz	Condensed milk [not evaporated]
1 lg	Egg
1 tsp	Vanilla
8 oz	Heath Toffee Bits [almond brickle chips]
1 cup	Pecans, chopped

Whisk sugar and flour together. Cut in the butter into the flour mixture with a pastry cutter or 2 knives until the mixture is crumbly or resembles coarse corn meal. Press the mixture into a 9x13-inch baking dish. Bake in a 350-degree oven for 15 minutes. While the crust is baking whisk the milk, egg, and vanilla. Stir in the toffee bits and nuts. Cool the crust slightly. Pour the egg mixture over the crust and bake in a 350-degree oven for 25 minutes or until it is a golden brown. Cool completely and cut into the desired number of servings.

PRALINE MACAROONS

Ingredients for 24 cookies

3 lg	Egg whites
1 cup	Brown sugar, firmly packed
1 cup	Pecans, coarsely chopped
24	Pecan halves
	Butter

Place a sheet of foil onto a cookie sheet and spread butter over the foil. Beat the egg whites until soft peaks form. Gradually add the brown sugar and beat until the peaks are very stiff. Fold in the chopped nuts with a large spoon. Spoon heaping spoonfuls onto the foil, leaving at least 1 inch between the cookies. Press the cookies to form a flat top. Place a pecan half on top of each cookie. Bake in a 275-degree oven for 30–35 minutes, or until the cookies are firm but are still shiny. Serve with ice cream or sherbet.

NEVERLAND COOKIES

Ingredients for 12 dozen

2 1/4 cups	All-purpose flour
1 tsp	Baking powder
1 tsp	Baking soda
1 tsp	Salt
1 1/2 cups	Creamy peanut butter [14 oz]
1 cup	Butter, softened
1 cup	Sugar, granulated
1 cup	Brown sugar, firmly packed
1 tsp	Vanilla
2	Eggs, slightly beaten
12 oz	White morsels [about 2 cups]
6 1/2 oz	Macadamia nuts [about 1 1/3 cups], coarsely chopped

Whisk the flour, baking powder, baking soda, and salt together in a small bowl. Set aside. In a large mixing bowl, beat the butter, peanut butter, sugar, brown sugar, and vanilla until blended with an electric mixer. Add the eggs and mix well. Gradually add the flour mixture. Stir in the morsels and nuts. Drop the batter with a very small ice cream scoop or with a teaspoon onto an ungreased cookie sheet about 1 1/2 inches apart. Bake in a 350-degree oven for about 15 minutes. Cool for 5 minutes and remove to a rack to cool completely.

POTATO CHIP COOKIES

Ingredients for 5 dozen

3 sticks	Butter, softened
1 1/2 cups	Sugar
1 lg	Egg

1 tsp	Baking soda
3 cups	All-purpose flour
6 oz	Pringles Original Potato Chips, crushed

Cream the butter and sugar. Add the egg and cream. Whisk the flour and soda together and mix. Add the crushed chips and mix. Drop onto a cookie sheet and bake in a 350-degree oven until lightly brown [12–15 minutes].

POUND CAKE COOKIES

Ingredients for 5 dozen

2 sticks	Butter, softened
1 cup	Sugar
2	Egg yolks
2 1/2 cups	All-purpose flour
1 tsp	Vanilla
1/2 cup	Chopped pecans

Cream butter and sugar. Add egg yolks and beat. Add flour, vanilla, and nuts, mixing well. Roll into balls and place on a slightly-oiled cookie sheet. Press balls with a fork until about 1 1/2 inches. Bake in a 350-degree oven for 10 minutes or until edges are golden brown. These are good with or without pecans.

PUMPKIN BARS

Ingredients for 3 1/2 dozen

4 lg	Eggs
2 cups	Sugar
15 oz	Pumpkin [can]

2 cups	Flour, all-purpose
1 cup	Oil
1/2 tsp	Salt
1 tsp	Soda
2 tsp	Baking powder
2 tsp	Cinnamon

FROSTING

3 oz	Cream cheese, softened
1 stick	Butter, room temperature
1 tbsp	Milk
1 tsp	Vanilla
2 1/2 cups	Confectioners' sugar

Whisk the flour, salt, soda, and baking powder together and set aside. Mix the eggs lightly. Add the sugar to the eggs and beat well. Mix in the pumpkin and oil. Stir in the dry ingredients. Pour the batter into a lightly-oiled 15x10x1/2-inch baking sheet. Bake in a 350-degree oven for 30 minutes. Cool.

FROSTING: Cream the frosting ingredients together until smooth. Spread the frosting over the cooled cake. Refrigerate and cut into bars or squares.

TOFFEE-NUT COOKIES

Ingredients for 8 dozen

1 cup	Butter [2 sticks], softened
1 cup	Sugar
2 lg	Eggs
1 tsp	Vanilla
2 1/2 cups	Flour, all-purpose
1 tsp	Baking soda

1 pinch	Salt, optional
8 oz	Toffee bits
1 cup	Salted peanuts

Combine the butter, sugar, and eggs in a mixing bowl, beating until creamy. Whisk the dry ingredients together and slowly add to the butter mixture. Beat until well mixed. Stir in the toffee bits and peanuts with a large spoon. Drop the batter onto cookie sheets with a small ice cream scoop. Bake in a 350-degree oven for 10–12 minutes. Cool and store in an airtight container.

Desserts

ANGEL-CAKE ROLL

Ingredients for 8 servings

1 box	Angel food cake mix and ingredients required to make
	Powdered sugar
1 cup	Heavy whipping cream
3 tbsp	Cocoa [OR sliced strawberries]
1/3 cup	Sugar
1/4 tsp	Vanilla

Prepare one box of angel food cake mix according to directions. Oil the bottom of a jelly roll pan and line with wax paper. Pour 1/2 of the batter into the pan and spread evenly to the edges and corners. [Use the remaining batter for another dessert or cupcakes.] Bake 15–20 minutes and cool. Dust a clean, lint-free towel with powdered sugar. Loosen the edges of the cake and turn it onto the towel. Remove the wax paper. Roll the towel and cake. Whip the cream, adding the cocoa, sugar, and vanilla... whipping until stiff. Unroll the towel and spread the whipped cream over the cake. Roll up just the cake, using the towel as a guide. Chill several hours before slicing. Serve with a dollop of more whipped cream and chocolate curls or a sliced strawberry.

ANGEL FOOD AND STRAWBERRY DELIGHT

Ingredients for 8 servings

14 oz	Condensed milk [can], not evaporated
1/4 cup	Lemon juice
16 oz	Cool Whip [2 cartons, 8 oz each]
1 lg	Angel food cake
2 pts	Fresh strawberries, washed and blotted

Break the angel food cake into bite-size pieces. Place 1/2 of the cake pieces into a large, clear bowl. Mix the condensed milk and lemon juice together. Fold in the thawed Cool Whip. Fold in the sliced strawberries, saving some for the top. Cover the cake pieces with 1/2 of the mixture. Place the rest of the cake in the bowl and top with the remaining mixture. Top with the fresh strawberries. Cover and keep in the refrigerator. If using an oblong dish, layer only once.

Helpful hint: This dessert is pretty served in sherbet glasses.

APPLE DUMPLINGS

Ingredients for 8 servings

2	Granny Smith apples
1 stick	Butter, melted
1 pkg	Crescent rolls, in the dairy case
1 cup	Mellow Yellow or Mountain Dew
2/3 cup	Sugar
1/8 cup	Sugar and cinnamon mixture [or less]

Peel the apples, remove the seeds, and cut into quarters. Wrap each slice of apple with a crescent triangle, covering the apple completely, and place in a buttered casserole dish. Mix the liquid, sugar, and melted butter. Pour over the wrapped apples. Sprinkle with cinnamon-sugar mixture. Bake in a 350-degree oven for 30–40 minutes or until golden brown.

Helpful hint: More liquid can be used, if desired. Serve warm with a dollop of whipped cream or a scoop of vanilla ice cream.

APPLE JUICE DESSERT

Ingredients for 8 servings

1/2 cup	Sugar
2 cups	Apple juice, bottled
3 tbsp	Lemon juice or sherry
1	Envelope unflavored gelatin
	Dash of salt

Boil the sugar, gelatin, salt, and apple juice. Add the sherry. Pour into parfait glasses and chill. Top with whipped cream and orange zest or peel.

SAUCY APPLE PUDDING

Ingredients for 10 servings

1/4 cup	Butter, softened
3/4 cup	Sugar
1 lg	Egg
1 cup	All-purpose flour, heaping [1 cup and 2 tbsp]
1/4 tsp	Salt
1/4 tsp	Cloves, ground
1/2 tsp	Cinnamon
1 tsp	Baking soda
2 lg	Apples [Fuji], peeled and diced
1 tbsp	Milk [or cream]

	SAUCE
1 cup	Sugar
2 tbsp	Flour
1 cup	Apple juice or apple cider
1	Orange, zested and juiced

Whisk together the flour, salt, cloves, cinnamon, and baking soda. Cream the butter, sugar, and egg together in another bowl. Combine the two mixtures and the milk. Add the apples and mix. Pour the batter into a buttered 10-inch baking dish. Bake in a 350-degree oven 35–40 minutes or until a golden brown on top. Boil the sauce ingredients in a medium, heavy bottom saucepan until it begins to thicken. Pour the sauce over the baked pudding. Serve with a dollop of lightly sweetened whipped cream.

Helpful hint: This sauce is good served over other desserts such as ice cream.

ROSALIND'S BAKED ALASKA

Ingredients for 6 servings

1 qt	Ice cream [strawberry is good, but others are also]

SPONGE CAKE

5 lg	Eggs
3 cups	Flour, all-purpose
1 tbsp	Baking powder
2 cups	Sugar
1 cup	Vegetable oil
1 cup	Milk
1 tsp	Vanilla

MERINGUE

3 lg	Egg whites
1/4 tsp	Cream of tartar
6 tbsp	Sugar

Sift the flour and baking powder together. Beat together the eggs, vegetable oil, and sugar until light and pale in color. Add the vanilla to the milk. Add 1/3 of the flour mixture and beat. Add 1/3 of the milk and beat. Repeat with 2 more additions. Line a jumbo muffin tin with liners and fill 1/2 full [there will be enough batter left to do another batch, if desired]. Bake in a 325-degree oven for 25–30 minutes or until cakes spring back when touched. Cool and remove the liners. With a small, serrated knife cut rounds out of the centers and scoop out with a teaspoon, leaving containers for the ice cream. Line a baking sheet with foil. Fill the cakes with ice cream, place them on the foil, and freeze. Beat the egg whites until frothy and add the cream of tartar. Gradually add the sugar and beat until stiff peaks form. Cover the ice cream and cakes completely and return to the freezer for 6 hours or 2 days. When ready to serve, preheat the broiler to 450 degrees. Bake the desserts for about 3 minutes or until the tops are a golden brown. Serve immediately.

Caution: Every oven is different and bakes differently. It would be wise to test one of these before serving guests. Some ovens may require 500 degrees and some less. Also, before making the meringue make sure the beaters are clean and dry.

To keep ice cream from icing, place a layer of plastic wrap over the top before putting the cover back on.

BAKLAVA

Ingredients for 3 dozen

16 oz	Phyllo pastry, thawed
2 1/2 sticks	Butter, melted
1 cup	Pecans, chopped small or ground

1/2 cup	Almonds, chopped small or ground
2 tbsp	Dark brown sugar
1 1/2 tsp	Cinnamon, ground
1/4 tsp	Nutmeg, ground
1/4 cup	Honey
1/2 cup	Sugar
1/2 cup	Water
1 tbsp	Lemon juice

Oil a 9x13-inch baking pan. Cut the phyllo pastry in half and trim to fit the pan. Cover the phyllo with a damp towel to prevent it from drying. Layer 15 sheets of pastry in the pan, brushing each sheet with melted butter. Combine the pecans, almonds, brown sugar, nutmeg, and cinnamon together and mix well. Sprinkle 1/2 of the nut mixture over the phyllo in the pan. Drizzle a little of the melted butter over the top. Add 15 phyllo sheets over the top, brushing each sheet with melted butter. Distribute the remaining nut mixture over the top and drizzle with melted butter. Top with the remaining phyllo sheets, brushing with butter. Score the top, making diamond designs, with a sharp knife. Bake in a 350-degree oven for 45 minutes or until it is a golden brown. While stirring, bring the water, honey, and sugar to a boil in a small saucepan for about 10 minutes. Stir in the lemon juice and drizzle over the top. Cut the baklava along the scored lines. Let the baklava rest for 8 hours at room temperature before serving.

BANANAS FOSTER

Ingredients for 4 servings

4 ripe	Bananas, peeled and cut in half [lengthwise]
1 stick	Butter
1 cup	Light brown sugar [packed]

3/4 tsp	Cinnamon
1/4 cup	Banana liquor
1/4 cup	Dark rum or Kahlúa

Melt the butter in a heavy skillet. Add the brown sugar and cinnamon. Cook for 2 or 3 minutes, or until the sugar dissolves. Add the bananas and cook, turning, until they begin to soften and caramelize [about 3 minutes]. Add the banana liquor and carefully add the rum which is flammable. Remove from the heat and carefully ignite the rum [when ignited, flames will shoot up and above the skillet]. Place back on the burner and shake the skillet a little to let the rum burn. Baste the bananas as the flame dies. Place the bananas in 4 serving dishes and add a scoop of vanilla ice cream. Spoon the sauce over all. This can also be served over a slice of pound cake.

BANANA PUDDING [LIKE MAMA'S]

Ingredients for 8 servings

4 med	Ripe bananas, peeled and sliced	3 tbsp	Flour
		2 cups	Milk
3 lg	Eggs, separated	1 pinch	Salt
1 1/3 cups	Sugar, divided	1 tsp	Vanilla
		1 box	Vanilla wafers

Mix the egg yolks [save the whites for the meringue], 1 cup of the sugar, flour, and salt in a heavy saucepan and gradually add the milk and vanilla. Stir until well mixed. Cook over medium heat, while stirring, until thickened. In a Pyrex dish, make a layer of wafers and banana slices. Spread 1/2 of the custard over the top. Repeat the layers. Beat the egg whites until foamy and they begin to form peaks. Add the remaining sugar gradually and beat until shiny. Spread the meringue evenly over the top of the pudding. Bake in a 350-degree oven until golden.

BLUEBERRY BREAD PUDDING

Ingredients for 8 servings

4 cups	Day-old bread, cubed
2 1/2 cups	Milk
3/4 cup	Sugar
2	Eggs
1/4 tsp	Almond extract
1 pint	Blueberries

Whisk eggs in a medium-size bowl. Stir in the milk, sugar, and almond extract. Add the bread and set aside for 15 minutes, allowing the cubes to absorb the egg mixture. Gently stir in the berries. Spoon mixture into a lightly-greased 8x8-inch baking dish. Bake in a 350-degree oven for 45 minutes.

BLUEBERRY YUM YUM

Ingredients for 9 servings

2 cups	Blueberries, fresh or frozen	1 cup	Flour, all-purpose
		1 cup	Nuts, finely chopped
2 cups	Sugar, divided	1 stick	Butter, softened
1/4 cup	Cornstarch	8 oz	Cream cheese, softened
1/4 cup	Water		
3 tbsp	Water	9 oz	Cool Whip

Combine the blueberries, 1 cup of sugar, and 1/4 cup of water in a saucepan and cook on low heat until the berries are soft [about

15 minutes]. Mix the cornstarch with 3 tablespoons of water, stirring until dissolved. Add the mixture to the berries and cook slowly until thickened, stirring constantly. Set aside to cool. Combine the flour, butter, and nuts in a small bowl, mixing well. Press the dough evenly into an 8-inch Pyrex dish. Bake in a 350-degree oven for 20 minutes. Cool. Combine the cream cheese and 1 cup of sugar, whipping until smooth. Fold in the Cool Whip. Spread the cream cheese mixture over the baked and cooled crust. Pour the blueberry mixture over the top. Refrigerate. Cut into squares and top with a dollop of whipped cream.

BREAD CUSTARD

Ingredients for 8 servings

2 sticks	Butter	2 cups	Sugar
4	Hot dog buns	2 cups	Milk
6 lg	Eggs	2 tsp	Vanilla

Melt the butter in a 7x11-inch [approximately] Pyrex dish. Open 4 hot dog buns and place them in the dish of melted butter, cut-side down. Beat the eggs well and add the sugar, milk, and vanilla. Ladle [or pour] the mixture over the buns, making sure the all of the buns have some mixture poured over them. This helps the buns to brown evenly. Bake for 35–45 minutes [or until golden brown] in a 350-degree oven. Best served warm, but not necessary. Yummy!

Helpful hint: This custard does not require a water bath.

ROSALIND'S SAUCY BREAD PUDDING

Ingredients for 12 servings

2 cups	Hot water
1 1/2 cups	Sugar
12 oz	Evaporated milk [can]
4	Eggs, slightly beaten
1/2 cup	Raisins
	[1 cup of flaked coconut or 1/2 cup drained pineapple, optional]
1/3 cup	Butter, melted
1 tsp	Vanilla extract
1/2 tsp	Nutmeg
9	Slices of white bread [day-old bread is best], cut into 1/2-inch cubes

	SAUCE
1 cup	Light corn syrup
1/4 cup	Butter
1/4 cup	Bourbon
1/2 tsp	Vanilla extract

Combine hot water and sugar in a bowl, stirring until sugar dissolves. Whisk the eggs and evaporated milk into sugar water until blended. Add raisins, 1/3 cup of melted butter, 1 teaspoon vanilla, and nutmeg, mixing well. Stir in the bread cubes. Let stand for 30 minutes, stirring occasionally. Pour into a greased 9x13-inch baking dish. Bake in a 350-degree oven for 45 minutes or until firm.

SAUCE: Bring corn syrup to a boil in a saucepan. Cool slightly. Whisk 1/4 cup butter, bourbon, and 1/2 teaspoon vanilla in the hot syrup. Drizzle warm bourbon sauce over the warm bread pudding.

BROWN SUGAR SAUCE

Ingredients for 4 servings

1 stick	Butter	1 pinch	Salt
1/2 cup	Light brown sugar, packed	1/3 cup	Bourbon
		1/2 cup	Pecans, toasted
1/4 tsp	Cinnamon		

Melt the butter in a heavy saucepan and add the sugar. Cook the sauce over medium-low heat until the mixture thickens slightly [about 5 minutes]. Add the bourbon and cook until the alcohol is gone and the flavor remains. Stir in the cinnamon and salt. Add the pecans and serve over ice cream or fruit, such as bananas or mangoes.

BROWNIE CHOCOLATE DELIGHT

Ingredients for 8 servings

1 box	Brownie mix [cake-like brownies, with or without nuts]
5 oz	Instant chocolate pudding [1 package]
2 cups	Milk
8 oz	Cool Whip
4	Candy bars, crushed [Heath bars or Butterfingers]

Make the brownies according to the directions on the box. Cool. Break into chunks and put into a serving dish. Mix the chocolate pudding and milk. Spoon over the layer of brownies before it completely thickens. Spread the thawed Cool Whip over the pudding. Sprinkle the crushed candy bars over the top. Cover and keep in the refrigerator. This can be layered twice in a clear glass bowl or once in an oblong casserole dish. Sinfully delicious!

EASY AND DELICIOUS CHEESECAKE

Ingredients for 16 servings

CRUST
1 1/2 cups	Graham cracker crumbs
1 stick	Butter, melted
1/3 cup	Powdered sugar

CHEESECAKE
24 oz	Cream cheese, softened
4 lg	Eggs, room temperature
1 cup	Sugar
1 tsp	Vanilla

TOPPING
16 oz	Sour cream, room temperature
21 oz	Cherry, strawberry, or blueberry pie filling

Combine powdered sugar, crumbs, and butter together and press into the bottom of an 8-inch springform pan. In a large mixing bowl, beat the cream cheese, eggs, sugar, and vanilla until smooth. Pour the mixture onto the prepared crust. Bake in a 350-degree oven for 50 minutes or until the center is set. Remove the cheesecake from the oven and spread the [room temperature] sour cream over the top. Return the cheesecake to the oven and bake for an additional 5 minutes. Remove the cheesecake from the oven and allow it to cool. Spread the topping over the top. Chill overnight and carefully remove the sides from the pan.

Helpful hint: Place a small pan of hot water on the bottom rack of the oven while baking the cheesecake. The moisture will help to minimize the cracking on the cheesecake.

CAKE-N-CHEESE CAKE

Ingredients for 8 servings

	CHEESE MIXTURE	2 lg	Eggs
8 oz	Cream cheese,	1 tsp	Milk
	softened	1 tsp	Vanilla
2/3 cup	Sugar		
1/2 cup	Sour cream		**TOPPING**
2 lg	Eggs	1 cup	Sour cream
1 tsp	Vanilla	2 tbsp	Sugar
		1 tsp	Vanilla
	BATTER		
1 cup	Flour, all-purpose		**FRUIT TOPPING**
1 tsp	Baking powder	1 can	Cherry pie filling or
1/2 tsp	Salt		fruit topping of
1 stick	Butter, softened		choice
2/3 cup	Sugar		

CHEESE MIXTURE: Mix the sugar and cream cheese. Blend in the sour cream and vanilla. Add the eggs one at a time. Set aside.

BATTER: Blend the butter, eggs [one at a time], milk, vanilla, and sugar [mixing well]. Whisk the dry ingredients together and add to the butter and egg mixture. Grease and flour a pie pan or plate. Spread the batter, spreading it 2 inches up the sides of the pan [the batter will be thinner on the sides of the pan]. Spoon the cheese mixture over the batter. Bake in a 325-degree oven until set, 45 minutes or more.

TOPPING: Mix the topping and spread over the top and return to the oven for 5 more minutes. The topping will not be brown. Cool and top with a fruit topping. Chill before slicing.

APPLE CHEESECAKE

Ingredients for 8 servings

1 can	Apple pie filling [21 oz], divided	1/4 cup	Caramel topping Toasted pecans [chopped and/or whole], optional
16 oz	Cream cheese, softened		
1/2 cup	Sugar	1	Graham cracker crust, 9-inch
1/4 tsp	Vanilla		
2 lg	Eggs		

Place enough of the pie filling [not Comstock] in the piecrust to just cover the bottom. Beat the cream cheese, sugar, and the vanilla until smooth. Add the eggs and mix well. Pour the mixture into the pie shell and spread over the pie filling. Bake in a 350-degree oven until the center is set, about 30–35 minutes. Mix the remaining pie filling with the topping. Spoon the mixture over the cheesecake and spread. Bake another 2 or 3 minutes in the oven. Optional: Place whole pecans around the top of the cheesecake and sprinkle chopped pecans in the center and then bake the last 2 or 3 more minutes. Chopped pecans can be sprinkled over the entire cheesecake. Refrigerate.

CHOCOLATE CHEESECAKE

Ingredients for 8 servings

CRUST

1/2 cup	Graham cracker crumbs, finely ground
1/2 cup	Butter, melted
1/4 cup	Sugar

FILLING

2 cups	Sugar
3 lg	Eggs, beaten with a fork

2 lbs	Cream cheese, softened
1 lb	Semisweet chocolate pieces
1/4 cup	Heavy cream
3/4 cup	Sour cream
1/4 tsp	Cinnamon
1/4 tsp	Almond extract

TOPPING

| 1 box | Confectioners' sugar [10X] |
| 2 cups | Whipping cream |

Mix the crumbs, sugar, and melted butter together. Press into an oiled or sprayed 9-inch springform pan. Press evenly into the bottom only. Beat the cream cheese until fluffy. It is best to use a heavy-duty stand mixer. Gradually add the sugar and eggs to the fluffy cream cheese. Beat until smooth. Melt the chocolate in a bowl placed over hot water. Add the cream to the melted chocolate. Beat the chocolate mixture into the cream cheese. Add the sour cream, cinnamon, and almond extract. Whip with the wire attachment for another 20–30 minutes. Pour over the crust. Place a large pan of water on the lower rack of the oven. Place the batter in a 350-degree oven and bake for 55–60 minutes. Turn the oven off and open the door. Leave both pans in the oven for another 30 minutes. Refrigerate for one day before cutting. Beat the 2 cups of cream, adding the box of sugar and top the cheesecake.

CHEESECAKE SQUARES

Ingredients for 9 servings

1 cup	Flour
1/3 cup	Butter, softened
1/2 cup	Brown sugar, packed
1/2 cup	Nuts, chopped

FILLING

8 oz	Cream cheese, softened
1/4 cup	Sugar
1 lg	Egg
2 tbsp	Milk
2 tbsp	Lemon juice
1/2 tsp	Vanilla

Combine the flour, butter, and brown sugar. Mix for 2 or 3 minutes on low speed with a mixer until well blended. Stir in the nuts. Save 1 cup of the mixture and pat the remainder into a Pyrex dish [8x8 inch] or pan. Bake in a 350-degree oven for 8–10 minutes or until slightly brown. Blend the filling ingredients in a bowl until smooth. Spread evenly over the crust. Sprinkle the reserved crumbs over filling. Return to the 350-degree oven for 20–30 minutes or until golden brown. Cool and cut into bars. Cover and refrigerate.

MINI CHEESECAKES

Ingredients for 5 dozen

24 oz	Cream cheese [3 packages, 8 oz each]
1 cup	Sugar
5 lg	Eggs
1 tsp	Almond or vanilla extract

TOPPING

1 cup	Sour cream
1/4 cup	Sugar
1/4 tsp	Vanilla
	Strawberry or cherry jam or preserves
	[Muffin tin liners]

Cream the sugar and cream cheese together. Add the eggs one at a time. Add the flavoring. Fill the miniature muffin tins [use liners] 3/4 full. Bake in a 300-degree oven for 30 minutes. Cool slightly in the pans. Spoon 1 tablespoon of the topping on top of each cake. Cook in the 300-degree oven for 5 minutes. Remove from the oven and top with the preserves or jam. Refrigerate or freeze until ready to serve. This recipe makes 24 individual cheesecakes if regular size muffin pans are used.

Helpful hint: The topping can be made while the cakes are baking. Thanks, Charlotte.

CHOCOLATE CHIP SAUCE

Ingredients for 6 servings

12 oz	Milk chocolate chips
1/2 cup	Heavy whipping cream
2 tbsp	Coffee [perked]

Mix the cream and chocolate chips in a bowl. Place the bowl over a saucepan of simmering water until the chocolate melts. Add the coffee and stir until the mixture is smooth. Drizzle the sauce over chocolate or vanilla ice cream and sprinkle with salted peanuts.

CHOCOLATE FUDGE SAUCE

Ingredients for 4 cups

1 3/4 cups	Heavy cream
3/4 cup	Brown sugar
1/4 cup	Butter, cut into small pieces
2 3/4 cups	Semisweet chocolate chips
1/8 tsp	Sea salt
1 tsp	Vanilla

In a heavy bottom saucepan, slowly bring the cream to a slight boil. Add the sugar while stirring until it just dissolves. Add the small pieces of butter and mix until the butter is completely melted. Stir in the chocolate chips. Wait for 3–5 minutes for the chocolate to soften. Fold the mixture with a spatula. Stir in the salt and vanilla and blend well. Let the sauce cool for 15–20 minutes before serving.

Helpful hint: The sauce may be stored in the refrigerator in a glass jar with a lid for about a week. Before serving, heat until just warm, but do not boil.

CHOCOLATE DELIGHT

Ingredients for 12 servings

1 cup	Flour, all-purpose
1 stick	Butter, softened
1 cup	Nuts, chopped small
8 oz	Cream cheese, softened
1 cup	Confectioners' sugar
12 oz	Cool Whip, divided
2 pkgs	Instant chocolate pudding mix [3 1/2 oz each]
3 cups	Milk

Mix the butter and flour and add the chopped nuts. Press into a 9x13-inch baking dish. Bake in a 350-degree oven for 20 minutes. Set aside to cool. Mix the cream cheese and 4X sugar. Fold in 1 cup of Cool Whip. Spread carefully over the first layer. Mix the 2 packages of chocolate pudding mix with the milk until thickened, but not stiff. Pour over the cream cheese layer. Top with the remaining Cool Whip. Cover and place in the refrigerator until firm. Cut into squares and serve. Extra toasted nuts can be sprinkled over top, if desired.

Variation: The chocolate pudding layer can be omitted and a can of fruit pie filling can be spread over the cream cheese layer. Cherry, apple, peach, or blueberry Comstock can be substituted instead.

Variation: The chocolate pudding can be omitted and 2 packages [3.4 oz each] of instant lemon pudding mix can be substituted.

Variation: The chocolate pudding can be omitted. Toast 6 oz bag of coconut. Sprinkle 1/2 of it over the cream cheese layer. Mix 5.9 oz vanilla pudding mix with 2 cups of milk. Fold in the sour cream and 1 cup of Cool Whip. Spread. Add the remaining coconut to the remaining Cool Whip and spread. Sprinkle toasted nuts or coconut over the top.

CHOCOLATE FROSTIE

Ingredients for 20 servings

1 gal	Chocolate milk
1 can	Eagle Brand milk
	Cool Whip

Mix all of the ingredients and churn in an ice cream machine as you would any homemade ice cream.

QUICK CHOCOLATE MOUSSE

Ingredients for 8 servings

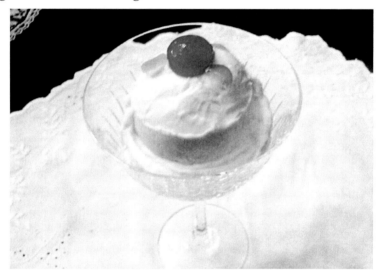

14 oz	Condensed [not evaporated] milk
5 oz	Instant chocolate pudding mix [white or dark]
1 cup	Cold water
1 cup	Whipping cream, whipped [1/2 pint]

Mix the milk, pudding mix, and cold water in a large bowl. Chill for 5 minutes. Fold in the whipped cream. Spoon into serving dishes. Keep chilled.

Helpful hint: During the holidays, decorate with red and green cherries for a festive touch. Place a half or whole cherry on top of the chilled dessert. Cut a green cherry in half and then into thirds. Place 3 slices around the red cherry to create a poinsettia.

CHOCOLATE MOLTEN CAKES

Ingredients for 8 servings

8 oz	Semisweet baking chocolate
2 sticks	Butter
2 cups	Powdered sugar, sifted
1/2 cup	Instant coffee [I use Suisse Mocha]
5 lg	Eggs
4	Egg yolks
3/4 cup	Flour, all-purpose

Oil 8 ramekins [6 or 7 oz] or custard cups and place them on a baking dish or tray. Microwave the chocolate and butter in a large bowl for 2 minutes or until the butter is melted. Whisk together until smooth. Add the powdered sugar and coffee, mixing well. Add the eggs and egg yolks, stirring until well blended. Stir in the flour. Pour the batter into the baking cups. Bake in a 400-degree oven for 15–20 minutes or until the edges are firm and centers are soft. The tops will be rounded and cake-like. Run a knife around the edges, place a dessert plate on top, and flip. Spoon any pudding left in the ramekin onto the top of the dessert. Add a scoop of ice cream and serve warm. This dessert may be garnished with berries and/or powdered sugar.

Helpful hint: These may be frozen before baking. Thaw and bake.

CHOCOLATE PUDDING

Ingredients for 6 servings

3 oz	Milk chocolate [a good quality], chopped fine
3 cups	Milk

1 oz	Unsweetened chocolate, chopped fine
6 lg	Egg yolks
1/2 cup	Sugar
3 tbsp	Cornstarch
1/2 tsp	Vanilla
	Sweetened whipped cream [optional]
	Milk chocolate shavings [optional]

Place the milk in a heavy saucepan and bring to a light simmer. Whisk the chocolates in the milk and heat until they melt and the mixture is smooth. Remove from the heat. Whisk the yolks, sugar, and cornstarch together in a large bowl. Add a little of the hot mixture into the eggs, whisking constantly. Add the two mixtures together and slowly heat in the saucepan, while whisking, until thickened [the mixture will coat a spoon and a finger run over the spoon will leave a clean line]. Remove from the heat and add the vanilla, mixing well. Pour into individual serving dishes and cover with plastic, placing the plastic directly on top of the pudding. After tightly covering the pudding, place in the refrigerator. Serve with a dollop of whipped cream and some chocolate shavings or your choice of garnish.

CRÈME BRÛLÉE

Ingredients for 8 servings

4 cups	Heavy cream
6 tbsp	Sugar
8	Egg yolks
3 tsp	Vanilla or vanilla bean
1 pinch	Salt
	Sugar in the Raw or light brown sugar

In a large, heavy bottom saucepan scald the cream [heat to just before boiling]. Remove from the heat and add the sugar. Stir the milk until the sugar is dissolved. Add the vanilla and stir well. In a large bowl beat the yolks until they are a light lemon color. Add the hot cream VERY slowly and carefully to the yolks while stirring. Add a pinch of salt. Strain the mixture into a 10-inch deep-dish pie plate or 8 ramekins [4 oz each]. Place the dish or dishes in a pan of hot water. Bake the ramekins in a 350-degree oven for 35–40 minutes or until a thin, inserted knife comes out clean. Bake the pie dish a little longer, about 50–60 minutes. Cool completely and refrigerate. When ready to serve, sprinkle the sugar evenly over the custard. Broil the custard about 4–6 inches from the heat [turning once, if necessary, to brown evenly] for 2–5 minutes or until the sugar has caramelized. A kitchen torch works great for this step of the recipe.

CRÈME DE MENTHE DESSERT

Ingredients for 6 servings

25 lg	Marshmallows
2/3 cup	Milk
1/3 cup	Crème de menthe [I like green]
1 pint	Whipping cream [heavy], whipped

Melt the marshmallows in the milk in the top of a double boiler. Let cool. Add the cool mixture to the whipped cream. Gently fold in the crème de menthe. Spoon into dessert dishes. Cover and chill until ready to serve. This dessert may be spooned into parfait glasses and layered with crushed chocolate cookies, starting and ending with the pudding. If desired, garnish the dessert with additional whipped cream, topped with a sprig of mint or a maraschino cherry or strawberry.

Helpful hint: For an easy dessert, crème de menthe is also good served over vanilla ice cream with a chocolate wafer. Remember, a little crème de menthe goes a long way.

CREAM SAUCE

Ingredients for 2 1/2 cups

2 cups	Whipping cream, heavy
1/4 cup	Sugar
1/4 cup	Irish cream liqueur
3 tbsp	Cornstarch
1 tbsp	Water
1 tsp	Vanilla

Mix the whipping cream, Irish cream liqueur, and sugar together in a saucepan and slowly heat. Mix the cornstarch and water together in a cup and add to the cream mixture. Stir over the heat until thickened. Add the vanilla. Serve over desserts such as bread pudding. Store leftovers in a covered container in the refrigerator for 2 or 3 days.

FRUIT DELIGHT

Ingredients for 8 servings

1 cup	Red seedless grapes, halved
1 cup	Blueberries, whole
1 cup	Strawberries, halved
1 cup	Nectarine halves or peaches
1 cup	Brown sugar, firmly packed
2 cups	Sour cream

Mix the fresh fruit together and sprinkle with the brown sugar. Fold in the sour cream. Chill for 3 or 4 hours before serving. Serve in a sherbet glass with a dollop of whip cream.

Variation: 1 1/2 cups of sliced fresh peaches, 1 cup grape halves, 1 cup blueberries, and 1 cup miniature marshmallows can be mixed with 8 oz of sour cream and sprinkled with 1/2 cup of light brown sugar.

Helpful hint: For the best results, make the day you plan to serve this. It does not keep well overnight.

GINGERBREAD

Ingredients for 9 servings

2 1/2 cups	Flour, all-purpose
1 1/2 tsp	Baking soda
1/2 tsp	Salt
1 tsp	Ginger
1 tsp	Cinnamon
1 tsp	Cloves
1 stick	Butter, softened
1/2 cup	Sugar
1 lg	Egg
1 cup	Molasses
1 cup	Hot water

	LEMON SAUCE
1/2 cup	Sugar
1 tbsp	Cornstarch
1 cup	Water
2 tbsp	Lemon juice, fresh
	Lemon zest

Whisk together the first 6 ingredients until well mixed. Cream the butter in a separate bowl, adding the sugar slowly, and beating on medium speed until light and fluffy. Add the egg and molasses, mixing well. Add the flour mixture alternately with the water, beginning and ending with the flour and mixing after each addition. Pour into a prepared 9-inch pan. Bake in a 350-degree oven for 35 minutes or until lightly brown on top.

SAUCE: Heat the cornstarch, sugar, and water in a saucepan and cook over medium heat until thickened. Add the lemon juice and zest. Serve warm over the gingerbread.

HUGUENOT TORTE

Ingredients for 12 servings

4 lg	Eggs
3 cups	Sugar
8 tbsp	Flour, all-purpose
5 tsp	Baking powder
1/2 tsp	Salt
3 lg	Granny Smith apples [2 cups], cored and cut into 1/2-inch pieces
2 cups	Chopped pecans
2 tsp	Vanilla
	Chopped pecans, lightly toasted
	Sweetened whipped cream

Beat the eggs until pale and thickened [about 4 minutes]. Add the sugar gradually. Sift the flour, baking powder, and salt together and add to the egg-sugar mixture gradually. Beat for 1 minute or until well incorporated. Add the apples, untoasted pecans, and vanilla. Mix well. Divide the mixture onto 2 sprayed [or prepared] baking trays with sides [approximately 17x11-inch pans]. Smooth the mixture evenly. Bake in a 325-degree oven until golden brown, about 45 minutes. Let cool 20 minutes and cut into 3- to 4-inch pieces. Remove from the pan with a spatula and stack onto serving plates, trying to keep the crust on top. The torte will break, but pile it onto the plate, crust side up. Top with whipped cream and sprinkle with the toasted nuts.

COFFEE ICE CREAM DESSERT

Ingredients for 8 servings

9 oz	Nabisco Famous Chocolate Wafers, finely ground
1/2 stick	Butter, melted
1 qt	Coffee ice cream, softened
1 pint	Whipping cream
2 tbsp	Sugar
1 tsp	Vanilla
7 oz	Crisp almond cookies [almond macaroons], finely ground
1/2 cup	Slivered almonds, broken and lightly toasted

CHOCOLATE SAUCE

1 1/2 cups	Heavy cream
2/3 cup	Dark brown sugar, firmly packed
8 oz	Chocolate chips, special dark
1/2 stick	Butter, room temperature
3 1/2 tsp	Amaretto

Mix the melted butter and chocolate crumbs together until well blended. Pat the mixture into a 9-inch springform pan, pressing the crumbs 1 inch up the side. Freeze for 30–40 minutes. Spread the ice cream carefully over the crust. Freeze until firm. Beat the heavy cream with the sugar and vanilla until stiff peaks form. Gently fold in the almond cookie crumbs, reserving some to sprinkle on top. Smooth on top of the ice cream. Sprinkle with the reserved crumbs and toasted almonds. Freeze. Serve with hot chocolate sauce.

CHOCOLATE SAUCE: In a heavy saucepan combine the cream and brown sugar, bringing to a boil while whisking until the sugar is dissolved. Remove from the heat and add the chocolate [whisking until melted], butter [whisking until melted], and amaretto. Whisk until smooth. Refrigerate. May rewarm over very low heat while stirring.

ICE CREAM WITH EASY AND YUMMY SAUCE

Ingredients for 6 servings

1 stick	Butter
3/4 cup	Light brown sugar, lightly packed
3 tbsp	Grand Marnier
1/2 gal	Vanilla ice cream

Slowly melt the butter and brown sugar in a heavy saucepan. Add the liqueur and boil, while stirring, for a couple of minutes to allow the alcohol to evaporate. Scoop a couple of dips of ice cream into a footed dessert dish. Spoon some of the sauce over the ice cream. Serve with a couple of fancy cookies.

Helpful hint: I like Pepperidge Farm's Pirouettes.

ICE CREAM SANDWICH DESSERT

Ingredients for 10 servings

17	Ice cream sandwiches
12 1/4 oz	Caramel topping [jar]
3/4 cup	Fudge topping, heated
1 1/4 cup	Chopped pecans, lightly toasted
12 oz	Cool Whip, thawed

Place 8 1/2 sandwiches in a 13x9 inch dish. Spread caramel topping over all of the sandwiches. Sprinkle with 1 cup of the pecans. Top with 2 cups of the Cool Whip. Layer the remaining sandwiches. Spread the remaining Cool Whip over the sandwiches. Sprinkle with the remaining 1/4 cup of nuts. Cover and freeze for 2 hours or more. Let the dessert stand at room temperature before cutting into squares. Drizzle the squares with heated chocolate syrup.

Helpful hint: This dessert can be made smaller by not adding the second layer of sandwiches.

Variations: Other toppings can be used, such as pineapple along with bananas to create a banana split version. Add the bananas just before serving, however.

LEMON-CAKE DESSERT

Ingredients for 12 servings

1 box	White cake mix and ingredients to make the cake
1 pkg	Lemon instant pie filling [3.4 oz] and ingredients to prepare the pudding
8 oz	Lemon frosting [can, near the cake mixes]
4 oz	Cool Whip, thawed

Prepare the cake mix according to the directions. Spread the batter in a sprayed or oiled 13x9-inch pan. Prepare the lemon pudding. Mix according to the directions on the package. Pour or drop the pudding evenly over the cake batter. Bake in a 350-degree oven for 30–40 minutes or until the cake is golden brown and the edges pull away from the sides of the pan. Cool completely. Blend the frosting and Cool Whip and spread over the cooled cake. Refrigerate.

LEMON FLUFF

Ingredients for 6 servings

1 1/2 cups	Hot water
1 sm pkg	Lemon Jell-O [3.4 oz]
1 cup	Sugar
1/2 cup	Lemon juice
13 oz	Evaporated milk [can]
	Whipped cream, lightly sweetened

Place the evaporated milk into the freezer until icy. Dissolve the lemon gelatin in the hot water and chill until it begins to thicken. Beat the gelatin with an electric mixer. Beat the icy milk with the electric mixer until it triples in volume. Beat in the sugar and the lemon juice. Fold in the whipped gelatin. Pour into a Pyrex dish or individual serving dishes such as sherbets. Chill until serving. Top with a dollop of whipped cream.

Helpful hint: Vanilla wafer crumbs can be used to line the Pyrex dish or serve a good cookie with it. This dessert can also be frozen.

LEMON PUDDING/CAKE

Ingredients for 6 servings

3/4 cup	Sugar, fine [divided]
1/4 cup	Flour
1/4 tsp	Baking powder
1/8 tsp	Salt
3/4 cup	Milk
1 tbsp	Butter, melted
2 tbsp	Lemon juice
1 tsp	Lemon zest or grated rind
2 lg	Eggs, separated

Sift the flour, baking powder, and salt together with 1/2 cup of the sugar. In another bowl, beat the egg yolks until lemony color. Add the melted butter, lemon zest, milk, and lemon juice and beat until smooth. Stir in the sifted dry ingredients and beat until smooth. In another bowl, beat the egg whites with clean beaters until stiff. Add the remaining 1/4 cup of sugar to the egg whites. Fold the two mixtures together. Pour into a buttered casserole dish. Place the casserole into a pan of warm water. Bake in a 375-degree oven for 40 minutes or until golden brown on the top. This is better served warm. The pudding on the bottom of the cake is mellow while warm.

LEMONADE ICE CREAM

Ingredients for 10 servings

1/2 gal	Vanilla ice cream
6 oz	Frozen lemonade, undiluted

Break pieces of the vanilla ice cream into a large mixing bowl. Pour the lemonade concentrate over all. When the ice cream is softened, beat well with a mixer. Pour into a container, cover, and refreeze.

VARIATION: For a lighter dessert, mix 1/2 gallon of vanilla ice cream, 12 oz can of lemonade concentrate, and 12 oz Cool Whip and refreeze. Serve with fresh berries, sweetened with a little sugar.

MERINGUES AND FRUIT

Ingredients for 8 servings

6 lg	Egg whites
1/4 tsp	Salt
1/4 tsp	Cream of tartar
1 1/2 cups	Sugar
1 tsp	Vanilla
1/2 cup	Nuts, chopped fine [optional]
2 qts	Vanilla ice cream
	SAUCE
1 can	Cherry pie filling
1/2 cup	Orange marmalade

Draw circles [3 1/2 inches each] on the back of parchment paper. Turn the paper over and place on a baking sheet. Beat the egg whites until foamy. Add the salt and cream of tartar, beating until soft peaks form. Slowly add the sugar, beating after each addition until all of the sugar is added and meringue is stiff. Add the vanilla and nuts. Place the meringue on the circles, shaping with the back of a spoon, forming shells. Bake in a 250-degree oven for 1 hour and 20 minutes. Turn off the oven and let cool. Leave the oven light on to help the meringues become crispy. Leave them in the oven for several hours. Store in an airtight container until ready to use. When ready to serve, heat the pie filling and marmalade in a saucepan. Place a scoop of ice cream in each shell and warm sauce over the top. Fresh fruit is good [raspberries, strawberries, blueberries, or a combination of bananas and passion fruit] with the ice cream.

Helpful hint: If parchment paper is not available, use foil.

OREO COOKIE DESSERT

Ingredients for 20 servings

15 oz	Oreo cookies [package], divided
1 stick	Butter, melted
8 oz	Cream cheese, softened
1 cup	Powdered sugar
12 oz	Cool Whip, divided
6 oz	Instant chocolate pudding
2 1/2 cups	Milk

Crush all of the cookies [may use a food processor]. Set aside 1/4 cup of the crumbs. Mix the rest of the crumbs with the melted butter. Press into the bottom of a 9x13-inch pan. Bake in a 325-degree oven for 5–7 minutes. Let cool. Blend the cream cheese and powdered sugar with a mixer until smooth. Fold in 1/2 cup of the Cool Whip. Spread the mixture over the crust. Refrigerate for 30 minutes. Mix the pudding and milk together until smooth. Spread the pudding over the cream cheese layer. Refrigerate for 1 hour. Spread remainder of Cool Whip on top of pudding. Sprinkle with the reserved cookie crumbs. Cover and refrigerate. Cut into squares.

OREO ICE CREAM

Ingredients for 12 servings

18	Oreo cookies
12 oz	Cool Whip
1/2 gal	Vanilla ice cream

Crush cookies. Add Cool Whip and softened ice cream. Whip all together and refreeze. Serve with leftover Oreo cookies.

OREO MOUSSE

Ingredients for 12 servings

15 oz	Oreo cookies [bag]
5 oz	Chocolate pudding mix [instant]
2 cups	Milk
1/2 cup	Sour cream
1/2 cup	Condensed milk [not evaporated]
8 oz	Cool Whip, thawed

Crush the cookies [may use a food processor]. Set aside 1/4 cup of the crumbs and cover the bottom of a 9x13-inch casserole dish with the rest. Mix the milk and the pudding mix together with a whisk or a hand mixer for 1 minute. Blend in the condensed milk, sour cream, and 1/2 of the thawed Cool Whip. Pour the mixture over the cookie crumbs. Let the mixture set for a couple of minutes and spread the remaining whipped topping over the top. Sprinkle the reserved crumbs over the top. Refrigerate for 6 hours before serving.

PINEAPPLE FLUFF

Ingredients for 8 servings

20 oz	Crushed pineapple, drained
14 oz	Condensed milk [not evaporated]
1/4 cup	Lemon juice
1 cup	Chopped nuts, lightly toasted
10 oz	Cool Whip

Mix the milk and lemon juice. Add the pineapple and nuts. Fold in the Cool Whip. Chill overnight in the refrigerator. Serve in a sherbet glass with a cherry, strawberry, pineapple bit, or mint leaf on top.

PUMPKIN SQUARES

Ingredients for 12 servings

15 oz	Pumpkin, can
1 cup	Sugar
1 tsp	Nutmeg
1 tsp	Cinnamon, ground
1 tsp	Ginger, ground
1 tsp	Salt
1/2 gal	Vanilla ice cream, softened
1 cup	Chopped pecans, lightly toasted
	Gingersnaps

Beat the pumpkin, sugar, and spices together until well blended. Add the softened ice cream and blend. Stir in the nuts. Line the bottom of a 9x13-inch dish with gingersnaps. Spread 1/2 of the ice cream mixture over the gingersnaps. Repeat the layers and freeze until firm. Cut into desired squares and serve with a dollop of sweetened whip cream and a toasted pecan on top or top the whip cream with some crushed gingersnaps.

RAINBOW DELIGHT

Ingredients for 10 servings

1 lg	Angel food cake
1/2 gal	Vanilla ice cream [or more if pan is large]
3 oz	Lime Jell-O [1 box]
3 oz	Strawberry Jell-O [1 box]
3 oz	Orange Jell-O [1 box]
1 can	Blueberries, drained [not Comstock]
1 pkg	Frozen strawberries [slightly thawed]
1 can	Mandarin oranges, drained [or crushed pineapple, drained]

Cut the cake into 3 sections and break into bite-size pieces into 3 bowls. Set aside. Place a small amount of softened ice cream into tube cake pan and freeze. Place 1 bowl of cake over ice cream layer and sprinkle with DRY orange Jell-O. Arrange orange sections over Jell-O and spread 1/3 of the remaining softened ice cream. Freeze. Place another bowl of cake pieces in the pan and sprinkle with the DRY lime Jell-O, and then the blueberries. Cover with 1/2 of the remaining ice cream. Freeze. Add the last bowl of cake pieces and sprinkle with the DRY strawberry Jell-O. Top with the partially thawed strawberries and cover with the remaining ice cream. Freeze for 24 hours. Invert on a flat dish or tray. This dessert slices best with an electric knife. A serrated knife will work if dessert is not frozen solid.

Helpful hint: My tube pan is a 2-piece pan. A plastic liner may be helpful if the tube pan is one piece. This dessert is a little extra work to make but it is delicious and pretty. It can be made several days in advance.

RICE PUDDING

Ingredients for 10 servings

1 1/2 cups	Sugar
1 cup	Hot water
12 oz	Evaporated milk [can]
4	Eggs, slightly beaten
1/3 cup	Butter, melted
1 tsp	Vanilla
1/2 tsp	Nutmeg
4 cups	Cooked rice
1/2 cup	Raisins [optional]
	LEMON SAUCE [optional]
1 cup	Water
1/2 cup	Sugar
2 tbsp	Cornstarch
1/2 cup	Lemon juice, fresh
	Lemon zest
	Pinch of salt
3 tbsp	Butter

Dissolve the sugar in the hot water. Melt the butter in the hot mixture. Add the vanilla to the milk and whisk into the mixture. Blend in the eggs and add the nutmeg. Stir in the rice and raisins. Pour into a buttered casserole dish. Place the casserole dish into a slightly larger pan. Pour water into the larger pan. Bake in a 350-degree oven for 45 minutes to 1 hour. The center should be set.

Helpful hint: Be cautious taking the hot water out of the oven. Once a hot pad gets wet, the heat penetrates immediately!

SAUCE: Combine the water, sugar, cornstarch, and salt in a small saucepan. Cook over medium heat, whisking, until slightly thickened. Add the butter, lemon juice, and zest and whisk over the heat until desired consistency. Serve warm over rice pudding or ginger bread.

CREAMY STRAWBERRY DESSERT

Ingredients for 8 servings

1 cup	Graham cracker crumbs
3 tbsp	Sugar
1/4 cup	Butter, melted
	FILLING
10 oz	Frozen strawberries [in syrup], thawed
1/4 cup	Cold water
1 pkg	Unflavored gelatin
8 oz	Cream cheese, softened
1/2 cup	Sugar
1 cup	Whipping cream, whipped
2 tbsp	Sugar
	Sliced strawberries

Combine crumbs, 3 tablespoons of sugar, and melted butter together in a small mixing bowl. Press the mixture into the bottom of an 8-inch springform pan. Bake in a 350-degree oven for 10 minutes. Cool. Drain the strawberries over a bowl and reserve the juice. Combine the reserved juice, cold water, and gelatin in a small saucepan. Cook over low heat, stirring constantly, until the gelatin dissolves. Cool for 10 minutes. In a mixing bowl, blend the cream cheese and sugar together. Add the strawberries and gelatin mixture until thoroughly blended. Chill in the refrigerator until partially set. Do not let the mixture get firm. Whip the cream, adding the 2 tablespoons of sugar. Gently fold the whipped cream into the gelatin mixture. Spoon the mixture onto the cooled crust. Chill overnight. Before serving run a thin knife around the sides of the pan to loosen and remove the sides of the pan. Slice and serve with sliced strawberries. If desired, extra whipped cream may be added on top of the slices.

Helpful hint: Other berries may be substituted instead of the strawberries.

STRAWBERRY PIZZA

Ingredients for 12 servings

1 pkg	Sugar cookie roll, in the dairy section
1/4 cup	Sugar
1 tsp	Vanilla
8 oz	Cream cheese, softened
13 1/2 oz	Strawberry glaze
1 1/2 qt	Fresh strawberries [washed, blotted, and sliced]

Press the cookie dough into an unoiled pizza pan. Bake in a 350-degree oven for 20 minutes or until done. Cool. Mix the cream cheese, sugar, and vanilla, blending well. Spread over the cooled cookie crust. Combine the strawberries and the glaze. Spread over the cream cheese layer. Top with a layer of Cool Whip and garnish with strawberries. Refrigerate.

STRAWBERRY SAUCE

Ingredients for 2 cups

2 pints	Strawberries, washed and trimmed
1/2 cup	Raspberry jam [seedless]

Cut the clean strawberries into quarters and put into saucepan. Add the jam. Cook over medium heat for 6–8 minutes or until the strawberries have cooked to desired consistency. Serve warm or cool over dessert. Cover and store in the refrigerator for several days.

TOFFEE SAUCE

Ingredients for 2 cups

3/4 cup	Dark brown sugar, heaping
2 tbsp	Dark corn syrup
3/4 stick	Butter
2/3 cup	Cream, heavy

Put the sugar, syrup, and butter in a heavy saucepan and slowly bring to a boil, allowing the butter and sugar to dissolve. Let the mixture bubble for a couple of minutes. Slowly add the cream. Cook over low heat, while stirring, for another 2 or 3 minutes until thick and glossy. Serve over vanilla ice cream or other desserts.

INDIVIDUAL TRIFLES

Ingredients for 6 servings

1 pkg	Ladyfingers
1/4 cup	Raspberry jam [seedless]
2 tbsp	Dry sherry

2 tbsp	Orange juice
1 pkg	Vanilla pudding mix, instant [3.9 oz]
2 cups	Milk
2 tbsp	Slivered almonds, toasted
	Heavy whipping cream, whipped and lightly sweetened

Split the ladyfingers in half lengthwise. Spread 1 teaspoon of the raspberry jam on the inside bottom half of each of the ladyfingers. Place the tops back on the bottoms of the ladyfingers and cut each one in half. Arrange 4 of the filled halves in each individual serving dish. Drizzle each with 1 teaspoon of sherry and 1 teaspoon of orange juice. Mix the pudding and milk together. Pour the pudding into the serving dishes and chill. Just before serving, top with whipped cream and a sprinkling of toasted slivered almonds.

Helpful hint: Whipped topping may be used, but I like the real whipped cream. Whipped cream may be sweetened with powdered sugar or granulated sugar. Also, it can be flavored with a very small amount of vanilla, almond, etc. extract.

VANILLA ICE CREAM

Ingredients for 4 servings

2 cups	Milk
2 cups	Whipping cream
3/4 cup	Sugar
6 lg	Egg yolks
1	Vanilla bean

Split the vanilla bean lengthwise and scrape the seeds with a small knife. Combine the milk, cream, sugar, vanilla bean, and seeds in a heavy saucepan. Bring the ingredients to a gentle boil. Remove from the heat. Beat the egg yolks with a mixer until they appear frothy and are lemon colored, about 2 or 3 minutes. Slowly whisk 1 cup of the hot mixture into the beaten egg yolks. Gradually add the tempered egg mixture to the hot cream while whisking constantly. Cook over medium-low heat, while stirring, until the mixture thickens. Strain through a fine mesh strainer into a Pyrex bowl and place a piece of plastic wrap directly on top of the custard [to prevent a skin from forming]. Refrigerate until chilled, 2 or 3 hours. Churn in ice cream maker of choice, according to the directions. Spoon into an airtight container and freeze until serving time.

CREAMY VANILLA SAUCE

Ingredients for 1 1/2 cups

| 2 lg | Egg yolks |
| 2 1/2 cups | Vanilla ice cream |

Whisk the egg yolks in a small mixing bowl for a couple of minutes. Slowly heat the ice cream in a small saucepan until it is hot. Slowly drizzle a little [about 2 tablespoons] of the hot cream into the beaten yolks while whisking the yolks. Drizzle the rest of the hot cream into the yolks, while whisking. Pour the mixture back into the pan and place it on very low heat. Stir occasionally until serving.

Helpful hint: Serve over fresh or baked fruit.

Frostings

CARAMEL FROSTING

Ingredients for 1 cake

1 lb	Brown sugar, box
5 oz	Evaporated milk, small can
1 stick	Butter

Mix brown sugar, milk, and butter in a saucepan. Allow to simmer on low heat for 4 or 5 minutes, stirring occasionally. Cool slightly. Beat for a few minutes until the frosting is of spreading consistency.

CARAMEL TOPPING

Ingredients for 1 1/2 cups

1 cup	Sugar
1/2 cup	Butter
1/2 cup	Buttermilk
1/2 tsp	Baking soda

Combine all of the ingredients in a medium saucepan. Bring to a boil. Reduce the heat and cook for 20 minutes, stirring constantly. Remove from the heat and beat until smooth. Pour over warm cake or dessert.

CREAM CHEESE FROSTING

Ingredients for 1 cake

2 sticks	Butter, softened
16 oz	Cream cheese, softened
4 cups	Confectioners' sugar, sifted
1 tsp	Vanilla
3/4 cup	Pecans, chopped small [optional]

Beat the cream cheese until smooth. Add the vanilla and butter. Add the sugar slowly and mix well. Increase the speed of the mixer and beat until light and fluffy. Frost a carrot cake or red velvet cake. If desired, sprinkle the chopped pecans over the top and press pecans around the sides of the cake. For an added touch, garnish a carrot cake with 2 or 3 carrot curls in the center of the carrot cake or 3 fresh strawberries in the center of a red velvet cake.

CREAMY CHOCOLATE FROSTING, TOO

Ingredients for 1 cake

1 stick	Butter
4 tbsp	Cocoa
6 tbsp	Milk [or half and half]
1 box	Confectioners' sugar
1 tsp	Vanilla

Melt the butter in a saucepan. Add the cocoa and milk. Bring to a boil. Remove from the heat and add the vanilla. Add the confectioners' sugar and beat until creamy. Add 1 cup of chopped nuts, if desired. This frosts a layer cake or halve the recipe to frost a pound cake.

Two cups of sugar weigh one pound, and four cups of flour weigh one pound. For larger recipes, weigh your ingredients instead of measuring by the cupful.

GRANNY SUE'S CHOCOLATE FUDGE FROSTING

Ingredients for 1 cake

2 cups	Sugar
1/3 cup	Cocoa [powder]
1 stick	Butter
5 oz	Evaporated milk, or a small can
1 tsp	Vanilla
1 pinch	Salt

Mix the milk, sugar, and cocoa in a heavy saucepan. Heat to boiling, stirring slowly to avoid scorching. Let mixture boil a rolling boil until it reaches the soft ball stage. [Have a small glass of water handy and drop frosting into it until a soft ball forms.] Add the vanilla, butter, and salt. Remove from the heat and beat until cooled and creamy enough to spread. This is enough frosting to frost a 2-layer cake or a 3-layer cake.

Helpful hint: This is good on the Eight-Layer Cake. Double the recipe. Good and impressive!

EASY CHOCOLATE FROSTING

Ingredients for 1 cake

1 stick	Butter
1/2 cup	Milk
1/4 cup	Cocoa
12 large	Marshmallows
1 box	Confectioners' sugar

Mix the first four ingredients in a saucepan and mix until the butter and marshmallows have melted. Blend the mixture and add the confectioners' sugar slowly. Stir until smooth. Pour over a baked 9x13-inch cake or frost a 2-layer cake.

CHOCOLATE GANACHE

Ingredients for 7 cups

4 cups	Heavy cream
2 lbs	Semisweet chocolate, finely chopped
1/4 cup	Light corn syrup
1/4 tsp	Salt

Heat the cream in a heavy bottom saucepan until steaming. Add the chocolate and move the pan around to cover all of the chocolate with the cream. Melt the chocolate until smooth. Add the corn syrup and salt. Stir until incorporated.

GERMAN CHOCOLATE FROSTING

Ingredients for 1 cake

1 cup	Evaporated milk
1 cup	Sugar
3 lg	Egg yolks
1 stick	Butter
1 tsp	Vanilla
1 cup	Nuts, chopped
1 1/2 cups	Coconut

Place the first 5 ingredients into a boiler and cook over medium heat while stirring until the mixture is thickened, about 12 minutes. Remove from the heat and add the nuts and the coconut. Beat until spreading consistency. Frosts 1 cake.

COCONUT FILLING

Ingredients for 1 cake

1 cup	Sugar
1 cup	Milk
12 oz	Coconut, grated
12 lg	Marshmallows [10 miniature marshmallows equal 1 large]
1 tsp	Vanilla
1/2 cup	Pecans, finely chopped, optional

While cake is baking, place the sugar and milk in a saucepan and bring to a boil. Add the marshmallows and coconut. Boil for 5 minutes, stirring constantly. Add the vanilla. Spread on the warm cake.

Helpful hint: This is good spread in between layers of the 8-layer chocolate cake recipe. Bake 3 layers only, spreading this between 2 layers. Frost the cake with Granny Sue's Chocolate Fudge Frosting and you have a delicious MOUND CAKE.

CHOCOLATE WHIPPED CREAM

Ingredients for 4 cups

2 cups	Heavy whipping cream
1 cup	Confectioners' sugar, sifted before measuring
1/2 cup	Cocoa, sifted before measuring

Place the beaters and a metal mixing bowl into the refrigerator to chill. Sift the dry ingredients and measure. Whip the cream about 2 minutes until it starts to thicken. Add the sugar and cocoa and continue beating until the cream holds stiff peaks. Frost cooled cake or cover and keep in the refrigerator for several hours.

LEMON FILLING

Ingredients for 3 cups

2 cups	Sugar
3 tbsp	Flour [not self-rising]
1 cup	Butter, melted
1 cup	Milk
8	Egg yolks, beaten until the color of lemons
3 lg	Lemons, juice and zest

Mix the sugar and the flour well with a wire whisk. Place all of the ingredients in the top of a double boiler. Cook, while stirring or beating, until thick enough to spread over cake layers. The mixture will hang from the beater when it thickens. This is enough filling for the top and sides of a 3-layer cake, or it can be piped into puffs. Save any extra filling in a jar to be used as lemon curd with angel food cake and fresh strawberries.

Helpful hint: A small grater can be purchased to zest fruit with. The job is much easier with one of these.

ROSALIND'S MERINGUE

Ingredients for 1 pie

3 lg	Egg whites
1/4 tsp	Cream of tartar
6 tbsp	Sugar

Beat the egg whites until frothy and add the cream of tartar. Gradually add the sugar and beat until stiff peaks form. Cover the pie filling with the meringue, making sure that the meringue seals with the crust around the pie. Bake in a 350-degree oven until lightly brown, about 15 minutes.

PINEAPPLE CURD

Ingredients for 3 cups

7 lg	Egg yolks
3/4 cup	Sugar
1/2 cup	Pineapple juice
1 stick	Butter, cut into small pieces
1	Lemon, juiced and strained [or 1 tablespoon]

Whisk the egg yolks and sugar in a stainless steel bowl until smooth. Slowly whisk the pineapple and lemon juices into the mixture. Place the bowl over simmering water and continue to whisk until thick, about 8 minutes. Remove from the heat and add the butter. Beat until smooth. Cover with plastic wrap and gently press it onto the top of the curd to prevent a skin from forming.

PRALINE FROSTING

Ingredients for 2 cups

1 stick	Butter
1 cup	Brown sugar, firmly packed
1/4 cup	Whipping cream
3/4 cup	Pecans, whole or coarsely chopped

Melt the butter in a small saucepan. Add the whipping cream and brown sugar. Bring to a boil. Boil, while stirring, for 2 or 3 minutes or until the sugar is dissolved. Add the pecans. Use as a topping for a cake, ice cream, or desserts.

ROLO FROSTING

Ingredients for 2 cups

6 pkgs	Rolo candy [1.7 oz each]
1/2 stick	Butter
7 oz	Condensed milk [1/2 can], not evaporated
1 cup	Chopped pecans, optional

Melt 1/2 stick of butter and Rolo candy. Add the condensed milk. Add the pecans to melted ingredients and stir. Pour over a baked 9x13-inch cake, brownies, or frost between layers of a cake.

RUM WHIPPED CREAM

Ingredients for 8 servings

1/2 pint	Heavy cream, cold
3 tbsp	Sugar
1/2 tsp	Vanilla
1 tbsp	Dark rum

Whip the cream until it begins to thicken. Add the sugar, vanilla, and rum. Continue to whip until stiff peaks form. Keep cold. Serve over a slice of pie or as a dessert topping.

SEA FOAM ICING

Ingredients for 1 cake

2 lg	Egg whites
1 1/2 cups	Sugar
1/4 tsp	Cream of tartar
1/4 tsp	Salt
1/3 cup	Water
2 tsp	Light corn syrup
1 tsp	Vanilla

Cook all of the ingredients, except for the vanilla, over boiling water in a double boiler. Cook for 7 minutes over boiling water, beating with an electric mixer. Remove from the heat and add the vanilla. Beat for another minute. Frosts a 2-layer cake liberally.

Helpful hint: If a double boiler is not available, use a heatproof bowl over boiling water instead.

SEVEN-MINUTE FROSTING

Ingredients for 1 cake

3 lg	Egg whites, room temperature
2 1/2 cups	Sugar
1 tsp	Cream of tartar
1/4 cup	Water
1/4 cup	White corn syrup
1 pinch	Salt
1 tsp	Vanilla

Beat the egg whites and sugar together. Mix all of the ingredients together, except for the vanilla, in the top of a double boiler. Beat with a mixer. Cook over boiling water while mixing for 7 minutes. Remove from the heat and add the vanilla. Frost a cooled cake.

Helpful hint: Sheila says that her mother fills Cream Puffs with this. Yummy!

WHITE CHOCOLATE FROSTING

Ingredients for 1 cake

1 cup	Whipping cream [or evaporated milk]
1 1/4 cups	Sugar, granulated
4 oz	White chocolate, chopped small
1 stick	Butter
1 tsp	Vanilla

Bring the sugar and milk to a boil in a heavy saucepan, stirring constantly. The heat should be high enough to bring the mixture to a boil, but not hot enough to scorch. Reduce the heat and cook slowly for 5 more minutes, while stirring. Remove from the heat and add the chocolate, butter, and vanilla. Beat with a hand mixer until creamy and thick enough to spread. This frosting is good on the chocolate chip pound cake.

Pastries

BEIGNETS

Ingredients for 1 batch

1 loaf	Bread dough, frozen
	Powdered sugar
	Cooking oil

Place the frozen dough in a cake keeper with a glass dome [or a deep bowl and cover with a cloth] the night before preparing. The next morning the dough will have doubled in size and will be sticky. Place the dough on a heavily-floured surface and knead. Knead 4 or 5 times until it is no longer sticky. Roll out very thin and cut into 2-inch squares. Cover with a slightly damp cloth and let rise. Heat oil to 375 degrees in a deep fryer. When the dough has doubled in size [about 30 minutes or more], drop the squares into the preheated deep fryer. When done, drain the beignets on paper towels placed on top of a brown paper bag. Sprinkle generously with powdered sugar.

To hasten the ripening of avocados, place them in a paper bag with a banana or an apple. The gases released from the banana or apple will lessen the time it takes for avocados to ripen.

CINNAMON ROLLS

Ingredients for 24 servings

1 pkg	Yeast
1/2 cup	Warm water
1/2 cup	Crisco [solid]
1/2 cup	Sugar
1 tsp	Salt
2/3 cup	Potato Buds [next to instant potatoes]
1 cup	Boiling water
2 lg	Eggs
1 cup	Milk, scalded
6 cups	Flour, all-purpose [divided]

FILLING

1 stick	Butter, room temperature
2 cups	Light brown sugar [packed]
	Cinnamon

GLAZE

1 1/2 cups	Powdered sugar
2 tbsp	Water

Dissolve the yeast in the warm water. Mix the Potato Buds in the boiling water. Combine the shortening, sugar, salt, potatoes, and scalded milk [steaming but not boiling]. Put a little of the mixture into the eggs to temper them and add the eggs to the mixture. Let the mixture cool to lukewarm and add the yeast water, stirring well. Add 1/2 of the flour and stir well. Add the remaining 3 cups of flour and knead well for 8–10 minutes [the dough will become elastic and will hold together]. Place the dough into a greased bowl, cover, and let it rise for about an hour or until doubled in size. Punch the dough down and knead again for a couple of minutes. Cut the dough in half. On a floured surface, roll the dough into a rectangle with a rolling pin. Spread liberally with some of the softened butter. Sprinkle cinnamon over the butter, sprinkle a cup of light brown sugar over the cinnamon, and sprinkle more cinnamon over the brown sugar. Carefully roll up and slice 1/2-inch rounds with a thin, sharp knife. Place the rounds into greased pans. Repeat the procedure with the remaining dough. Dot with a little butter, cover, and let rise. Bake in a 375-degree oven for 15 minutes or until lightly brown. Cool slightly and drizzle the glaze with a fork.

Helpful hint: This dough makes very good rolls. Increase the salt to 2 teaspoons. After covering and letting them rise until doubled in size, place them in a 400-degree oven for 10 minutes, reduce the heat to 325 degrees, and let them bake until they are a golden brown.

EASY MINI CINNAMON ROLLS

Ingredients for 40 rolls

2 cans	Crescent rolls [Pillsbury], in the dairy case
1 stick	Butter, softened
1/4 cup	Sugar
1 tsp	Cinnamon
1/4 cup	Chopped nuts, optional
1/4 cup	Raisins, optional
1/4 cup	Maraschino cherries, chopped, optional
	GLAZE
1 cup	Confectioners' sugar
2 tbsp	Milk [or apple juice]

Separate each of the crescent rolls into 4 rectangles, pressing the seams together. Spread the butter [or the butter may be melted and brushed on with a pastry brush]. Combine the sugar, cinnamon, and the desired nuts or fruit and sprinkle over the butter. Roll the rectangles from the short ends. Cut each roll into 5 slices. Place into an ungreased baking dish, cut-side down. Bake in a 350-degree oven for 20–25 minutes, or until golden brown. While the rolls are baking, mix the glaze and pour over the warm rolls. These are great for a morning party.

CREAM PUFFS

Ingredients for 40 portions

6 tbsp	Butter
3/4 cup	Water
3/4 cup	Flour, all-purpose
3 lg	Eggs

Bring the water and butter to a boil. Reduce the heat and add all of the flour, stirring rapidly. Cook and stir until the mixture leaves the sides of the pan [about 30 seconds]. Remove from the heat. Add the eggs one at a time, beating well after each addition. Beat until the mixture looks like satin and breaks off when the spoon is raised. Drop by teaspoonfuls onto an ungreased baking sheet. Bake in a preheated 425-degree oven for 20–30 minutes or until brown. Let cool and fill or freeze until using.

Helpful hint: These can be filled with chicken salad [or other salads and spreads] as an appetizer, or they can be filled with lemon curd [check Lemon Curd Tassies recipe], creams [Seven-Minute Frosting], or a variety of puddings for a sweet treat.

CREAM PUFFS AND CUSTARD FILLING

Ingredients for 8 servings

1 cup	Water
1 stick	Butter
1 cup	Flour [all-purpose], sifted
4 lg	Eggs

CUSTARD FILLING

1/2 cup	Sugar
1/2 tsp	Salt
1/3 cup	Flour, all-purpose
4 lg	Egg yolks
2 cups	Milk
2 tsp	Vanilla

Heat the water to a rolling boil and melt the butter in the water. Add the flour, stirring. Stir over lowered heat [about 1 minute] with a wooden spoon until the mixture rolls up into a ball while stirring. It will leave the sides of the pan and cling to the spoon. Remove from the heat. Add the eggs 1 at a time, beating thoroughly after each addition. Beat well until the mixture is velvety and smooth. Line a baking tray with parchment paper and drop the mixture with a spoon or a scoop. Bake in a 350-degree oven for 45 minutes or until a golden brown. Cool in the oven slowly so the puffs can continue to dry. Cut off the tops with a serrated knife and remove the soft dough. Fill and place the tops back on. Sprinkle with powdered sugar.

CUSTARD: Mix the sugar, salt, and flour in a saucepan. Stir in the milk and cook over medium heat until the mixture boils. Boil for 1 minute and remove from the heat. Add a little of the mixture to the egg yolks to temper them. Blend the yolks in the hot mixture and bring just to the boiling point. Add the vanilla. Cool and fill the puffs.

GRAHAM CRACKER CRUST

Ingredients for 1 pie

1 pkg	Golden graham crackers, crushed fine [1 2/3 cups]
1/4 cup	Sugar
1/3 cup	Butter, softened
	Egg white, beaten with a fork

Combine the crumbs, sugar, and butter. Mix well with a fork or a pastry blender. Using the back of a large spoon, press the mixture evenly into a 9-inch pie plate [covering the sides and bottom of the plate]. Brush the egg white lightly over the surface with a pastry brush or a small paintbrush [for kitchen use only]. Bake in a 350- to 375-degree oven for 6–8 minutes. Cool and fill. For a no-bake crust, leave off the egg white and chill in the refrigerator for 30 minutes before using.

Helpful hint: A package of graham crackers can be easily crushed in a plastic bag.

LEMON CURD TASSIES

Ingredients for 2 dozen

3 oz	Cream cheese, softened
1 stick	Butter, softened
1 1/2 cup	Flour, all-purpose
1 pinch	Salt

	LEMON CURD
3 lg	Lemons, zest and juice
1 cup	Sugar
4 lg	Eggs
1 stick	Butter, melted

Place all of the ingredients in a food processor and pulse until a ball is formed. Wrap in plastic and chill for 1 or 2 hours. Divide the pastry into 24 balls. Press the balls into the bottoms and sides of miniature muffin tins. Bake in a 350-degree oven until lightly brown, about 20 minutes.

Helpful hint: If not using a food processor, use the paddle on a regular mixer.

LEMON CURD: Mix the lemon zest and sugar. Add the lemon juice and eggs; mix well. Slowly add the melted butter and mix. Place the mixture in the top of a double boiler and cook over lightly boiling water, whisking constantly until it is thickened and the sugar is dissolved. [The mixture will hang from the spoon or whisk.] Remove the pastry shells from the tins and fill with the curd. Add a small dollop of sweetened whipped cream on the tops or serve plain.

Helpful hint: Lemon curd can be stored in an airtight container in the refrigerator for several weeks.

ORANGE RUSKS

Ingredients for 39 servings

13 slices	Thin, white bread
1 stick	Butter
1/2 cup	Sugar
2 lg	Oranges

Cut the crusts off of the bread and slice into thirds. Remove the skin from the oranges with a zester. Melt the butter and sugar in a saucepan. Add the orange zest. Line a cookie sheet with foil. Place the slices of bread on the foil and spread the orange mixture over all. Bake in a 250-degree oven for an hour. Store in an airtight container.

Helpful hint: The bread may be cut into any shapes desired. This recipe is easily doubled.

QUICKY PASTRY CRUSTS

Ingredients for 2 dozen

24 slices	Thin sliced white bread [or more]
1/2 stick	Butter, melted [or more]

Place slices of the bread on a cutting board and cut out circles with a 2-1/4- or 2-1/2-inch cookie cutter. Melt the butter and brush it on one side of the bread. Press the buttered side of the bread into miniature muffin tins, shaping them. Bake in a 250-degree oven for one hour or until lightly brown. Cool and store in an airtight container.

Helpful hint: Great for filling with chicken salad or other party salads.

SUGARY PASTRY STRIPS

Ingredients for 8 servings

15 oz	Refrigerated piecrusts [2 crusts]
3 tbsp	Brown sugar [light or dark], packed
1 tsp	Cinnamon, ground
1/4 cup	Nuts [pecans or walnuts], chopped small

Bring the piecrusts to room temperature. Place 1 piecrust onto an ungreased cookie sheet. Press and seal any cracks. Mix the brown sugar and cinnamon together and crumble evenly over the crust. Sprinkle the nuts over the mixture. Place the second piecrust on top and press with the palm of your hand. Press around the edge with fingers and then the tines of a fork. Bake in a 375-degree oven until light brown [about 11 minutes]. Cut with a pizza cutter or a sharp, thin knife. Drizzle while hot with honey or confectioners' sugar dissolved in a little milk and 1/4 teaspoon of vanilla.

Variation: May add 1/2 cup of raisins with or instead of the nuts. Also, the amount of nuts may be increased to 1/2 cup.

To keep egg yolks centered while cooking hard-boiled eggs, stir the water while cooking.

NO-ROLL PECAN CRUST

Ingredients for 1 crust

1 cup	All-purpose flour
1/4 cup	Pecan meal
1/4 cup	Confectioners' sugar
1/2 cup	Butter, softened

Place all of the ingredients in a bowl and mix until soft and pliable. Spread evenly against the bottom and sides of pie plate or pan. Bake in a preheated 400-degree oven for 15 minutes or until golden brown. Fill with cream or chiffon pie filling. Also good with lemon or lime filling.

DO-AHEAD PIECRUSTS

Ingredients for 5 crusts

4 cups	Flour, all-purpose
1 tbsp	Sugar
1 tsp	Salt
1 lg	Egg
1 3/4 cups	Crisco
1/2 cup	Water
1 tbsp	Vinegar

Whisk the flour, sugar, and salt together. Add the Crisco, mixing with a pastry blender. Mix the water, egg, and vinegar together, beating gently with a fork or a small whisk. Make a well in the flour and add the egg mixture, stirring gently with a fork. Work the flour gently with hands until a ball is formed. Divide the dough evenly into 5 portions. Wrap the portions in plastic wrap, place in a freezer bag, and freeze until needed. When needed, remove from the freezer 20 minutes ahead of time. Roll on a floured surface and place in a pie plate or pan.

EASY AND TASTY PIECRUST

Ingredients for 1 crust

1 1/2 cups	All-purpose flour
1 1/2 tbsp	Sugar
1/4 cup	Oil [vegetable]
1 tsp	Salt
2 tbsp	Milk

Sift the flour, salt, and sugar together. Stir the milk and oil together, mixing well. Add the liquid to the dry ingredients and mix. Make into a ball and press onto the bottom and sides of the pie pan. Prick the bottom and sides with the tines of a fork. Bake in a 400-degree oven for 10 minutes or until golden brown.

Helpful hint: The dough may have to be shaped with your hands. Also, place the crust on the top rack for the last few minutes of baking.

PETITE PIE SHELLS

Ingredients for 4 dozen

1 stick	Butter
1 cup	Flour, all-purpose
3 oz	Cream cheese, softened

Mix all of the ingredients together, cover, and chill for 1 hour. Pinch off small amounts [about the size of a marble], roll, and press into miniature muffin tins. Bake in a 325-degree oven for 10–12 minutes. Fill with chicken salad or dessert fillings.

PRALINE PIECRUST

Ingredients for 1 crust

9 inch	Pie shell
1/3 cup	Brown sugar
1/3 cup	Butter
1/2 cup	Pecans, chopped small

Lightly bake the pie shell in a 400-degree oven for 4 or 5 minutes, pricking it with the tines of a fork to prevent bubbling. Combine the sugar and butter in a small saucepan and heat until the mixture boils and bubbles, melting the sugar. Remove from the heat and stir in the nuts. Spread the mixture evenly over the bottom of the crust. Bake in a 450-degree oven for 5 minutes or until bubbly. Cool and fill with a pie filling of choice.

STRAWBERRY TARTS

Ingredients for 6 tarts

2 pts	Fresh strawberries, cleaned and sliced lengthwise

PASTRY CREAM

1/4 cup	Cornstarch
3/4 cup	Sugar
2 cups	Milk
4 lg	Egg yolks, lightly beaten
2 tbsp	Vanilla
2 tbsp	Butter, unsalted
1 pinch	Salt

TART DOUGH

1 stick	Unsalted butter, room temperature
1/4 cup	Sugar
1 lg	Egg yolk
1 1/2 cups	Cake flour, sifted
	Extra flour, if needed, for rolling dough

GLAZE

1/2 cup	Strawberry jam

To make the CREAM, combine the cornstarch with 1/4 cup of sugar in a mixing bowl. Stir in 1/2 cup of milk. Blend the egg yolk into the sugar mixture, stirring until smooth. Combine the remaining 1 1/2 cups of milk with the remaining 1/2 cup of sugar and the salt in a heavy saucepan. Cook over medium-low heat and bring to a boil, stirring constantly. Remove from heat and add a little of the hot mixture to the eggs, whisking constantly. Add the remaining milk mixture to the eggs. Place the mixture back into the saucepan and cook over medium heat, whisking constantly to prevent scorching until the mixture comes to a boil [5–7 minutes]. The mixture will cling to the whisk and the whisk will leave a trail on the cream. Remove from the heat and add the vanilla and butter. Place the pan in ice water and cover the top of the cream with plastic wrap.

To make the DOUGH, cream the sugar, butter, and vanilla until smooth and light in color [about 2 minutes]. Add the egg yolks and blend until smooth [about 1 or 2 minutes]. Add the flour and mix on low speed until just blended. Press the dough into a log and wrap tightly with plastic wrap. Refrigerate 30 minutes, cut into 6 portions, and roll to fit tart pans. [At this point the pastries can be placed back into the refrigerator for 30 minutes to re-chill, to prevent shrinking.] Dock the dough [pricking with fork tines], line the tops with parchment paper, add pie weights or dry beans, and bake in a 350-degree oven for 10 minutes or until golden brown. Remove from the oven and let cool.

For the GLAZE: Heat the jam in a small saucepan and strain to remove any seeds. Set aside. When the tart shells are cool, remove from the pans and fill with the cream. Arrange the strawberries around the custard tops in a petal design. Brush the jam onto the strawberries with a pastry brush. Place the tarts in the refrigerator for a few minutes to let them set.

Helpful hint: This recipe can be made into one larger tart.

TEA TIME TASSIES

Ingredients for 24 servings

3 oz	Cream cheese, softened
1 cup	Flour, all-purpose
1/4 cup	Butter [1/2 stick]

FILLING

3/4 cup	Brown sugar, firmly packed
3/4 cup	Nuts, chopped small
1 lg	Egg, slightly beaten
1 tbsp	Butter, softened
1 tsp	Vanilla
1 dash	Salt

Mix the tart ingredients and divide into 24 balls. Chill for 5 or 10 minutes. Press into miniature tart or muffin pans, covering the bottoms and sides of the cups. Mix all of the filling ingredients well. Fill the tart shells 3/4 full. Bake in a 350-degree oven for 20 minutes or until browned. May dust with powdered sugar. Store in an airtight container. This recipe doubles well.

Helpful hint: Other fillings may be used such as lemon curd. Simply bake the empty pastry shells for about 20 minutes in a 350-degree oven or until lightly browned. Cool and fill.

GAIL'S APPLE PIE

Ingredients for 8 servings

6	Tart apples
1 cup	Sugar
3 tbsp	Flour
1 tsp	Cinnamon
1/4 tsp	Salt
1 tbsp	Lemon juice
1/2 stick	Butter

	PIECRUST [makes ONE piecrust]
1 3/4 cup	Flour
1/2 cup	Oil
1 tsp	Sugar
	Buttermilk
	Dash of salt

Peel, core, and slice apples [thin slices]. Mix apple slices with lemon juice. Mix flour, cinnamon, sugar, and salt together and add to apples. Fill a 9-inch pastry-lined pie plate or pan with apple mixture. Dot with 1/2 stick of butter and cover with top pastry crust. Cut slits to allow steam to escape. Bake at 375 degrees for 50 minutes or until done.

PIECRUST: Mix dry ingredients together. Make a well in the center. Add just enough buttermilk to oil to measure 3/4 cup and pour into the well. Mix with a fork and mix thoroughly. Roll out between wax paper.

Helpful hint: Place pie plate on a cookie sheet while baking to prevent boiling over into oven. This pie requires 2 piecrusts.

UPSIDE DOWN APPLE PIE

Ingredients for 8 servings

2	Piecrusts [15 oz package in the dairy case]

GLAZE

1/4 cup	Brown sugar, firmly packed
1 tbsp	Corn syrup
1 tbsp	Butter, melted
1 tsp	Flour
1/2 cup	Pecans, whole or coarsely chopped

FILLING

6 med	Apples, peeled, cored, and thinly sliced [Gala or yellow delicious]
2/3 cup	Sugar, granulated
2 tbsp	Flour
1/2 tsp	Cinnamon

TOPPING

Ice cream or whipped cream

Melt the butter in a small saucepan and add the flour, brown sugar, and corn syrup. Lightly oil a 9-inch pie plate or pan. Spread the glaze mixture over the bottom of the pie plate and arrange the nuts over all. If using whole nuts, place them upside down. Place one crust over the mixture and fit it to the size of the pan. Combine the filling mixture in a small bowl. Mix well until lumps of sugar and flour are gone. Arrange 1/2 of the apple slices evenly over the crust. Sprinkle 1/2 of the filling mixture over the apples. Repeat the procedure with the rest of the apples and filling mixture. Top with the remaining crust, sealing the crusts together and fluting the edges by pinching with fingers. Cut several slits on the top crust with a pointed knife. Place on a larger pan. Bake in a 425-degree oven for 8 minutes. Reduce the heat to 375 degrees and bake for an additional 40 minutes [or more] until golden brown. Loosen the edges with a blunt knife and invert onto a serving plate. Serve warm or cold.

Helpful hint: If using tart apples, increase the sugar accordingly.

BANANA CREAM PIE

Ingredients for 8 servings

8 oz	Cream cheese, softened
1 cup	Powdered sugar
4 cups	Cool Whip, divided
3 lg	Bananas [ripe but firm], sliced
3 oz	Instant vanilla pudding mix
1 1/4 cups	Milk
	Extra crushed pretzels for garnish

PRETZEL CRUST

1 cup	Flour, all-purpose
3/4 cup	Crushed pretzels [butter-flavored pretzels, if possible]
1/2 tsp	Salt
9 tbsp	Butter, room temperature [or butter-flavored shortening]
3 tbsp	Ice water

Combine the flour, crushed pretzels, salt, and butter in a bowl until the mixture is crumbly. Add the water and mix well. Place between wax paper and roll until the dough is thin and large enough for a deep-dish pie plate. Place in the pie plate. [If the crust breaks, pinch it back together and press it into the pie plate.]

Using a fork, flute the edges and prick the bottom of the crust several times. Bake in a 350-degree oven for 12 minutes. Cool.

FOR THE FILLING, combine the cream cheese, powdered sugar, and 1 cup of the whipped topping. Spread the mixture over the cooled crust. Slice the bananas over the cream cheese mixture. Mix the milk and pudding mix together and pour over the bananas. Top with the remaining whipped topping. Refrigerate for 1 hour or longer. Before serving, sprinkle pretzel crumbs over the top.

Helpful hint: I have used the pretzel crust in my strawberry-pretzel salad recipe for this pie. Deelish!

BLUEBERRY PIE

Ingredients for 8 servings

1 can	Condensed milk, not evaporated
1 can	Blueberries, not Comstock
	Juice of 2 lemons
3 tbsp	Sugar
3 tbsp	Cornstarch
	Piecrust [graham cracker or your choice]

Drain blueberries, saving the liquid. Mix the milk and lemon juice. Add the drained blueberries and pour the mixture into a piecrust. Chill. Add 3 tablespoons of sugar and 3 tablespoons of cornstarch to the blueberry juice. Cook over medium heat until thick, stirring while it cooks. Pour the mixture over the first layer and chill. Top with whipped cream or Cool Whip when served.

KENTUCKY BOURBON PIE

Ingredients for 1 pie

9 inch	Pie shell	1 pinch	Salt
1 stick	Butter, softened	2 tbsp	Kentucky bourbon
1 cup	Sugar		[or 1 tsp vanilla]
2 lg	Eggs, beaten	1 cup	Pecans, chopped
1/2 cup	Flour, all-purpose	1 cup	Chocolate chips

Bake the pie shell in a 350-degree oven for about 5 minutes or until it begins to puff. Prick lightly with the tines of a fork. Cream the butter and sugar. Add the beaten eggs, flour, salt, and bourbon [or vanilla] and mix. Add the chocolate chips and nuts, stirring until well mixed. Pour the mixture into the partially baked pie shell. Bake in a 350-degree oven until the center is set, about 30 minutes. Cool and slice, serving with a dollop of whipped cream or a scoop of ice cream.

Helpful hint: Place the pie on a cookie sheet while baking to catch any overflow.

BROWNIE CHEESE-CAKE PIE

Ingredients for 8 servings

15 oz	Pillsbury Thick n' Fudgy Swirl Deluxe Brownie Mix	3 lg	Eggs, divided between mixtures
		1/4 cup	Oil
8 oz	Cream cheese, softened	2 tbsp	Water, divided
		1/2 cup	Chopped pecans
3 tbsp	Sugar	1	Unbaked piecrust
1 tsp	Vanilla		

Mix the cream cheese, sugar, vanilla, and 1 egg in a bowl. Cream until smooth. In another bowl combine the brownie mix, one tablespoon of water, and the remaining 2 eggs. Beat with a large spoon, about 50 strokes. Prick the piecrust with a fork to release steam while baking. Pour 1/2 of the brownie mixture into the pie shell and spread. Spoon the cream cheese mixture over the brownie layer and spread it carefully. Pour the remaining brownie mixture over the cream cheese layer and smooth it. Sprinkle the chopped pecans over all. Bake in a 350-degree oven for 40 minutes or until the center is puffed. Place strips of aluminum foil around the crust after 15 minutes to prevent it from burning. Open the foil package and squeeze the fudge into a small bowl. Add 1 tablespoon of water to the fudge. Heat, and stir. Drizzle the fudge and water mixture over the baked pie. Chill before slicing.

BUTTERMILK PIE

Ingredients for 16 servings

3 3/4 cups	Sugar
4 tbsp	Flour, all-purpose
6	Eggs
1 cup	Buttermilk
1 cup	Butter, melted
2 tsp	Vanilla
2	Pie shells, unbaked

Combine the sugar, flour, eggs, buttermilk, butter, and vanilla. Mix until well blended. Pour into the pie shells. Bake in a 450-degree oven for 10 minutes. Reduce the heat to 350 degrees and bake for 40–50 minutes or until center is firm.

Helpful hint: If crusts brown too quickly, cover the crusts with foil. Don't let the foil touch the filling. Also, it is good to place the pies on a cookie sheet to prevent any filling from spilling in the oven.

BUTTERMILK CHESS PIE

Ingredients for 8 servings

1 1/2 cups	Sugar
1/2 cup	Bisquick
3 lg	Eggs
1 cup	Buttermilk
1/3 cup	Butter, melted [plus butter for the pie plate]
1 tsp	Vanilla
	Whipping cream, optional

Coat a pie plate generously with butter. Mix all of the ingredients in a bowl with an electric mixer for a minute or 2. Pour the mixture into the buttered pie plate. Bake in a 350-degree oven for 50 minutes or until an inserted toothpick comes out clean. Cool before slicing. Serve with a dollop of lightly sweetened whipping cream.

CARAMEL COCONUT PIES

Ingredients for 24 servings

3	Graham cracker piecrusts
8 oz	Cream cheese, room temperature
16 oz	Cool Whip
1 can	Condensed milk [not evaporated]
1 cup	Pecans, chopped
7 oz	Coconut [can]
	Caramel Sundae Syrup [squeeze bottle]

Blend the cream cheese and Eagle Brand milk until smooth. Gently fold in the Cool Whip. Lightly toast the coconut and chopped pecans and combine. Cover the bottom of the 3 piecrusts with the cream cheese mixture. Add some coconut and pecan mixture. Drizzle caramel syrup over the coconut mixture. Add the remaining coconut mixture and top with more caramel syrup. Freeze.

EASY CHOCOLATE FUDGE PIE

Ingredients for 8 servings

1 stick	Butter
2 oz	Chocolate, unsweetened squares
2 lg	Eggs
1 cup	Sugar
1/4 cup	Flour, self-rising
1/4 tsp	Vanilla
1 pinch	Salt

Melt the butter and chocolate squares in a small, heavy bottom saucepan. Set aside. Beat the 2 eggs slightly. Add the sugar, salt, and vanilla to the eggs. Next, add the slightly cooled chocolate/butter mixture while beating. Mix in the flour. Pour the batter into an oiled pie plate. Bake in a 350-degree oven for 25–30 minutes, or until the center is set. Serve warm or cold with ice cream.

CHOCOLATE SUNDAE PIE

Ingredients for 8 servings

6 oz	Chocolate morsels, semisweet
3/4 cup	Evaporated milk
1 1/2 cup	Miniature marshmallows
1 qt	Vanilla ice cream
1 cup	Roughly chopped pecans, toasted
1	Chocolate cracker crust

Place the ice cream in refrigerator to let soften enough to spread. In a saucepan, melt the chocolate, milk, and marshmallows over low heat and blend well. Cool. Spread a layer of the ice cream over the piecrust. Cover the ice cream with a layer of the chocolate. Sprinkle 1/2 of the nuts over the chocolate. Repeat the procedure. Freeze. After pie is frozen, cover with plastic wrap. Keep frozen.

Helpful hint: The crust may be baked for 4 or 5 minutes in a 300-degree oven and cooled before using.

CHOCOLATE PIE

Ingredients for 1 pie

3 lg	Egg yolks	9 inch	Pie shell, baked
1 cup	Sugar		
3 tbsp	Cornstarch		**MERINGUE**
3 tbsp	Cocoa [heaping spoonfuls]	3 lg	Egg whites
		1/4 tsp	Cream of tartar
1/8 tsp	Salt [or a pinch]	6 tbsp	Sugar
1 cup	Boiling water		

Beat the egg yolks until light and lemon colored. In another bowl whisk together the sugar, salt, cornstarch, and cocoa. Slowly add the boiling water to the dry mixture, whisking well. Add a little of the hot mixture to the egg yolks and beat well before adding the remainder to the yolks. Cook, while stirring constantly, in a double boiler [or in a heatproof bowl over boiling water] until the mixture is thickened. Cool and pour into a baked piecrust. Beat the egg whites until frothy and add the cream of tartar. Gradually add the sugar and beat until stiff peaks are formed. Cover the filling completely, sealing the meringue to the crust. Bake in a 350-degree oven until lightly brown, about 15 minutes.

CHOCOLATE-BUTTERMILK PIE

Ingredients for 8 servings

7	Eggs
1 cup	Buttermilk
2 1/2 cups	Sugar
1 tsp	Vanilla
1/8 tsp	Salt [or a pinch]
6 oz	Semisweet chocolate chips
	Unbaked piecrust [Mrs. Smith's deep dish]

Beat eggs. Add sugar and mix well. Blend milk, salt, and vanilla into mixture. Melt chocolate chips in the microwave. 40 seconds…then 30 seconds…and 20 seconds more if needed. Add chocolate to other ingredients, mixing well, and pour into unbaked pie shell. Bake in a 325-degree oven for 1 hour. Cool and chill before slicing.

Helpful hint: Place pie on a larger baking sheet to prevent any spilling in the oven.

CHOCOLATE CHIP PIE

Ingredients for 8 servings

1 lg	Egg
1 cup	Sugar
1/2 cup	Flour, all-purpose
1 tsp	Vanilla
1 cup	Chocolate chips [semisweet]
1 stick	Butter, melted
9 inch	Piecrust

Mix the first 6 ingredients together thoroughly [starting with the egg, sugar, and butter]. Pour into the unbaked piecrust. Place the unbaked pie onto a baking sheet to catch any spills. Bake in a 350-degree oven until golden brown on top, about 35–45 minutes. Serve with a dollop of lightly sweetened whip cream.

Helpful hint: Any chocolate chips may be used. If using sweet chips, cut the amount of sugar to 1/2 cup, or to taste.

CHOCOLATE CREAM PIE

Ingredients for 8 servings

2 tbsp	Cocoa
1/4 cup	Cornstarch, sifted
2/3 cup	Sugar
1/4 tsp	Salt
1 cup	Milk
1 cup	Half and half
3 lg	Egg yolks, beaten with fork
2 tbsp	Butter
1 tsp	Vanilla
9 inch	Pie shell, baked
	MERINGUE
3 lg	Egg whites
1/4 tsp	Cream of tartar
6 tbsp	Sugar

Heat the milk and half and half slowly in a boiler until scalded [just before boiling]. Mix the cocoa, cornstarch, 2/3 cup of sugar, and salt together. Gradually add the milk and the half and half to the dry ingredients. Cook over medium heat, stirring constantly, until the mixture thickens and begins to boil. Cook, while stirring, for another 2 minutes and remove from the heat.

Add a little of the hot mixture to the egg yolks to temper them. Stir the yolks into the hot mixture and cook for 1 minute. Pour into the baked pie shell.

MERINGUE: Beat the egg whites until frothy and add the cream of tartar. Gradually add the sugar and beat until stiff peaks form. Cover the chocolate pie filling with the meringue, making sure the meringue seals with the crust all of the way around. Bake in a 350-degree oven until lightly brown, about 15 minutes.

CHOCOLATE-PEANUT BUTTER PIE

Ingredients for 6 servings

1 qt	Chocolate ice cream
1/2 cup	Peanut butter [creamy]
4 oz	Cool Whip, thawed
6 oz	Graham cracker pie shell

Blend thawed whipped topping and peanut butter. Fold into softened chocolate ice cream. Pour mixture into pie shell. Cover and freeze. Top with more whipped topping and a cherry or chocolate shavings.

Helpful hint: To keep a crumb crust from becoming soggy, brush the crust with egg white and bake it in a 350-degree oven for 4 or 5 minutes and cool. A Hershey bar and a potato peeler will work for quick chocolate shavings.

COCONUT CREAM PIE DELUXE

Ingredients for 8 servings

1 cup	Sugar
2 tbsp	Cornstarch, heaping
5 lg	Eggs, separated and whites reserved
2 1/2 cups	Milk
1/4 cup	Butter
1 tsp	Vanilla
1/2 cup	Flaked coconut
1	Piecrust, baked

	MERINGUE
7 tbsp	Sugar
3 tbsp	Confectioners' sugar
1 pinch	Salt
1/2 tsp	Cream of tartar
1 tsp	Vanilla
2 tbsp	Coconut
5 lg	Reserved egg whites

Combine 1 cup of sugar and cornstarch in a heavy bottomed saucepan. Add the egg yolks and combine. Add the milk slowly and whisk to remove any lumps. Cook over medium heat, while stirring, until thick. Remove from heat and add the butter in small pieces, stirring until butter is melted. Add the vanilla, 1/2 cup of coconut, and stir well. Pour the filling into the baked pie shell.

MERINGUE: Mix the 2 sugars and salt together in a small bowl. Place the reserved egg whites in a mixer bowl. Beat on medium speed until frothy. Add the cream of tartar and increase the speed to medium high. When soft peaks form, begin to add the sugar gradually. When the peaks are firm, add the vanilla. Beat on high speed until the mixture is stiff, about 30 seconds. Place the meringue on top of the filling and seal the edges of the meringue to the pie shell. Sprinkle the 2 remaining tablespoons of coconut over the meringue. Bake the pie in a 350-degree oven until the meringue is lightly browned, about 8 minutes. Cool at room temperature before serving. Store leftovers in a refrigerator.

CREAMY CUSTARD PIE

Ingredients for 8 servings

8 oz	Cream cheese, softened
1/2 cup	Sugar
3 lg	Eggs
1/2 cup	Milk
1 tsp	Vanilla
9 inch	Pie shell
	Nutmeg

Bake the pie shell in a 425-degree oven for 5 minutes, pricking the bottom with the tines of a fork. Place the softened cream cheese in a bowl and beat until smooth. Blend in the sugar. Beat the eggs slightly and add the milk and vanilla. Slowly add the milk mixture to the cream cheese and blend. Pour the custard mixture into the lightly baked pie shell. Sprinkle generously with nutmeg [freshly grated is great]. Bake in a 350-degree oven for 25 minutes or until the custard is set.

ROSALIND'S EGG CUSTARD PIE [ALMOST LIKE MAMA'S]

Ingredients for 8 servings

9 inch	Pie shell, unbaked
5 lg	Eggs

1 1/2 cups	Sugar
1 3/4 cups	Milk
1/8 tsp	Salt
1 tsp	Vanilla
	Whole nutmeg

Beat the eggs on medium speed with the mixer until well blended. Add the sugar, milk, salt, butter, and vanilla. Mix. Pour the mixture into the pie shell. With a rasp, grate the nutmeg over the top of the mixture. Place the pie shell on a cookie sheet and place it into a 325-degree oven. Bake for 45–55 minutes or until a thin inserted knife is clean when removed.

Helpful hint: Prick the bottom of the pie shell with a fork before filling. Strips of aluminum foil may be lightly placed on the crust if it gets brown before the pie is firm.

FRIED PIES

Ingredients for 1 batch

3 cups	Flour, all-purpose
1/2 tsp	Baking soda
1 tbsp	Baking powder
1/3 cup	Crisco [not oil]
1 cup	Buttermilk
1 lg	Egg

Measure the dry ingredients, stir with a whisk, and sift all together. Mix in the Crisco and keep mixing until it resembles coarse meal. Mix the milk and egg together and add to the dry mixture. Mix well and knead until it is smooth. Roll the pastry on a floured surface until it is 1/4 inch thick. Cut into 5- to 6-inch circles, using a cereal bowl or saucer as a guide. Fill 1/2 of the pastry circle with chilled fruit. Moisten the filled side's edge with a little water. Fold the other half over the fruit and press the edges together. Prick each pie once in the center with a fork to allow the steam to escape. Heat the cooking oil to 375 degrees and fry in 1/2-inch deep oil. Turn once. Drain on paper towels placed on top of a brown grocery bag. Use 1 quart of sweetened fruit [fresh or dried] which has been cooked the day before. Chill well before using in the pies.

EASY FRUIT COBBLER

Ingredients for 8 servings

1 cup	Self-rising flour
1 cup	Sugar
1 cup	Milk
1 stick	Butter or oleo
1 can	Fruit pie filling [21 oz can Comstock or 2 cups of fresh fruit with 1 cup of sugar and some water]

Melt butter in a [8x8- or 9x9-inch] Pyrex dish. Mix the flour, sugar, and milk until well blended. Pour the batter evenly over the butter...do not stir. Dot the fruit evenly over the flour mixture...do not stir. Bake in a 350-degree oven for 1 hour. Can be spooned into dessert dishes and topped with sweetened whipped cream or ice cream.

FUDGE PIE

Ingredients for 8 servings

1 cup	Sugar
2 1/2 tbsp	Cocoa

1/4 cup	Flour
1 stick	Butter, melted
2 lg	Eggs
1 tsp	Vanilla
1 pinch	Salt
1/2 cup	Pecans, chopped
1	Pie shell, unbaked

Mix the flour, cocoa, sugar, and salt together. Add the melted butter. Beat in the eggs and vanilla. Add the nuts. Pour into the unbaked pie shell. Bake in a 350-degree oven for 35–45 minutes. If desired, serve warm with a dollop of lightly sweetened whipped cream or a scoop of ice cream.

Helpful hint: This recipe can also be baked in a buttered Pyrex pie dish without a crust…yummy either way.

GRAHAM CRACKER PIE

Ingredients for 8 servings

3 lg	Egg whites
1 cup	Sugar
1 tsp	Baking powder
1 cup	Pecans, chopped
1 cup	Graham crackers, crushed
1 tsp	Vanilla

Beat the egg whites until fluffy. Gradually add the baking powder and sugar to the egg whites. Add the vanilla. Beat until stiff. Gently fold in the crushed graham crackers and nuts. Pour into a lightly-oiled glass pie plate. Bake in a 350-degree oven for 25–30 minutes. Cool and serve with Cool Whip or lightly sweetened whipped cream.

GRASSHOPPER PIE

Ingredients for 8 servings

1/4 cup	Butter [1/2 stick], melted
2 cups	Oreos, finely crushed
8 oz	Cream cheese, softened
14 oz	Condensed milk [not evaporated]
1 tbsp	Lemon juice
1/4 cup	Green crème de menthe liquor
8 oz	Cool Whip, thawed

Mix the crumbs and melted butter. Press onto the bottom and sides of a lightly-oiled or sprayed 9-inch pie dish, forming a crust. Chill. In a mixing bowl, beat the cream cheese until fluffy. Gradually beat in the condensed milk. Stir in the crème de menthe and lemon juice. Fold in the whipped topping. Spoon the mixture into the chilled crust. Chill for 6 hours before slicing. Garnish with mint leaves, chocolate curls, or crushed Oreos.

Helpful hint: A chocolate bar can be shaved with a vegetable peeler to create curls.

HERSHEY BAR PIE

Ingredients for 8 servings

8 bars	Hershey candy [without nuts]
12 oz	Cool Whip
1	Graham cracker crumb piecrust

Thaw Cool Whip. Microwave the Hershey bars just long enough to melt them. Mix the chocolate into the Cool Whip, working fast. Pour the mixture into the piecrust and refrigerate. Can shave a little chocolate from a candy bar to decorate the top.

HERSHEY BAR PIE TOO

Ingredients for 8 servings

6 sm	Hershey bars with almonds
16 lg	Marshmallows
1/2 cup	Milk
1 cup	Whipping cream
9 inch	Piecrust, baked

Slightly chop the candy bars in a small chopper. In the top of a double boiler, melt the marshmallows and chocolate bars in the milk. Cool completely. Whip the cream until stiff. Fold in the cool chocolate mixture. Place in the refrigerator or freezer until ready to serve. Whip extra whipping cream and lightly sweeten to serve on top of the slices of the pie. Shave an extra chocolate bar on top of the dollop of whipped cream.

Helpful hint: A graham cracker crust can be used instead of a rolled pastry shell.

CREAMY LEMON PIE

Ingredients for 2 pies

1 can	Sweetened condensed milk [not evaporated]
8 lg	Eggs, separated
1/2 cup	Lemon juice, fresh
2 tbsp	Lemon zest, stirred into the lemon juice
1 tbsp	Cornstarch [rounded tablespoon]
1 tbsp	Flour, all-purpose [rounded tablespoon]
1/2 tsp	Salt
1/2 tsp	Cream of tartar
1/3 cup	Sugar
	All of the pie ingredients at room temperature

LEMON CREAM TOPPING

Topping ingredients at refrigerator temperature

1/4 can	Sweetened condensed milk
2 1/2 tbsp	Lemon juice, fresh
1 tbsp	Lemon zest, stirred into lemon juice
8 oz	Sour cream
1/8 tsp	Salt
1 pkg	Dream Whip or Cool Whip
2 small	Piecrusts or 1 large piecrust

In a medium mixing bowl, beat the egg yolks until light and creamy. Slowly add the can of milk and lemon juice and continue beating. Gradually add the cornstarch, flour, and salt. Set aside. Beat the egg whites at a slow speed until foamy. At a high mixer speed, add the cream of tartar and sugar until peaks form. Fold the yolk mixture into the meringue until blended. Fill the piecrusts with the filling. Bake in a 325-degree oven for 30 minutes. Reduce the heat to 300 degrees and continue baking for another 30 minutes or until the top is lightly brown and springy. Set aside and cool completely. Dust with powdered sugar or top with the following: For the topping, beat the condensed milk until creamy. Drizzle in the lemon juice and beat well. Spoon in the sour cream and beat gently. Whip the Dream Whip topping according to directions on the package. Fold the whip into the creamed topping until blended. Spread the topping over 2 small pies or 1 large pie.

Helpful hint: Thawed Cool Whip may be used instead of the Dream Whip.

LEMON MERINGUE PIE

Ingredients for 8 servings

3 lg	Egg yolks
1 cup	Sugar
1/4 cup	Cornstarch
1/4 tsp	Salt
	Zest of 1 lemon
1/3 cup	Lemon juice or 2 lemons juiced
2 tbsp	Butter
1 1/2 cups	Water

	MERINGUE
3 lg	Egg whites
6 tbsp	Sugar
1/4 tsp	Cream of tartar
1	Baked pie shell

Mix all of the pie filling ingredients together in a heavy saucepan. Cook over medium heat, stirring constantly, until thickened. [The mixture will thicken when it reaches the boiling stage.] For the meringue, place the egg whites in a mixing bowl and beat until frothy. Add the cream of tartar and keep mixing. Add the sugar in small amounts while beating. Beat until stiff peaks form. Add 2 heaping tablespoons of the meringue to the pie filling, folding it in. Pour the pie filling into a baked pie shell. Top the filling with the meringue, sealing the edges of the pie with the meringue. Bake in a 350-degree oven for 15 minutes or until the meringue is a golden brown.

FROZEN LEMONADE PIE

Ingredients for 1 pie

6 oz	Frozen lemonade concentrate [in the frozen foods section]
14 oz	Condensed milk [not evaporated], chilled
12 oz	Cool Whip, thawed

CRUST

2 cups	Graham crackers
1/4 cup	Sugar
7 tbsp	Butter, melted

Combine the cracker crumbs, 1/4 cup of sugar, and the melted butter. Press the mixture on the bottom and sides of a pie plate, pressing well. Bake in a 350-degree oven for 7 minutes and let the crust cool completely. In a bowl, mix the frozen lemonade concentrate and the chilled milk. Fold the Cool Whip in gently, not mixing too much to avoid mixture from becoming soupy. Pour the mixture into the cool piecrust and freeze overnight.

EASY KEY LIME PIE

Ingredients for 8 servings

8 oz	Cream cheese, softened
8 oz	Cool Whip, thawed
1 cup	Sugar
3 oz	Lime juice

Mix cream cheese, sugar, and lime juice well. Mix the Cool Whip in the mixture and pour into a graham cracker crust. Freeze. Thaw 10–15 minutes before slicing. Garnish with a sprig of mint or a slice of lime.

Helpful hint: Run knife under hot water before slicing a frozen pie. Double the recipe for three pies!

FROZEN KEY LIME PIE

Ingredients for 10 servings

1 cup	Whipping cream [heavy]
2/3 cup	Sugar
12 oz	Condensed milk [not evaporated]
3/4 cup	Key West lime juice [or fresh-squeezed Key limes]
2 cups	Half and half

	CRUST
2 cups	Graham cracker crumbs
1/4 cup	Brown sugar [packed]
1 stick	Butter, melted

Mix the crumbs, brown sugar, and melted butter together. Press the mixture together in a 10-inch springform pan. Bake in a 350-degree oven for 8–9 minutes. Cool. Whip the whipping cream in a large bowl until thickened. Add the sugar gradually until soft peaks form. Add the condensed milk and beat. Add the lime juice and half and half. Mix and pour the mixture into the cooled pie shell. Cover and freeze for 4 or more hours, or for a couple of days. Serve with additional sweetened whipping cream, sprinkled with a little lime zest.

Helpful hint: When pressing the crumb mixture into the springform pan, use the bottom of a 1-cup, flat-bottomed measuring cup. The edge of the cup will press the mixture up the sides of the pan more easily.

EASY LIME PIES

Ingredients for 12 servings

12 oz	Frozen limeade [or lemonade] concentrate [2 cans, 6 oz each], thawed
14 oz	Sweetened condensed milk, can [not evaporated]
8 oz	Frozen whipped topping, thawed
8 oz	Cream cheese, softened
2	Graham cracker crusts [6 oz each]

Mix limeade and milk together. Whip mixture and cream cheese until blended. Fold in the whipped topping and pour into the cracker crusts. Keep refrigerated.

Helpful hint: Easy Lime Pie is also good in the No-Roll Pecan Crust.

MACADAMIA NUT PIE

Ingredients for 8 servings

7 oz	Cream cheese, softened
1 cup	Sugar
1/3 cup	Heavy cream
3/4 cup	Heavy cream, whipped soft
6 oz	Premium white chocolate
1/2 tsp	Orange zest
2/3 cup	Macadamia nuts, chopped and lightly toasted
1	Deep-dish pie shell, baked

GANACHE

1/2 cup	Semisweet chocolate chips
1/4 cup	Milk chocolate chips
1/2 cup	Heavy cream

GARNISH

1 1/2 cups	Heavy cream
1/4 cup	Confectioners' sugar
	Chopped macadamia nuts

Melt the white chocolate in a small heatproof bowl over [but not touching] hot water. Beat the cream cheese and granulated sugar together until smooth. Scrape down the sides with a spatula and beat in the 1/3 cup of cream. Add the melted chocolate, orange zest, and nuts. Stir until incorporated. Fold in the whipped cream. Pour into the baked and cooled pie shell. Place in the freezer for 1 hour, or until the top is firm and cold. For the ganache, put the chocolate chips in a small heatproof bowl over [but not touching] hot water. Put the cream in a small saucepan and heat slowly. Add the heated cream to the melted chips and mix. Cool. Pour the ganache over the pie and place in the refrigerator. For the garnish, beat the 1 1/2 cups of cream. Add the confectioners' sugar and beat until stiff peaks form. Sprinkle chopped nuts over the top of the pie. Pipe the whipped cream onto the pie.

Helpful hint: If desired, serve the pie with a dollop of whipped cream instead of piping the cream on top. A crumb crust, such a Keebler's shortbread crust or graham cracker crust, can be used.

MILLIONAIRE'S PIE

Ingredients for 16 servings

1 can	Eagle Brand milk
1 sm can	Coconut
1 sm can	Crushed pineapple, drained
1/4 cup	Lemon juice
1 cup	Pecans, chopped
12 oz	Cool Whip

| 2 | Graham cracker piecrusts |
| 1 | Egg white |

Beat the egg white in a small bowl with a fork and brush over the piecrusts with a pastry brush. Bake in a 350-degree oven for 5 minutes. Cool. Mix the lemon juice and milk together. Reserve about 2 ounces of the Cool Whip to garnish the pie slices. Add the remaining ingredients together and divide evenly between the piecrusts. Chill before serving or they may be frozen.

Helpful hint: For a holiday appearance, use several drops of food coloring [green for St. Patty's Day, etc.].

FROSTY ORANGE PIES

Ingredients for 16 servings

2 cups	Orange sherbet, softened
8 oz	Cool Whip
6.8 oz	Instant vanilla pudding mix [2 boxes, 3.4 oz each]
2 cups	Cold milk
2	Shortbread crusts
1	Egg white

Slightly beat the egg white with a fork. Brush the egg white on each crust with a pastry brush. Bake the crusts in a 350-degree oven for 5 minutes. Cool. Add the milk to the pudding mixes and beat for a couple of minutes. Fold in 1/2 of the whipped topping. Spoon evenly into the crusts and smooth. Refrigerate. Add the remaining whipped topping to the softened sherbet. Stir with whisk until blended. Spoon over the pudding layer and freeze. May garnish with extra whipped topping and mandarin orange slices or swirl with orange sherbet over the top. Keep frozen until 30 minutes before serving, or place in the refrigerator 2–3 hours before serving.

ORANGE PIES

Ingredients for 2 pies

12 oz	Frozen orange juice [can], undiluted
14 oz	Condensed milk [not evaporated]
1 cup	Sour cream
9 oz	Cool Whip, thawed
2	Piecrusts [graham cracker or shortbread]

Mix the orange juice and the condensed milk together. Add the sour cream. Fold in the whipped topping until smooth. Divide between the 2 piecrusts. Chill for 6 hours or until firm. Serve with a dollop of Cool Whip and a mandarin orange slice or sprinkle the Cool Whip with zest from an orange.

PEAR PIE

Ingredients for 8 servings

1 1/4 cups	Sugar
1/4 tsp	Salt
3 tbsp	Flour
1 tsp	Cinnamon
7 med	Pears, peeled and sliced thin
1 tsp	Vanilla
1/4 cup	Butter, cut into small cubes
	Pastry for a 2-crust pie

Combine the 4 dry ingredients together in a small bowl, mixing well. Line a 9-inch pie plate with half of the pastry. Pour half of the dry mixture evenly over the pastry. Sprinkle the vanilla over the pears and mix. Place the pears over the layer of sugar mixture. Sprinkle the pears with the remaining sugar mixture and dot with butter. Cover with the top crust. Slit the crust in several places to allow the steam to escape. Place the pie plate on a baking sheet and bake in a 350-degree oven for 15 minutes. Reduce the heat to 300 degrees and continue baking for 40–50 minutes.

PECAN PIES

Ingredients for 16 servings

6 lg	Eggs
1 1/3 cups	Sugar
2 cups	Light corn syrup
3 cups	Pecans, chopped
1 pinch	Salt
2/3 cup	Butter, melted
2	Deep-dish piecrusts [I like Mrs. Smith's]

Bake the piecrusts in the hot oven for a minute and prick the bottoms with a fork to release the steam. Beat the eggs and sugar together. Add the other ingredients and mix. Pour the mixture into the pie shells. Bake in a 325-degree oven for 1 hour.

Helpful hint: Place the pies onto a baking sheet with sides to catch any overflow while they are baking.

CHOCOLATE PECAN PIE

Ingredients for 8 servings

1 stick	Butter, melted and cooled
1 cup	Sugar
3 lg	Eggs, slightly beaten

1/2 cup	Flour, all-purpose
6 oz	Chocolate chips [semisweet or milk chocolate]
1 tsp	Vanilla
1 cup	Chopped pecans
1	Deep-dish pie shell, unbaked

Combine the first 4 ingredients and blend with a wire whisk. Add the vanilla. Stir in the nuts and chocolate chips. Pour into the pie shell and bake in a 350-degree oven for about 35 minutes or until the center is set. Cool before slicing. Serve a slice of the semisweet chip pie with a scoop of vanilla ice cream...or serve the milk chocolate chip pie with a dollop of whipped cream.

Helpful hint: I usually bake the pie shell for a couple of minutes and prick the shell with the tines of a fork to prevent the pastry from bubbling.

PECAN-PUDDING PIES

Ingredients for 16 servings

2	Pie shells [9 inch], deep dish [I prefer Mrs. Smith's]
2 cups	Chopped pecans
6 oz	Cook and serve vanilla pudding mix [2 boxes, 3 oz each]
2 cups	Corn syrup, light
3/4 cup	Milk
3/4 cup	Whipping cream
2 lg	Eggs, beaten with a fork

Place 1 cup of the chopped pecans into each pie shell. Combine the pudding mixes, milk, whipping cream, corn syrup, and eggs until well blended. Ladle the mixture over the pecans. Bake in a

325-degree oven for 55–60 minutes or until done. Cool for 1 hour before slicing. Keep leftovers in the refrigerator.

Helpful hint: It's good to place the pies on a baking sheet to catch spills in the oven. Much easier to clean baking sheets than an oven.

PRALINE/CUSTARD PIE

Ingredients for 8 servings

1	Deep-dish pie shell [Mrs. Smith's, 9 inch]
2/3 cup	Butter
2/3 cup	Light brown sugar, firmly packed
1 1/4 cup	Chopped nuts, divided
1 pkg	Instant vanilla pudding [5.1 oz]
2 cups	Milk
1 1/3 cups	Cool Whip
1/2 tsp	Vanilla

Bake pie shell in a 400-degree oven for 5 minutes or until it is lightly browned. Combine butter, one cup of nuts, and sugar in a saucepan and cook over low heat until melted. Pour mixture into the pie shell and bake in a 450-degree oven for 5 minutes or until bubbly. Cool. Lightly toast 1/4 cup of nuts. Mix milk and the vanilla pudding mix. Spread 1/2 of the mixture over the cooled praline. Combine the whipped topping with the vanilla and remaining pudding. Spread over the pie. Sprinkle the toasted nuts over the pie and chill.

CREAMY PUMPKIN PIE [EASY]

Ingredients for 2 small pies

4 lg	Eggs
2 cups	Pumpkin [1 1/2 cans]

6 oz	Evaporated milk
3/4 cup	Milk
1 cup	Sugar
1 tsp	Vanilla
	Cinnamon to taste

Mix all of the ingredients together and pour into 2 small pie shells. Bake in a 350-degree oven for 10 minutes and bake an additional 45 minutes in a 325-degree oven.

CREAMY PUMPKIN PIE

Ingredients for 8 servings

4 oz	Cream cheese, room temperature
1 tbsp	Milk
1 tbsp	Sugar
1 1/2 cups	Cool Whip
1	Graham cracker crust [9 oz]
15 oz	Pumpkin [can]
1 cup	Milk
1 tsp	Cinnamon, ground
1/2 tsp	Cloves, ground
1/2 tsp	Ginger, ground
2 pkgs	Vanilla instant pudding mix [3.4 oz]

Mix cream cheese, milk, and sugar. Fold in Cool Whip and spread over bottom of the crust. Mix the pumpkin and milk. Add the spices and mix well. Add the dry pudding mix and beat with a whisk until well blended. Spread the pumpkin mixture over the cream cheese layer. Cover the pie and refrigerate for several hours or overnight. Garnish with additional whipped topping and finely toasted chopped walnuts.

RITZ CRACKER PECAN PIE

Ingredients for 8 servings

3/4 cup	Sugar
15	Ritz crackers, crushed
1 tsp	Vanilla
1 tsp	Baking powder
1 cup	Pecans, chopped small
3	Egg whites, beaten stiff

Combine and mix the first 5 ingredients. Fold into the stiffly beaten egg whites. Pour into a lightly oiled pie dish. Bake in a 325-degree oven for 35 minutes. Refrigerate for several hours before slicing. May serve with a dollop of whipped cream or a scoop of vanilla ice cream.

SALTINE CRACKER PIE

Ingredients for 8 servings

16	Saltine crackers, crushed fine
1 cup	Pecans, chopped small
16	Dates, chopped
1 cup	Sugar
1 tsp	Vanilla
4 lg	Egg whites

Beat the egg whites until stiff and add the sugar. Add the vanilla and mix. Fold in the pecans, saltines, and dates. Pour into an oiled 9-inch Pyrex pie plate. Bake in a 350-degree oven for 20–25 minutes. Cool. Serve with a dollop of lightly sweetened whipped cream.

FRESH STRAWBERRY PIE

Ingredients for 8 servings

1 qt	Fresh strawberries
1 1/2 cups	Water
1/4 cup	Cornstarch
1 1/2 cup	Sugar
3 oz	Strawberry Jell-O

Mix water, sugar, and cornstarch and cook until thickened. Add dry Jell-O to the mixture and stir until blended. Cool. Place strawberries into a baked 9-inch pie shell. Pour cooled mixture over the strawberries and refrigerate. Serve with whipped cream and garnish with strawberry slices.

SUGAR CREAM PIE

Ingredients for 8 servings

1 cup	Whipping cream
1/3 cup	Sugar
3/4 cup	Milk
1/2 cup	Flour, all-purpose
1 cup	Sugar
2 tbsp	Butter
	Nutmeg
9 inch	Pie shell, unbaked

Beat whipping cream, adding 1/3 cup of sugar gradually. Combine 1 cup of sugar with the flour and milk in a mixing bowl. Fold in whipped cream. Pour into pie shell. Dot with small pieces of butter. Sprinkle with freshly ground nutmeg. Bake in a 400-degree oven for 10 minutes. Reduce heat to 350 degrees and bake another 30 minutes. May reduce heat to 325 and bake another 10

508

minutes if needed. Cool and refrigerate. May garnish with extra whipped cream and fresh fruit.

SWEET POTATO PIE

Ingredients for 8 servings

2 cups	Sweet potato, cooked and mashed
1 cup	Milk [1/2 evaporated and 1/2 homogenized]
1 1/2 cups	Light brown sugar, lightly packed
1 stick	Butter, softened
2	Eggs, slightly beaten
1/2 tsp	Allspice
1/2 tsp	Cloves
1 tsp	Cinnamon
1	Piecrust, unbaked

Mix all ingredients well. Pour into an unbaked pie shell. Bake in a 350-degree oven for approximately 1 hour.

SUNDAE PIE

Ingredients for 8 servings

1	Chocolate crust
8 oz	Cream cheese, softened
3/4 cup	Confectioners' sugar
8 oz	Cool Whip
1 tsp	Vanilla
	LAYER 2
1 lg	Instant chocolate pudding mix [box]
2 1/2 cups	Milk

4 oz   Cool Whip
1   Chocolate candy bar, shaved or grated

Whip cream cheese and vanilla. Add the confectioners' sugar and blend well. Mix in the Cool Whip and spread into the piecrust. For the second layer, mix the milk and chocolate pudding until it begins to thicken. Pile onto the first layer and smooth. Top with more Cool Whip and sprinkle with chocolate curls or shavings. Refrigerate.

Helpful hint: To prevent a soggy crust, mix a spoonful of water with an egg white and brush over the crust. Bake in a 350-degree oven for 5 minutes. Cool before filling.

TANG PIE

Ingredients for 8 servings

14 oz   Sweetened condensed milk [not evaporated]
8 oz   Cool Whip
16 oz   Sour cream
1/2 cup   Tang
1   Baked deep-dish piecrust
                  [or 2 graham cracker pie shells]

Mix milk, Tang, sour cream, and add the Cool Whip. Pour into pie shell [or shells] and chill.

Everybody smiles in the same language.

- George Carlin

Index

V